The Global Impe

GLOBAL HISTORY SERIES

Bruce Mazlish, Carol Gluck, and Raymond Grew, Series Editors

---

*The Global Imperative: An Interpretive History
of the Spread of Humankind,* Robert P. Clark

Global History and Migrations,
edited by Wang Gungwu

Conceptualizing Global History,
edited by Bruce Mazlish and Ralph Buultjens

FORTHCOMING

Global Civilization and Local Cultures,
edited by Wolf Schäfer

The Global Imperative

An Interpretive History of the Spread of Humankind

Robert P. Clark

GEORGE MASON UNIVERSITY

Global History Series

Copyright © 1997 by Westview Press, A Division of HarperCollins Publishers, Inc.

Published in 1997 in the United States of America by Westview Press, 5500 Central Avenue, Boulder, Colorado 80301-2877, and in the United Kingdom by Westview Press, 12 Hid's Copse Road, Cumnor Hill, Oxford OX2 9JJ

A CIP catalog record for this book is available from the Library of Congress.
ISBN 0-8133-3180-3—ISBN 0-8133-3181-1 (pbk.)

The paper used in this publication meets the requirements of the American National Standard for Permanence of Paper for Printed Library Materials Z39.48-1984.

10   9   8   7   6   5   4   3   2   1

To Anne, Kathleen, and Robert . . . at last

Contents

Tables and Figures

Foreword

BRUCE MAZLISH, CAROL GLUCK,
AND RAYMOND GREW, SERIES EDITORS

Unlike the previous volumes in the Global History series, Robert P. Clark's *The Global Imperative* seems to call for a foreword. It does so for at least three reasons. Clark's is the first single-authored volume in the series; others are multiauthored and generally on a single topic, such as migrations or food, where the introductions speak for themselves. With the present volume, we wish to make it clear that we encourage a multitude of ways in which contributions to global history, as we define it, can be made. Next, *The Global Imperative* takes globalization all the way back to the beginning and does so in an original and effective manner. It gives historical depth to the present-minded quality inherent in the study of the modern globalization process and encourages others to proceed in the same manner. Last, it sustains a tightly conceived, well-argued vision of global history in terms of a particular concept, entropy. In this sense, again, it differs from most volumes in our series, which do not so consistently build on a central theory.

Clark's ecological-materialistic views may not appeal to everyone. Yet, it is clear that the first four or five Episodes offer a perceptive and glorious overview of the human drive to globalization. In the later episodes, as he comes to the more modern period, Clark enters into even greater specificity and also strikes a more somber note: Is the human species running out of space? This tone accords well with the millennial year, 2000, fast approaching. It also raises the question as to the fine grain of the modern globalization process: Can it be summed up in this way? The authors of the other volumes in this series tend to be more concerned with detailed research on particular aspects of modern global history, but the development of this field of study will benefit from both focused empirical studies and expansive theory. With his vision of global history, Clark enters in an exciting fashion into a provocative discourse with the authors of other titles in this series while inviting yet other scholars to raise their voices as well.

Introduction:
Why Globalization?

Seen from a very great distance, our planet appears to be a single place—unbroken, integrated, whole. Geologists tell us that about 200 million years ago its land areas really *were* a single place (or nearly so), but for all of human time on Earth, the fragmented nature of the continents has prevented us from understanding this fundamental unity. Nevertheless, challenged by an imperative, the nature of which I describe below, we have steadily spread ourselves, our technologies, and our plant and animal companions across the planet in a process called globalization.[1]

The global spread of human beings is thought by many to be a phenomenon peculiar to the modern age, related to its technology and mode of production. I believe, however, that we humans have been compelled to extend our reach to every habitable part of the Earth ever since our hominid ancestors first walked upright. That globalization per se is most clearly visible in the past three to five centuries is a function of technological capabilities, but the global imperative already confronted our ancestors in East Africa 3 to 4 million years ago. Since about 1500, and with increasing speed in recent decades, we have used the technologies of transport and communication to liberate ourselves from the constraints of nature, to fashion global networks of production and consumption at once both remarkable to use and to enjoy and ominous for what they portend for our long-term future. A fragmented view of the world makes it difficult for many of us to think about things as enormous as global systems or processes as transhistorical as globalization. I believe we desperately need to instill a sense of unity in our perspective of the Earth—a perspective I call *global awareness.*

At the level of individual cognition, global awareness has two dimensions: simple knowledge of the world as a single place and a grasp of the interconnectedness of its parts (i.e., how change in one part of the global order affects other parts).[2] Awareness at the first level is largely a matter of information flow. We know the Earth is a single place because we have seen photographs of it taken from space and we have read accounts written by people who have seen it from a distance. Becoming aware of the interconnectedness of the world's component parts, on the other hand, is much more challenging, since it involves a paradigm shift, or transformation in one's worldview. As an educator, I am keenly aware of how difficult it is to transform one's own way of thinking about how the world works, let alone change the worldview of others.

The word *liberal,* as used in the phrase "the liberal arts," comes from the Latin, *liberalis,* meaning "of, or pertaining to, a free person." Thus, we teach and learn the liberal arts to liberate ourselves from the chains of falsehood and ignorance. Even though I was aware of this as the end of liberal education, I was never sure how to conceptualize the confinement from which we were trying to free ourselves until I read the following, by Albert Einstein: "The individual feels the nothingness of human desires and aims and the sublimity and marvelous order which reveal themselves both in nature and in the world of thought. He looks upon individual existence as a sort of prison and wants to experience the universe as a single significant whole."[3]

The essence of the human condition is a fundamental connectedness with other parts of the universe across both time and space. The goal of a liberal education must be to free ourselves from the falsehood of individual disconnectedness, from the myth that we are separate and discrete beings entitled to conduct our lives without an awareness of how we are affected by other parts of the universe and without due regard for how we affect them. The central objective of such an education must be to enable us to connect with each other, with others more distant in time or space, with sources of information, with technologies, and with the whole of the natural world. In addition, we must begin to understand the profoundly fragmenting impact of postmodern life and of higher education in particular. We must see that such fragmentation is a social and intellectual artifact not inherent in the nature of knowledge and also that its effects are potentially extremely harmful for us as individuals and for society as a whole. We must be sensitized to the need to overcome this fragmentation and acquire the tools necessary to do so, so we can begin to introduce some identity, meaning, and coherence into our lives.

To write a comprehensive history of globalization from the beginning to the present would be a daunting task, one far beyond the scope of this project.[4] I propose more modestly to sketch out my interpretation of the process by focusing on seven "episodes" of globalization: the migration of *Homo erectus* and *Homo sapiens* from our East African origins across and beyond the African continent, the Neolithic Revolution, the rise of ancient cities and trade routes, the Age of Discovery, the partnership of coal and steam, the union of petroleum and the internal combustion engine, and the Information Age. But before we encounter the seven episodes, we must examine the reason why all that they involve has been necessary: the global imperative.

✢   ✢   ✢

"The one true test of all living systems," writes James Beniger, "is the persistence of [their] organization counter to entropy."[5] In his book *The Control Revolution,* Beniger explores how the industrial production system of the

United States was able by means of new technologies and institutions of control to stave off the inescapable costs of entropy. Similarly, if we are to understand the imperative of humankind to become global, it is with the concept of entropy—and our attempts to persist against its effects—that I believe we must begin.[6]

For millennia, observers have commented on the apparent tendency of the world around them to deteriorate, decay, or fall into ruin. Cyprian, a Roman writer from the third century A.D., described the process in these words:

> The World itself . . . testifies to its own decline by giving manifold concrete evidence of the process of decay. There is a diminution in the winter rains that give nourishment to the seeds in the earth, and in the summer heat that ripens the harvest. The springs have less freshness and the autumns less fecundity. The mountains, disembowelled and worn out, yield a lower output of marble; the mines, exhausted, furnish a smaller stock of the precious metals: the veins are impoverished, and they shrink daily. . . . This is the sentence that has been passed upon the World . . . this loss of strength and loss of stature must end, at last, in annihilation.[7]

Since the mid-nineteenth century, scientists have believed that all systems exhibit an inevitable tendency to decay. Systems possessing order and information tend inevitably toward disorder and meaninglessness. In the process, energy held within the system's structure, and therefore available to us, becomes liberated. Each time work is performed, energy is liberated and becomes unavailable for future use. This process is inescapable and irreversible; once energy has been liberated from the structure of matter, it is lost to us forever. Kenneth Boulding refers to this process as the loss or diminution of a system's potential for work.[8] Such a loss or diminution invariably accompanies the performance of work. Thus, as work is performed, the potential for further work declines.

Of course, the liberated energy still exists somewhere in the universe; but it is dispersed in ways that make it unavailable to us. For example, the burning of coal to power steam engines results in the transformation of the molecular structure of the coal so that its energy can be liberated; this process is accompanied by heat as well as by work, and the lost energy can never be recovered. Falling water liberates energy to turn a waterwheel, but the energy cannot be recovered without raising the water once more, which requires the investment of new energy from outside the system.

The irreversible nature of these changes can be illustrated by an experiment. Imagine a large glass container separated into two compartments by a removable partition. On one side of the partition are 100 red Ping-Pong balls being kept in motion by jets of air; on the otherside, 100 white Ping-Pong balls similarly in motion. Thus arranged, these two populations possess structure, or order. Remove the partition and the balls begin to mix. In so doing, they lose the order, or structure, they possessed just a moment before.

Eventually, the balls become mixed randomly. No matter how long we observe the container, the balls will never again separate themselves into distinctive red and white groups. Their structure has been lost forever unless we intervene from the outside (the container's "environment"), replace the center partition, and separate them again.

Our understanding of this phenomenon is based on the second law of thermodynamics, aspects of which began to be known to scientists in the early nineteenth century. In 1811, Jean-Joseph Fourier of France described mathematically the propagation of heat in solids and showed that heat always moves from warmer to colder objects. In 1824, another Frenchman, Sadi Carnot, identified the heat lost from steam-driven engines as an inevitable cost of performing work. By the middle of the century, scientists in Great Britain and Germany had announced the principle of the conservation of energy: Energy can be neither created nor destroyed but only changed from one form to another.

In 1850, the German physicist Rudolf Clausius began to study systematically the energy losses observed in heat engines, and in 1865, he formulated the cosmological version of the two laws of thermodynamics: First, that energy in the universe is a constant; and second, that entropy in the universe increases to a maximum. (Boulding refers to the second law as the principle of diminishing potential.[9]) Although energy cannot be destroyed, it can be changed in form. But each time energy is changed from one form to another, a certain penalty is exacted. That penalty is the loss of some quantity of energy that might otherwise have been available for work in the future. To label this phenomenon, Clausius coined the term *entropy* as the measure of the amount of energy no longer available for conversion into work.

Since Clausius, entropy has also been used to denote the degree of disorder or disorganization or the loss of meaning in a complex system. The tendencies of any system toward energy loss, decay, and disorder are referred to as *entropic tendencies.* These tendencies lead to the inevitable degradation of all matter and energy in the universe into inert uniformity. The opposite of entropy, *negative entropy* (or *negentropy*), is the measure of available energy, order, or meaning in a system. These properties are sometimes referred to as *high entropy* and *low entropy.*

Although entropy is a property of matter and energy, it is inextricably linked to human values and thus is central to economic processes of production and consumption as well.[10] Energy transformed during work is still present somewhere in the universe; it is "lost" only in the sense that it is unavailable for future human use. Nature by itself does not discriminate between energy available for human use and energy not available. According to Herman Daly, however,

Matter/energy is not at all uniform in the quality most relevant to economics—namely, the capacity to receive and hold the rearrangements dictated by human purpose, the capacity to receive the imprint of human knowledge, the capacity to embody value added. . . . If the economic system is to keep going, it cannot be an isolated circular flow, as the textbooks suppose. It must be an open system, receiving matter and energy *from* outside to make up for that which is dissipated *to* the outside.[11]

If all systems tend toward energy loss, decay, and disorder, how is it possible for human beings to create and maintain systems as complex and as large as, say, a great city? How can cities and civilizations grow and prosper when the laws of thermodynamics say they should be decaying? The answer to these questions and the principal force compelling us to become a global species lies in *dissipative structures*.

Civilizations, cities—indeed, all large and complex systems—depend on dissipative structures. This term, coined by Ilya Prigogine, refers to the ability of complex systems to transfer their entropic costs to other parts of the universe.[12] Dissipative structures enable complex systems to achieve and maintain a high level of order by dissipating their entropic tendencies, that is, their tendencies to disorder, disorganization, and energy loss, to neighboring systems. (Boulding refers to this process as the *segregation of entropy*.[13]) Some of these systems may be nearby; others may be on the other side of the country; still others, on the opposite side of the world. Without the ability to dissipate the costs of complexity and growth to other populations, primitive peoples could never have developed agriculture, built cities, or sustained classes that lacked any role in the gathering or hunting of food.

The belief that entropy is inescapable, argues Prigogine, rests on several important assumptions, the central of which is that we are dealing with closed systems that are either at equilibrium or near it. Any change in such a system will be linear, bounded, slow, gradual, and predictable. Such systems will be relatively simple and have few important transactions with the outside world.

Suppose, argues Prigogine, we alter these assumptions fundamentally. We replace the relatively simple system with one that is highly complex, with numerous interconnected parts that are linked in ways that no one knows or understands. Instead of being closed, the system is open to interaction with the outside world. Then the pace of change speeds up, so that now change is nonlinear, or as Prigogine prefers, "far from equilibrium." Suppose also that we are dealing with purposeful, human-contrived systems that have the ability to reorder themselves and their relationships with surrounding systems by injecting a new ingredient—information—into the equation.[14] Under these circumstances, entropic tendencies, like change of any kind, may actually become the source of higher levels of organization—order out of chaos, as it were. Paul Davies and John Gribben put it this way:

> In open systems, entropy can decrease, but the increase in order in the open system is always paid for by a decrease in order [increase in entropy] somewhere

else. . . . Because the Universe as a whole is progressing from a state of low entropy to a state of high entropy, . . . we are able to dump entropy into the flow going past.

All of this [decrease in entropy] is possible because the Earth is an open system, through which energy and entropy flow. The source of almost all the useful energy we use is the Sun, which is a classic example of a system in thermodynamic disequilibrium—a compact ball of hot gas in a relatively low entropy state is irreversibly pouring huge amounts of energy out into the cold vastness of space. . . . [Reversing the flow of entropy has its] origin in our proximity to this great source of energy in the sky, which is like a bucket of negative entropy into which we can dip in order to create ordered systems on Earth.[15]

In recent years, scholars specializing in complexity theory, or the science of complex adaptive systems, have implied or even stated explicitly that the second law of thermodynamics may not apply to extremely complex, open, and highly adaptive systems like living organisms. The very existence of life, they argue, proves that order can emerge from disorder, that complex systems can self-organize, that the universe can harbor (as Stuart Kauffman puts it) "order for free."[16] Jack Cohen and Ian Stewart, for example, call the science of thermodynamics "a horrible trap for the unwary. Thermodynamics," they assert, "works beautifully in its original context, heat engines. In most other areas it is usually no more than a metaphor, one that has often been stretched far beyond its breaking point."[17]

Even these scientists, however, are forced to admit the validity of thermodynamics when they confront the necessity in self-ordering systems for disposing of entropy. Kauffman, for example, concedes that "order is not 'for free' thermodynamically. Rather, in these open systems, [order] is 'paid for' thermodynamically by exporting heat to the environment."[18] Cohen and Stewart ask how a chicken can create an ordered system (an egg) from a disordered one (chicken feed). Their answer: "A common explanation is that living systems somehow 'borrow' order from their environment by making it even more disordered than it would otherwise have been. Then they use their 'negative entropy'—order—to build an egg. *There's a certain amount of truth to this,* yet it seems that chickenkind has been borrowing an awful lot of negative entropy over the millennia."[19] To which we can only add: Exactly so. That is the function of dissipative structures. Nicholas Georgescu-Roegen puts it this way:

Given that even a simple cell is a highly ordered structure, how is it possible for such a structure to avoid being thrown into disorder instantly by the inexorable Entropy Law? The answer . . . : a living organism is a *steady-going concern* which maintains its highly ordered structure by sucking low entropy from the environment so as to compensate for the entropic degradation to which it is continuously subject. Surprising though it may appear to common sense, life does not feed on mere matter and mere energy but . . . on low entropy.[20]

Complexity theory can blind us to the reality of system building in a social context. When complexity theorists focus their attention at the atomic or molecular or cellular level, they cause us to lose sight of the fact that every system in the social order must be paid for by someone, somewhere, sometime. This essential reality is hidden from our view because human beings are very skillful at exporting the costs of their own behavior to others via dissipative structures. According to A. J. McMichael,

> In the long-term, the health and survival of a population cannot be sustained if the carrying capacity of its ecosystem is exceeded. For the human species . . . this criterion of living within the carrying capacity of ecosystems is less straightforward than for other species. We have a unique ability to adapt to environmental adversity, to extract additional energy and materials beyond those that flow naturally through ecosystems, and to offset a shortfall in ecological productivity in one location by trading with humans in another location. We can thus live at one remove from direct accountability to local ecosystems—as, for example, do rich urban populations eating year-round imported tropical fruits or dry-land farmers irrigating their crops. For the human species as a whole, however, we cannot sever the connection. Ecological debits may be displaced or deferred, but cannot be indefinitely ducked.[21]

Confronted with the problem of entropy, we have very few options. One obvious solution is simply to live surrounded by our own entropy, to put up with its costs. People who lived 20,000 years ago in the caves of northern Spain and southwestern France lived in the midst of their own entropy because they had no choice. They generated very little solid waste, but what they did create (e.g., the remains of animals they had eaten) was simply discarded near the cave where they lived. They had no solid waste disposal problem as we do, because they had no technology to move waste to a distant sink (one very common dissipative structure). Their waste disposal sites, or middens, found close to their cave sites, were in some instances as long and as wide as a football field and six to ten feet deep.[22]

Whether the problem is waste disposal or a dwindling resource base, living with one's entropy is not an easy solution to maintain. It is speculated, for example, that the people of Easter Island eventually came to ruin because after arriving on the island from Polynesian origins far to the west, they somehow lost the ability to leave and the island became their prison.[23] For a time, as they exploited the island's resource base, they flourished and their population grew. But without the ability to import an energy source (another way of dissipating entropy), they ran up against the limits of the island's timber supply and fell into violence and decline. Thus, without the option of mobility, a group must practice a considerable degree of self-restraint in both numbers and lifestyle. This option requires that we sharply restrict both our population and our individual consumption levels, something that few of us are willing to accept if we have other alternatives.

And, of course, we *do* have other alternatives. Historically, the first option was to use local resources and sinks to exhaustion and then move to fresh land (Episode 1). This alternative, seen in human behavior ever since our earliest ancestors began their long trek out of Africa, calls for the group to move from areas of resource scarcity and waste to areas of resource abundance and unspoiled landscape.[24] Such a solution leaves behind the entropic costs of the group's activities for the local ecosystem to absorb through its own recovery mechanisms. Slash-and-burn agriculture is one such technique still seen in many parts of the world today; pastoral nomadism is another.

Eventually, however, we ran short of fresh landscape, so we sought other alternatives that would appear to free us from the need for self-restraint. Our next option was to exploit local resources and sinks more extensively and intensively (Episode 2). Our objective here was to increase the quantity of resources (matter, energy, and information) available to human populations from nearby sources. One way to do this was to rearrange local resources to use them more intensively than is possible when they are in a natural state (e.g., domesticate animals and plants to increase and regularize food supply). A second was to rearrange the local ecosystem to extract from it new resources not exploited before (e.g., switch from falling water to burning biomass as an energy supply).

When this alternative (the Neolithic Revolution) reached its limit, we turned to the only other possible solution: to bring resources to us from far away (Episodes 3 through 7). This option in all its variants has one simple goal: to move scarce resources from where they are to where we want them to be (e.g., transport crude oil from Saudi Arabia to refineries in Houston).

For each of the options that we employ to increase available resources, there is a counterpart solution to discard waste: Rearrange the waste so that the local ecosystem can absorb more of it (e.g., wastewater treatment); rearrange the local ecosystem so that it can absorb more waste (e.g., build modern disposal sites); or move waste from where it is created to a distant sink (e.g., dump toxic materials into the ocean).

Unfortunately, our situation is complicated enormously by two facts: One, our great needs for resources and sinks cannot be met in the sparse concentrations and unusable forms in which they occur naturally on the Earth; and two, each solution is accompanied by costs associated with the creation, operation, and maintenance of increasingly large and complex systems. Thus, as we select and implement various options for acquiring, processing, consuming, and disposing of resources, we inevitably create even more entropy. The result is a vicious cycle of challenge and response, and most significant for this analysis, of expansion.

❧   ❧   ❧

A dissipative structure is anything—a technology, a social process, a cultural practice, an institutional arrangement—that shifts the entropic costs of a complex system from the persons and regions directly benefited to others more distant in time or space. Eric Jantsch describes how dissipative structures are essential to all self-organizing and self-maintaining systems:

> The metabolism of self-organizing matter systems would soon die down were the exchange processes with the environment left to chance encounters of the participants involved in the reactions. Entropy would accumulate in the reaction volume and move the system toward its equilibrium, at which all processes come to an end, except for thermal . . . motion. This is the way equilibrating systems run themselves down.
>
> Under conditions far from equilibrium, the processes within the system as well as its exchange processes with the environment assume a distinct order in space and time, called a *dissipative structure*. It constitutes the dynamic regime through which the system gains autonomy from the environment, maintains itself, and evolves. In particular, it is the dynamic regime that keeps the system self-regenerative.[25]

The problem we face is that complex human systems such as great cities consume huge quantities of critical resources, such as industrial energy, food, water, manufactured goods, and information, for which sources must be sought, and they produce huge quantities of goods, services, and wastes, including heat and garbage, for which markets and sinks must be found and maintained.[26] The more complex a system, the more inputs it needs simply to survive, let alone grow and prosper. Likewise, the more complex a system, the more wastes (the more entropy) it creates, because of the additional resources it must expend simply to coordinate and control itself. Thus, as cities grow they must spread their networks of inputs and waste disposal farther and farther afield, dissipating their entropy, or costs, to others. As Lester Brown and Jodi Jacobson put it,

> Cities require concentrations of food, water, and fuel on a scale not found in nature. Just as nature cannot concentrate the resources needed to support urban life, neither can it disperse the waste produced in cities. . . . Cities are . . . larger than their municipal boundaries might imply: As urban material needs multiply through the effects of sprawl and mismanagement, they eventually exceed the capacity of the surrounding countryside, exerting pressure on more distant ecosystems to supply resources.[27]

If the notion of dissipative structures is to be more than simply a suggestive metaphor, we must extend its insights to specific social systems and begin to assemble empirical data to describe specific dissipative processes at work. To facilitate the description of these processes, I adopt the literary convention of the *center* and the *periphery*, where the center is the city or other system that is dissipating its entropy and the periphery comprises all of the neighboring systems that are the recipients of the center's disorder, decay, and energy loss.[28]

How do complex social systems actually dissipate their entropic tendencies? How can the center force periphery systems to absorb the cost of its development "counter to entropy"? Such processes take place frequently in social systems directed by the will, or volition, of purposeful intelligence. The will of the dissipating center is not sufficient, however, to spread its entropic costs to others; for this to happen, there must be a power imbalance in favor of the center over its periphery(ies). In other words, dissipation of entropy occurs when one system has the will and the ability to force others to absorb the costs of its own growth and prosperity. Such an asymmetrical power relationship is one of the defining characteristics of colonial systems, which suggests that the absorption of entropic costs is one of the functions a colony performs for its metropole.

How does such "forcing" actually occur? The most obvious way is through conscious decisions made by elites at the center. We can identify in the abstract a number of these processes. Two of these require the state's monopoly of legitimate force: First, by annexation a city or nation-state can acquire neighboring territory to which entropy can be dissipated against the will of the periphery; and second, by coercion, or the repression of resistance by force or threat of force, the objections of the periphery to being used this way can be suppressed. Other processes involve deception by the center to conceal such dissipation from those on the periphery who must bear the cost. One way to do this is to filter the dissipation through impersonal market mechanisms so that victims on the periphery are not aware of what is being done to them, or why, or by whom. Another is a national accounting system that counts entropy-producing activity as a plus to gross national product while undercounting (or not counting at all) the costs of the entropy produced (e.g., the degradation of the soil or water). Alternatively, the center may simply reward or pay neighboring systems to absorb their entropy. Or by making commitments that obligate future generations to absorb entropy that they did not create, the center may pass entropic costs on to populations that are peripheral in time rather than space. When the costs of a particular entropy-producing transaction have been passed on to other species, distant human populations, or future generations (none of whom, presumably, are parties to or benefit from the transactions), then we say (following the economists) that these costs have been "externalized."[29]

The knowing, informed, and purposeful displacement of entropy by the center to its neighbors is only one possible way in which a complex social system dissipates its entropy to other systems to facilitate its own higher order and organization. In a second process, where disorder already exists in the periphery (e.g., revolution in Central America, which forces refugees into the global population flow), the center may be able to take advantage of this disorder to achieve for itself a level of order that it could not otherwise attain. This does not mean that residents in a prosperous U.S. city stimulate instability in, say, El Salvador, just so they will have a ready supply of cheap

Salvadoran labor for their construction industry. But they are more than ready to take advantage of the supply of such labor when it occurs. The city may not *cause* Third World instability (at least, not for such indirect reasons), but it does *benefit* from it.

A third mechanism is at work when a carrier of entropy, or disorder, moves from the center to a periphery system (frequently but not always one that is at an earlier stage of industrial development) and carries the entropic tendencies from the place where they were generated to some other place. Some of these processes occur through natural forces, such as when wind or water carries pollutants or toxic substances from their origin to a neighboring ecosystem where they are deposited and absorbed. Sometimes, however, the carriers are human. When unemployed construction workers move from the center because of the collapse of the local construction industry, for example, they become the responsibility of the welfare and unemployment support system of their new home on the periphery, which may be quite far from the origin of their unemployment.

In his book *Plagues and Peoples,* William McNeill describes the historical impact of diseases and human predation in terms that are strikingly similar to what we are calling dissipative structures.[30] Throughout history, McNeill writes, human beings have been locked in a struggle for survival that involves microparasites (microorganisms that seek out human hosts, spreading disease as they do so) and macroparasites (other large animals that prey on humans for food). Long ago humans had much to fear from large predators such as lions, but in the last 10 to 30 millennia the macroparasite that has done the most damage to human populations is *Homo sapiens* itself, through war, slavery, pillaging, and other acts of intrahuman violence.

For McNeill, human beings and their macro- and micro-parasites are all part of an intricate system of energy flows. He describes microparasites draining energy from their human hosts just as macroparasites drain energy from their slaves, conquered subjects, or peasants from whom they exact food and other resources. In our terms, McNeill's macroparasites occupy the system's core and use their superior power to dissipate their entropic costs to a submerged population of slaves or peasants. The population of microparasites moving invisibly through the environment has also frequently staked its claim to the energy of the human hosts, however, and with greater success than the macroparasites. Thus, the energy drained off by the microorganisms represents a reduced pool of energy available to be exploited by other humans.

Both sets of parasites have had to proceed cautiously, for when either exploited the energy supply too much, the human population was so weakened or reduced that the parasites' own existence was threatened as well. A rough energy balance had to be worked out repeatedly across the millennia as humans interacted with each other and with other organisms, some large and others microscopic. For microparasites, of course, these adaptations took place without awareness or conscious direction. If a disease was too virulent and killed off its entire host population, it too would perish. Macroparasites, on the other hand, were more likely to be aware of the dangers of overexploitation of their human subjects and thus had the chance to control their exploitative drives before they exhausted the human energy sources on which they depended. In our terms, the elites at the system's core must be careful not to dissipate so much entropy to the periphery that they destroy the very people on whom they so hugely depend. The fact that many core elites have failed to control their own appetites and have exploited a subject population to exhaustion may have been a function of their greed or perhaps a lack of understanding of their own self-interest.

҈   ҈   ҈

The need of cities, city-regions, and nation-states to connect with global systems is a direct consequence of their growing complexity. According to Joseph Tainter, "Complexity is generally understood to refer to such things as the size of a society, the number and distinctiveness of its parts, the variety of specialized social roles that it incorporates, the number of distinct social personalities present, and the variety of mechanisms for organizing these into a coherent, functioning whole. Augmenting any of these dimensions increases the complexity of a society."[31]

Scholars from different fields disagree about the origins of complexity.[32] Adaptationists follow Darwinian thinking and assert that complex structures evolve in gradual, minute changes as systems respond to environmental conditions. Structuralists, such as scientists who study complex adaptive systems, believe that there are fundamental laws that allow such systems to self-organize "out of chaos." Whichever school is correct, it is clear that evolving systems could not increase their complexity without dissipative structures, or the ability to dissipate the costs of their complexity to other systems.

Complex systems enjoy certain advantages in competition with more simple systems, and up to a point (difficult to know before the fact), the more complex a system becomes, the greater these advantages appear. Some of these advantages show up in competition between two contemporary systems, in real time as it were. Ian Stewart offers several examples:

> Perhaps chaos and complexity are so common because they bestow advantages on the things that contain them. Chaotic systems can respond to an outside stimulus far more rapidly than non-chaotic ones can. . . . A nervous system that has developed from . . . an underlying sea of chaos could offer definite advantages to an evolving organism. It's reasonable to believe that prey whose nervous systems incorporate chaos are harder for predators to catch. . . . It is advantageous for an eco-system to evolve into a state of high diversity, for a diverse ecology has many more ways to recover from disaster. Everybody knows that a one-crop economy is a mistake, and so is a one-crop ecology.[33]

In addition to these contemporary advantages, complex systems also have a long-term, future-oriented edge over less complex opponents. Complex systems have an evolutionary advantage because they enjoy a heightened opportunity or potential for the random occurrence of characteristics that are positive or favorable for survival or for winning out in a struggle with less complex systems. Carl Sagan and Ann Druyan assert that this is the reason why organisms that reproduce asexually are at a disadvantage versus organisms that reproduce sexually.[34] Because sexual reproduction yields novel genetic combinations with each generation, there is greater likelihood that some genetically transmitted characteristic that favors survival will emerge; organisms that reproduce asexually must plod slowly along with only occasional, random mutations, perhaps waiting millennia before a "survival-friendly" characteristic appears. John Holland contends that complexity makes organisms "fitter" in the Darwinian sense by equipping them with more adaptable procedures for discovering the rules of the ecosystem in which they happen to find themselves.[35]

Jack Cohen and Ian Stewart have argued that the increasing complexity of systems is for the most part the inevitable outcome of evolution and the struggle for competitive advantage. There are two reasons, according to Cohen and Stewart, behind the trend toward increasing complexity: First, it is easier for a system

> to add stages onto an already effective sequence than it is to modify earlier steps in the sequence. So most innovations that offer a competitive edge are refinements that complicate (and often enlarge) the *adult* stage of organisms. The second idea concerns the kind of innovation. It is more likely that competitive advantage will be gained by adding something than by removing it. Neither idea is universally valid, but both are true much more often than they are false.[36]

Finally, notes Murray Gell-Mann, complex systems tend toward increasing complexity because of what he calls "frozen accidents." As a system evolves, it confronts moments in which the direction chosen is a matter of chance or accident. Some of these accidents become "frozen as rules for the future," and as these accumulate, "the number of possible regularities keeps increasing with time, and so does the possible complexity [of the system]."[37]

The advantages enjoyed by complex systems exact quite a price, however. Extraordinary amounts of energy are needed to sustain complex systems due to their greater requirements for coordination and control as compared with simple systems. Warm-blooded creatures, for example, enjoy much greater adaptability to changing environmental constraints and much greater mobility than cold-blooded animals, but they must consume much more energy to "pay for" these advantages. Since humans cannot ingest many energy sources (such as grass) directly from nature, we must acquire this energy indirectly, as part of a food chain in which the energy is processed by herbivorous animals before it reaches us. For this reason, the food necessary to supply a growing population could not be achieved until animals and plants were domesticated, which explains why dense human populations depended on the invention of agriculture.

Tainter has raised this insight to a general law concerning society as a whole:

> Human societies and political organizations, like all living systems, are maintained by a continuous flow of energy. . . . Not only is energy flow required to maintain a sociopolitical system, but the amount of energy must be sufficient for the complexity of that system. . . . More complex societies are more costly to maintain than simpler ones, requiring greater support levels per capita. As societies increase in complexity, more networks are created among individuals, more hierarchical controls are created to regulate these networks, more information is processed, there is more centralization of information flow, there is increasing need to support specialists not directly involved in resource production, and the like. . . . The result is that as a society evolves toward greater complexity, the support costs levied on each individual will also rise, so that the population as a whole must allocate increasing portions of its energy budget to maintaining organizational institutions.[38]

To make matters worse, Tainter goes on, investments in increasing complexity are subject to a law of diminishing returns. In many crucial sectors of society, including agricultural production, information processing, sociopolitical control and specialization, and overall economic productivity, "continued investment in sociopolitical complexity reaches a point where the benefits for such investment begin to decline, at first gradually, then with accelerated force. Thus, not only must a population allocate greater and greater amounts of resources to maintaining an evolving society, but after a certain point, higher amounts of this investment will yield smaller increments of return."

To cope with these problems, the complex system is forced to grow or expand its boundaries. Rapidly changing systems need time to adjust to the onrushing limits to growth. The more complex a system is, the more it tries to push back the natural limits to growth to give itself more time to react to changing circumstances and thus avoid the damage of overshoot.[39] Natural system growth is one of the consequences of such a measure. Complex systems also need to acquire additional resources, particularly energy, and access to additional sinks where they can discard waste. These dual processes lead inescapably to system growth. So the central problem with complexity is this: The more complex a system becomes, the more it is compelled to grow or expand its boundaries.

The expansion of complex systems can only be a short-term palliative, however, for as David Ruelle has demonstrated, "The entropy of a system is proportional to its size."[40] For example, all other things being equal, a metropolitan region of, say, 1,000 square miles generates twice as much entropy as a city of only 500 square miles. Hence the unavoidable dilemma: Systems face an imperative to become more complex, but greater complexity leads to system growth, which in turn produces proportionately greater entropy, which must be dissipated to other systems, which requires another round of expansion, and so on until the system collapses of its own size and complexity or because it can no longer force other systems to absorb its entropic costs.

If these observations are true for systems in general, they must be even more true for one of the most complex of all human-contrived systems: the city. The study of globalization is the study of the evolution of global systems and the technologies and social institutions needed to create and operate them. But we cannot understand global systems without studying the cities they were created to serve. These two institutions—cities and global systems—exist in a symbiotic relationship.

Cities are not a natural habitat for human beings; *Homo sapiens* did not evolve to live in such dense concentrations in nature. But more to the point here, cities cannot supply their own needs from local resources, so they require the support of systems to transport what they need from where it exists naturally. Cities take in huge quantities of matter, energy, and information; process them (i.e., disassemble them into their component parts and reassemble these parts into something different); and then send them back out to other systems. To achieve this goal, cities require bulk flow technologies (to be discussed shortly), since other modes cannot transport sufficient quantities of matter, energy, and information fast enough to be of use.

Just as cities need global bulk flow systems, however, global systems also need cities. Human beings have faced a global imperative from our beginnings. The constant battle to "persist counter to entropy" has forced us to devise dissipative structures to transport our entropy some distance from where it was created. We began to develop bulk flow technologies for doing this perhaps as long ago as 10,000 years. About 5,000 years ago, these systems reached a stage of complexity where they required a growing number of specialized operators who lived and worked in close proximity to each other. The more complex and global these systems have become, the greater must be the population of specialized support workers. Hence the vicious circle: Human societies require the support of bulk flow systems; the larger these systems become, the more people are required to operate and support them, and therefore the larger cities must become; but the bigger cities become, the more their support systems must expand. Thus, the rate of urbanization rises along with the rate of population growth generally and the advance of globalization. In other words, the more of us there are, the more urban is our habitat and the more global are the systems on which we rely for survival.[41]

These observations are especially pertinent for cities in the Information Age. Cities in highly industrialized countries are—and by their nature *must be*—connected to systems that are extremely complex and global in scope.

They must become "global cities,"[42] even if no local elites expressed a preference for establishing such linkages, no public policy decisions were directed at bringing them about, and there was no historical precedent for doing so. Cities become enmeshed in global systems not because of conscious policy decisions, but because of the global imperative. This feature of cities appears frequently in my discussion of the episodes in global history because of the critical role cities played in all those episodes (save the first two, of course).

ᕯᐤ   ᕯᐤ   ᕯᐤ

Roland Robertson reminds us that globalization is not a particularly new phenomenon:

> Human history has been replete with ideas concerning the physical structure, the geography, the cosmic location and the spiritual and/or secular significance of the world . . . ; movements and organizations concerned with the patterning and/or the unification of the world as a whole have intermittently appeared for at least the last two thousand years; . . . Even something like . . . the 'global-local nexus' . . . was thematized as long ago as the second century BC when Polybius, in his *Universal History,* wrote with reference to the rise of the Roman Empire: "Formerly the things which happened in the world had no connection among themselves. . . . But since then all events are united in a common bundle." However, . . . it has not been until quite recently that considerable numbers of people living on various parts of the planet have spoken and acted in direct reference to the problem of the "organization" of the entire, heliocentric world.[43]

Today's globalization process differs from that of earlier times in four ways: The distances covered are longer; the volume of materials moved is larger; the speeds with which they are moved are faster; and the diversity of materials moved is greater, including not just matter and energy, but information as well.

Becoming conscious of, or experiencing, the world as a *single* place is not the same as seeing it as an *integrated* structure. In other words, "globalism" is not the same as "one-worldism." The planet can be seen as a single place and still be subdivided into hundreds, or even thousands, of competing or warring factions. Globalism is also not a prediction of universal homogenization, or what social scientists call convergence theory.[44] Actually, the contrary seems to be happening: Greater global interdependence is bringing about heightened cultural self-awareness and thus greater ethnic, religious, racial, and linguistic conflict.[45]

The ability of people to experience the world as a single place depended in the first instance on the availability of technologies and organizations able to move large quantities of matter, energy, and information over great distances. Steven Vogel points out that to function complex systems need to move large quantities of materials and there are only two means of doing so: diffusion and bulk flow (see Table I.1).[46] Diffusion, the direct transfer of

TABLE I.1 Diffusion and Bulk Flow Compared

	Diffusion	*Bulk Flow*
Speed	Slow	Fast
Distance	Limited to proximate	Long Distance
Volume	Low	High
Cost	High	Low
Intermediary or linking technologies required	None	Containers
		Packing
		Loading
		Conveyance
		Unloading
		Unpacking

matter, energy, or information from one part of the system to another without intermediaries, is satisfactory when speed is unimportant, distances to cover are small, and the objects to be moved are tiny. But where distances are great, speed is critical, and quantities to be moved are large, diffusion is too slow and inefficient. For the movement of large quantities over large distances at high speeds, bulk flow is required. But bulk flow requires the capacity to package the materials, load them into some container, transport that container, and unload and unpackage the materials at destination. This is as true for the circulatory system of a warm-blooded animal as it is for a nation's economic system, a global information network such as Internet, or the dissipative structures of a city.

Critical components of any bulk flow system are the central switching units. These components sit at the center or hub of a radiating network of spokes or fibers in a web. They receive shipments of matter, energy, or information bound for many different destinations; unload and repackage them according to their destination; and send them out again. Without such central switch points, every source would have to be connected with every destination, a requirement that would overload any bulk flow system at very low volumes. Central switches can be as large as an entrepôt city like Amsterdam in the seventeenth and eighteenth centuries or as small as the switchboard of a metropolitan telephone company.

Globalization was made possible by society's ability to fashion the bulk flow technologies necessary to move matter, energy, and information to virtually every inhabited space on the planet. These components include people (immigrants, refugees, tourists), manufactured goods (automobiles, clothing, television sets), services (insurance, data processing, accounting), raw materials (petroleum, iron ore, food stuffs), information and images (news reports, entertainment, broadcasts of sporting events), cultural objects (film, television, music), financial capital (corporate stocks, national currencies, government bonds), technology (computers, steel mills, farming implements), and the waste created by production and consumption (air and water pollution, toxic substances, radiation).

For millennia, the ability of humans to move matter, energy, and information around the planet was blocked by three obstacles. The first of these was conceptual, or "knowledge dependent"; that is, first, human beings were unconscious of the world as a single place, a barrier that began to lift about 1500 when Europeans established their first connections with Western Hemisphere native peoples and rudimentary global systems began to take shape. For about the next 300 years, from 1500 to 1800, materials could be moved increasingly to distant parts of the world, but only at speeds and in volumes dictated by natural forces (wind, water, animal and human power). The two remaining barriers were the absence of the technology and organization required for bulk flow. The initial phase of globalization (driven by sail technology) was followed after 1800 by three successive stages, during which society developed the institutions, modes of thought, and control mechanisms needed to absorb the technologies to be unleashed over the course of the next two centuries (coal and steam, electricity, oil, nuclear energy).[47]

From 1840 on, the technologies and institutions of globalization diverged, depending on whether they were moving physical objects or ideas and images. For moving objects, from 1840 to 1910 the dominant technology was the coal-fired steam engine and its application to rail and ship transport; after 1910, steam was joined (and eventually replaced) by the internal combustion engine and petroleum, and railroads and ships by automobiles, trucks, and airplanes. For the movement of information and images, the principal technologies from 1840 to 1940 were the telegraph, telephone, film, recorded music, and radio; from 1940 to the present, these have been joined by computers, television, satellites, fiber optics, and many others.

We cannot separate the globalization process from the spread throughout the world of the industrial system as the dominant mode for organizing the power of production, a process that has resulted in what Nigel Harris calls the global manufacturing system.[48] Highly industrialized societies have experienced a steady shift of resources from the primary and manufacturing sectors to both advanced services (engineering, design, accounting) and basic services (secretarial and clerical, retail sales). Meanwhile, the manufacturing role has shifted steadily to the newly industrializing countries such as South Korea, Taiwan, and Brazil, which increasingly produce manufactured goods for markets in Europe, North America, and Japan. As capital, information, people, products, languages, and cultural objects (and diseases, waste, and toxic substances as well) flow with increasing speed and ease across space, the old "Three Worlds" paradigm seems increasingly inaccurate as a descriptor of the world as it actually functions.

Globalization holds major implications for all complex institutions, but especially for cities. For one thing, the component parts of global systems can be moved in greater volume and over greater distances than ever before, and they can be combined and recombined in new packages that are more complex than ever. These developments increase the complexity and diversity of any given local system and the number of variables that must be considered by local decisionmakers. In addition, the components of global systems can be moved at much greater speeds than ever before, thereby increasing the uncertainty of unpredictability of complex system behavior and reducing the response time available to local decisionmakers. Thus, the more global our society becomes, the greater is the need for decisionmakers who are flexible and able to respond to rapid and unexpected change.[49]

The ability of a city to establish global connections is a function of what Donald Janelle calls "space-adjusting technologies."[50] For example, the time required to travel from Boston to New York has dropped from 4,700 minutes in 1800 (by stagecoach) to 300 minutes in 1965 (by car), a decline of 27 minutes per year for 165 years. Delivery of a piece of mail from New York to San Francisco declined from 600 hours in 1858 to under 12 hours in 1990 (or almost instantaneously, if one considers electronic facsimile delivery the equivalent of paper copy). Travel by air from Paris to New York took 7 hours in 1950, but it takes only 4 hours at Concorde speeds. To place a call from New York to San Francisco in the 1920s took 14 minutes; with direct dialing and Touch-Tone phones, the time has been reduced to 30 seconds. As the speed with which information, people, and objects move about the globe has decreased, so has the cost as well and the volume of such global transactions has risen sharply.

Information Age cities are the site of production, but they are also an essential part of the world's distribution and consumption systems. As hyperconsumer societies, such cities are driven to exploit increasingly distant sources of energy, manufactured products, and cheap labor to satisfy their huge needs for mobility, goods, services, entertainment, cultural objects, and amenities. As an earlier quotation from Brown and Jacobson suggests, all cities do this to some degree. The bigger, wealthier, and more complex cities become, however, the farther afield they must go to meet their consumption needs.

It is tempting to lay the responsibility for consumption-driven globalization at the doorstep of the Information Age. I argue in the following pages, however, that the roots of globalization run extremely deep, back in time before the Wright brothers and powered flight, before James Watt and the steam engine, before Columbus and the age of sail, before ancient cities and the Silk Road, even before the Neolithic Revolution (see Table I.2). Three to four million years ago, animals not yet fully human stood erect, surveyed the East African savanna, and took the first steps on a journey that is not yet completed and that may yet take us to distant worlds in a postglobal future.

TABLE I.2 Seven Episodes of Globalization and Related Bulk Flow Systems

Episode	Title	Approximate Dates	Available Bulk Flow Systems (representative examples)
1	Out of Africa	100,000–10,000 ybp*	human beings
2	The Neolithic Revolution	10,000–5,000 ybp*	domesticated animals and plants pottery, basketry sledges, canoes
3	Ancient Cities and Trade Routes	3000 B.C.–A.D. 1400	draft animals, human porters trade diasporas, camel caravans maritime cities wheeled vehicles sail-driven ships, amphora jars writing, paper, maps
4	The Age of Discovery	1400–1800	Chinese treasure fleet Portuguese caravel trading companies
5	The Partnership of Steam and Coal	19th century	coal and steam engine steamship, railroad telegraph, telephone
6	Petroleum and the Internal Combustion Engine	20th century	gasoline engines automobile, truck, airplane
7	The Information Age	1960–?	digitalization of analog information computers, satellites, lasers, fiber optics, television

*ybp=Years before present.

Episode One

Out of Africa

Although no humans were around to witness the sight, there was a time, between 200 and 250 million years ago, when the world actually was a single place, or very nearly so.[1] Until relatively recently, earth scientists regarded the familiar fragmented pattern of the continents as permanent and immobile: The continents had always been the way we see them today; they would forever be so. Then, in 1912, a German geophysicist and meteorologist named Alfred Wegener advanced the theory that the continents had at one time been joined together in a single supercontinent, which he named Pangaea.[2] Pangaea consisted of two connected landmasses: Laurasia, which included what is today North America, Europe, and Asia (minus India); and Gondwana, which contained South America, Africa, India, Australia, and Antarctica. Wegener based his theory on the observed fit of the continents (e.g., the way the bulge of Brazil nestles neatly into the west coast of Africa), as well as the presence of matching mineral deposits, climatic histories, and fossils on either side of the Atlantic Ocean. Missing from his theory, however, was an explanation of the mechanism by which such a change could have occurred.

To say that Wegener's theory was greeted with skepticism by the scientific community would be an understatement. At a 1926 symposium in New York sponsored by the American Association of Petroleum Geologists, Wegener (who was absent from the proceedings) was harshly criticized for engaging in pseudoscience and manipulating the facts to fit his theory. Within a few years after his untimely death in 1930, Wegener's theory had few supporters left among geophysicists or geologists.

Between 1930 and 1960, however, technological advances in a number of specialized fields provided the evidence that would not only confirm Wegener's hypothesis but also supply the explanation for how such a change could have taken place. Cartographers improved greatly their understanding of the structure of the Earth's landmasses, while seismologists made great strides in mapping the internal structure of the Earth.[3] The field of geological oceanography was born, leading to a much improved understanding of changes in the ocean floor. Geologists, using Ernest Rutherford's idea that radioactivity could be used as a geological clock, achieved much more precise chronologies of Earth dynamics. The discovery that the magnetic field of the Earth periodically changed polarity in regular patterns and that these changes could be detected in the volcanic debris on the ocean floor led a new group of scientists, called paleomagneticians, to the theory of seafloor spreading, a process they identified first in the Atlantic Ocean and then in the Pacific.

In the 1960s, these and other advances came together to produce the theory of plate tectonics. Far from being stationary, the continents are now understood to be floating on gigantic plates pushed slowly outward from continuously erupting fissures in the ocean floor.[4] Where these plates meet each other, the surface is disrupted by earthquakes; where they are separating, by volcanoes. At last, the paradigm shift begun by Wegener was complete and the theory of continental drift was firmly established as the accepted convention among geologists.[5]

The idea that Pangaea represents a kind of primordial global unity is a metaphor to help us begin the story of how we became a global species. But the fate of Pangaea is much more than simply a metaphor, for the fragmentation of the Earth's landmasses can be seen as the beginning of the process of globalization.

The splitting apart of the Earth's surface, and the separating of its landmasses, created gradients where none had been before. Gradients are lines that divide space into zones of unequal distribution of material objects, energy flows, or ideas. These lines are created by boundaries, both physical and conceptual, that impede the movement of matter, energy, or information. For example, the wall of a building is a barrier to the movement of heat and thus forms a gradient between the temperatures outside and inside the building.[6] Different resource endowments and demand curves create a gradient between the price of grain in New York City and on an Iowa farm. The vertical distance between a mountain peak and the adjacent valley creates a gradient of potential energy to be exploited by falling water. In the mass media, the role difference between a news reporter and her or his audience, as well as the different preparations each has experienced, create a gradient in information.

Much of the movement we witness in the world stems from nature's dislike of gradients. Air attempts to penetrate the building's wall to even out the temperatures on either side. The trade in grain moves the product from Iowa to New York to exploit its higher price in the latter, thus tending to even out its value in both places. Water falls from high points to low, turning mill wheels or hydroelectric turbines to convert potential to kinetic energy. Reporters transmit news of the day's events; the rest of us receive and absorb it. As if in pursuit of uniformity, mobility works to reduce the differential distribution of matter, energy, or information on either side of a gradient. (These are specific examples of Fourier's law on the propagation of heat in solids or Clausius's law that entropy increases in the universe to a maximum.)

When the Earth's landmasses were still connected, the planet's organisms faced relatively few barriers to movement and hence there existed few gradients. Alfred Crosby has written that Pangaea represented a degree of global biological unity unknown after the continents separated: "Two hundred million years ago the continents of the earth were parts of one immense world continent in which physical contiguity minimized the development of biological diversity. That is to say, the world's land biota, though it varied from one region or even neighborhood to another, was more homogeneous than at any time since, because true geographical isolation was very rare, except for ocean islands."[7]

In his book *The Columbian Exchange*, Crosby argued that the splitting apart of Pangaea 200 million years ago created a number of gradients (mostly water barriers, or as he refers to them, "the seams of Pangaea") separating the planet's flora and fauna and creating much more diversity than there had been prior to the movement of the continents. What Crosby calls the Columbian exchange involved the massive movement of plants, animals, and diseases around the world in the centuries following 1492, a movement whose effect was to eliminate gradients and restore some degree of the global unity and homogeneity that had existed in primordial times: "The two worlds, which God had cast asunder, were reunited, and the two worlds, which were so very different, began on that day [October 12, 1492] to become alike. That trend toward biological homogeneity is one of the most important aspects of the history of life on this planet since the retreat of the continental glaciers."[8]

Since virtually all of the species we know today emerged after the fragmentation of the Earth's landmasses into separate continents, their evolution along separate paths served to increase their diversity and the differences between and among them. Both Europeans and Native Americans were astonished at their differences and contrasts when first they laid eyes upon one another and the animals and technologies each was accompanied by. For Crosby, the great impact of 1492 was the centuries-long process of global exchange and homogenization that ensued from the Columbian encounter, a process continuing today at a greatly accelerated pace. It is almost as if humankind has been striving mightily to restore the global unity lost when Pangaea split apart.

Plate tectonics and continental drift are important to our story in yet another way, for they explain how our species came to be the way it is. It was one of the geologic collisions described and explained by the theories of continental drift and plate tectonics that led to the emergence of humans on the Earth. More important, the *way* in which *Homo sapiens* evolved, a conse-

quence of this geologic event, led more or less directly to the global imperative of our species, our need to spread ourselves and our cultures to every
spot on the planet, no matter how remote the place or daunting the journey.

⋄   ⋄   ⋄

Paleoanthropologists are today engaged in a great debate over which of two
models more accurately describes how humans came to occupy the entire
Earth.[9] Both models recognize that there were two great migrations out of
Africa; and they agree that the first, between 1 million and 700,000 years ago,
took *Homo erectus* to the limits of Europe and Asia. Here the models di-
verge. The first theory, dubbed the "out of Africa" model, asserts that we are
all descended from a common ancestor, a species that originated in a single
place in eastern Africa about 200,000 years ago. According to this single-ori-
gin theory, modern humans evolved in East Africa and then 100,000 years ago
began to spread across the rest of Africa and the other continents, displacing
all competing populations, such as the Neanderthal, that they encountered
(see Figure 1.1). The second model is called the "multiregional model." It
holds that humankind's ancestors arose at different places around the world
and gradually blended themselves with other species with which they came
into contact, producing thereby the mix of traits that we label as "modern
human." Thus, local populations of *Homo erectus* in Europe, Asia, and Australia evolved toward *Homo sapiens* with a significant gene flow between
them. This evolution lasted from about 100,000 to about 35,000 years ago.[10]

Fortunately for our purposes here, we do not have to choose between
these models. In either case, the critical characteristic of modern humans that
made expansion *both* necessary *and* possible was what set us apart from
other primates: our mobility. (It has been remarked that human beings are
the only animal that can swim five miles, run twenty miles, and climb a tree.)

The birthplace of humankind is now conventionally accepted to be East
Africa, more specifically the Rift Valley.[11] More than 8 million years ago, the
valley was much more shallow and less irregular than it is today, so equator-
ial Africa constituted one homogeneous biogeographical region from the
Atlantic to the Indian Ocean. The valley was home to the common ancestors
of both the genus *Homo* and that of our nearest cousin, the genus *Pan*, the
chimpanzee. About 8 million years ago, a tectonic event occurred that
brought about two important alterations in the Earth's surface: Sinking produced the Rift Valley, and rising brought into existence the line of peaks that
make up the western rim of the valley.

These geologic changes significantly altered the environment by disrupting the prevailing circulation of air. To the west of the rift, the air masses remained moist, fed by the Atlantic, whereas to the east the weather system
evolved into the monsoon, or seasonal, pattern we see today. Consequently,
the west remained humid; the east, less so. The west retained its forests and
woodlands, but the east evolved into open grasslands, or savanna.

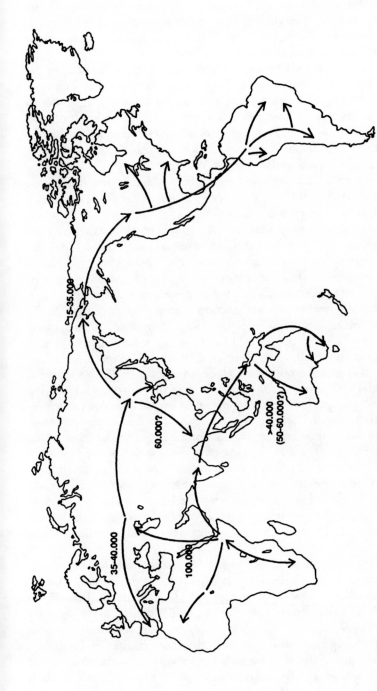

FIGURE 1.1   Map showing the probable expansion routes of anatomically modern humans (*Homo sapiens sapiens*) from their original birth place in East Africa to the rest of Africa and the other continents, including the probable date of arrival.

Source: Cavalli-Sforza, *The Great Human Diasporas*, Translation © 1995 Addison-Wesley Publishing Company Inc. Postscript © Luigi Luca Cavalli-Sforza. Reprinted by permission of Addison-Wesley Longman Publishing Company, Inc.

The common ancestors of humans and chimpanzees thus found themselves divided into two populations. The more numerous, those who remained to the west of the rift, continued to adapt to a humid, arboreal environment. Still tree dwellers, these primates found little need to change the way they moved about. Today, their evolution has led to the *Panidae*, or the chimpanzee. The eastern descendants of these same common ancestors were forced to invent a different repertoire of behaviors and physical attributes to adapt to a more open environment with few trees and different kinds of food and predators. These were the *Hominidae*, of which *Homo sapiens* is the sole surviving member. This theory has been labeled the "East Side Story" by its originator, the French paleoanthropologist Yves Coppens.

Coppens's theory tells us why and where humankind began; it does not explain why humans should be virtually everywhere on the Earth for at least the last 10,000–12,000 years. When Europeans began to arrive in lands previously unknown to them, they were met in virtually every instance by people. Early explorers did not regard this fact as remarkable, since cultural traditions, both literary and folkloric, had forecast it.[12] Nevertheless, if *Homo sapiens* is the only species that occupies virtually all the habitable portion of the planet, we need to ask how this expansion came about and why.

The mobility of human beings is a function of three important characteristics of our species: anatomy, technology, and social organization. In the long first stage of the emergence of humankind, our mobility derived from certain anatomical structures, such as our knee joint, which made bipedalism possible. The second source of mobility, which began to make itself felt somewhat later, between 40,000 and 10,000 years ago, was our capacity for making things (technology) and for organizing ourselves in social groups (which required communication). These skills also had an anatomical origin: the opposing thumb; the peculiar human structure of the tongue, palate, and throat that made speech possible; and the long-term dependence of the young on external care, leading to family structure and monogamy. Although all three characteristics are important for the physical mobility of individual humans, the latter two are also of critical importance for later episodes in our story because they gave us the power to impart mobility to material objects, to energy, and to information by means of the construction and operation of bulk flow systems.

Much of what we know about our earliest ancestors comes from examination of the oldest hominid remains yet discovered,[13] the famous "Lucy" skeleton discovered by Donald Johanson and his associates in Ethiopia in 1974.[14] Lucy was a tiny female who lived about 3.5 million years ago. Her ability to walk upright gave her and her species a competitive advantage over other apes, including chimpanzees. Although other primates dragged their knuckles on the ground as they walked, Lucy's anatomy—the structure of her arms, pelvis, legs, and (perhaps most important) knee joint—made it possible for her to walk upright.[15]

Some anthropologists have argued that the switch to bipedalism did not free the hands so much as enslave the feet. In other words, losing the ability to grasp objects with all four appendages was a lot to give up for the mobility of walking upright. This might have been so had Lucy continued to live in the forests, but living in open grasslands as she did, through mobility she and the others of her species gained several great advantages in the competition for scarce resources.

Lucy and others like her could walk long distances in search of food, and their greater speed and mobility enabled them to escape predators. Upright walking exposed a smaller area of the skin's surface to the sun's heat, so they could remain active into the heat of midday when other animals had settled down in the shade. Eventually, after millennia of evolution, hunting bipedal humans would be able to chase, outlast, catch, and kill running quadrupeds. (The human ability to sweat profusely also gave us greater endurance in the chase by dissipating metabolic heat more efficiently than the prey could do.) Finally, walking upright freed the hands of early hominids to make, carry, and use tools; reach for and carry food back to a central distribution point; and carry infants as they moved.

Our earliest ancestors were not distinguished by their intelligence. The size of Lucy's skull was only about one-third that of modern human skulls (about 400 cc versus 1350 cc). Intelligence, enlarged brain size, and a more complex brain organization would emerge as important human traits only sometime later, between 1.8 and 2.5 million years ago.[16] Our expanded intelligence manifested itself in the emergence of speech (made possible as well by changes in our throat and mouth) and in the fabrication and use of stone tools.[17] By about 1.7 million years ago, the next link in the chain of humankind, *Homo erectus*, appeared as the first of the large-brained species. (*H. erectus* was also the first species with a lower back structure that enabled running for long periods.) The brain of *Homo erectus* was too big for babies to pass through the narrow pelvis of a bipedal female, however; the forces of evolution solved this problem by ensuring that most of a child's brain development occurs after birth.[18] Although human and chimpanzee brains grow about the same proportion of body weight before birth, the brain of a human newborn is only 25 percent the size of what it will be as an adult, whereas that of a chimpanzee infant is about 46 percent of its adult size.[19] These characteristics of human brain anatomy had significant consequences for the social behavior of the species. With the delay of much of their brain growth until after birth, human infants were much more helpless and dependent on adults for their survival. The family and its division of labor was the solution to this problem.

There was a price to pay for the advantages of mobility, however. It presented itself in the form of an increased demand for food energy.[20]

First, there were the heavy energy requirements of bipedalism.[21] The problem we faced was not in going from apelike quadrupedalism to human bipedalism. Chimpanzees are only about half as energy efficient as humans when walking on the ground, whether they move quadrupedally or (as they can do occasionally for brief periods) bipedally. But chimpanzees remained primarily arboreal. Hominids evolved bipedally as an adaptation to forage for an apelike diet that was more sparsely distributed over savanna terrain. In comparison with other quadrupeds, however, such as horses, gazelles, deer, or dogs, bipedal humans are clearly energy inefficient. Humans burn more calories covering the same distance at top speed than do these quadrupeds and quadruped top speeds are greater than are those of humans. (One of the key reasons why humans had to learn to hunt in groups was for their effort to produce a positive energy balance.)

Then, there were the increased energy costs of our large brains. The brain of *Homo erectus* was three times larger than that expected for a typical mammal of the same size and the brain of *Homo sapiens* is five times that of a mammal of equal size.[22] The energy cost of the human brain eventually reached three times the level for chimpanzees. According to Richard Leakey,

> As every biologist knows, brains are metabolically expensive organs. In modern humans, . . . the brain constitutes a mere 2 percent of body weight, yet consumes 20 percent of the energy budget. Primates are the largest-brained group of all mammals, and humans have extended this property enormously: the human brain is three times the size of the brain in an ape of equivalent body size. . . . This increase in brain size could have occurred only with an enhanced energy supply: the early *Homo* diet . . . must have been not only reliable but nutritionally rich. Meat represents a concentrated source of calories, protein, and fat. Only by adding a significant proportion of meat to its diet could early *Homo* have "afforded" to build a brain beyond australopithecine size.[23]

Although it is impossible to construct the exact energy budget of individuals who lived so long ago, the available evidence suggests that *Homo erectus* probably needed to consume as many calories per day as do today's adult humans, that is, 2000 to 2700.[24] The six African specimens of *erectus* complete enough to allow estimates of weight and height all fall within the top 17 percent of modern human males and their brain size (about 900 cc) suggests fairly heavy energy drain in this department as well. Moreover, *erectus* was a very mobile animal, ranging far and wide across three continents, and adapting to great changes in terrain and climate.[25] In a conversation with Donald Johanson, the archeologist Rob Blumenschine assessed the food energy value of the marrow from the bones of an impala at about 1500 calories, or as he put it, about 60 percent of a hominid's daily caloric requirements. This calculation shows that early hominids needed about 2500 calories daily, almost exactly what an adult human requires today.[26] The obvious next question, then, is from where could early hominids have obtained such large quantities of food energy?

◆ ◆ ◆

To meet their increased needs for more food energy, *Homo erectus* became omnivores, that is, they ate virtually everything. To their established diet of berries, nuts, fruits, insects, and grains, they added meat.[27] Early hominids became meat eaters probably from scavenging the remains of kills by other animals and breaking the bones for precious marrow. Their life as active hunters probably came somewhat later, when they had worked out the social requirements for such a complex collective enterprise. Many anthropologists believe that adding meat to their diet was the crucial breakthrough for *erectus* because it gave our ancestors the ability to tap food energy supplies that would otherwise have been denied them, by first processing them through the bodies of other large mammals. Later on, when we reached the stage of herding animals, we reaped great advantages by giving mobility to a large part of our food supply as well.

The initial breakthrough was more apparent than real, however, for two reasons. The first was local: The apparently lush food supply of East Africa was still largely inaccessible to ground-dwelling hominids. The second was universal: Inescapable energy inefficiencies are involved in long food chains.

Vaclav Smil has argued that "both gathering and hunting were surprisingly unrewarding in species-rich tropical and temperate forest environments."[28] Most of the food energy found in these ecosystems is stored in tall tree trunks that cannot be digested by humans. Energy-rich seeds and fruits are a small percentage of the local biomass, scattered sparsely through the forest and usually inaccessible in high tree canopies. Seeds are often protected by hard shells that hominid jaws cannot crack and many of the forest's small animals, such as monkeys, are nocturnal tree dwellers largely out of reach to diurnal, ground-dwelling hominids. In contrast, open grasslands offer much better food prospects for bipedal meat eaters. Food energy through seeds or tubers is more accessible to gatherers. Mammals grow larger and move about in herds, making them easier to hunt or scavenge. Thus, according to Smil, the earliest hominids moved from tropical forest to open savanna in search of more accessible food energy.

At this point, the entropic costs of the food chain intervened. The basis for all life on Earth is photosynthesis, the only way the energy from solar radiation can be introduced into the planet's food supply.[29] A very small portion (often as low as 0.2 percent) of the sun's energy that makes its way to Earth is converted into matter, however, and there is no way this efficiency can be improved. The photosynthesizers (plants, trees, grasses) are at the base of the food chain. Upon their death, they decompose and their elements return to the soil for other photosynthesizers to use. Photosynthesizers are also eaten by animals (herbivores) able to extract energy from the plants; carnivores able to extract energy from the flesh of other animals eat the herbivores; and so on until the energy reaches the top carnivore of all: *Homo sapiens*.

As the sun's energy makes its way up the chain, there are huge and inescapable losses. A cow, for example, is able to store only 0.6 percent of the energy available in the grass on which it is grazing. This feature of the food network helps explain why meat eating is such a rare phenomenon in nature. Donald Johanson explains:

> In an average African game park, . . . only 1 or 2 percent of the animals eat meat. The reason for this lies in the nature of the food pyramid. The occupants of each layer in the food pyramid obtain only about 10 to 20 percent of the total energy of the occupants of the next lower level. By the time we get to the carnivores, who are perched precariously at the very top, the amount of packaged energy available is much smaller than that available to the herbivores they consume. Their numbers must of necessity be lower, to reflect their more limited feeding opportunities.[30]

In sum, our need for mobility derives from our high consumption of food energy. As a species, we consume a very high proportion of our body weight in food, so our need for food could not be met by supplies available naturally within easy reach of a sedentary population or that could regenerate themselves easily. The Earth's resources, although abundant, were not sufficiently concentrated to satisfy our needs, and they were limited by weather, uncertainty of harvest, and competition by other animals. Early hominids' search for secure food supplies, especially meat, brought them into direct competition with other meat eaters, which increased greatly the level of threat or challenge they faced from their environment. It also meant that they quickly exhausted the food supplies available from nature within a short distance of their habitat. In other words, even at this early date, we were eating ourselves out of our niche in the ecosystem.

Researchers from a variety of disciplines have pointed out two important characteristics of early hominid populations that derive from their need for large quantities of food energy: One, these populations were scattered very sparsely across the available landscape; and two, they were on the move almost constantly in search of food supplies.

For example, the Italian demographer Massimo Livi-Bacci has estimated that an area of slightly more than 120 square miles (a circle roughly 12.5 miles in diameter) of subtropical savanna could have supported no more than 136 persons who were surviving on what they could hunt and gather (slightly more than one person per square mile), and if the area in question were grassland, no more than 54 could have lived there (less than half a person per square mile).[31] (Livi-Bacci also estimates that at the beginning of the Neolithic Revolution, about 10,000 B.C., after several hundred millennia of growth, the total population of the Earth stood at only about 6 million.[32]) Smil reports research findings that average foraging densities ranged from just one person to several hundred people per hundred square kilometers (38.6 square miles).[33] Clive Gamble estimates that a group of twenty to fifty East African hominids living 100,000 to 200,000 years ago would have needed a "lifetime range" of more than 120 square miles to ensure their survival.[34] John Pfeiffer reports that a band of twenty-five prehistoric men (presumably augmented by some number of women and children) would have needed a "home range" of 500 to 1,500 square miles.[35] Roger Lewin notes that cave sites in southwestern France and northern Spain dating from about 30,000 years ago appear to sit in the middle of a "sphere of influence" nearly 20 miles in diameter, which meant that a typical population of fifty or so cave dwellers needed more than 300 square miles to sustain themselves.[36]

Even with such a large ecosystem to sustain them, however, *Homo* still was forced to keep on the move, to find and exploit new food sources, simply to survive. In his book *Stone Age Economics*, Marshall Sahlins interprets this imperative in terms of the "imminence of diminishing returns":

> Beginning in subsistence and spreading from there to every sector, an initial success seems only to develop the probability that further efforts will yield smaller benefits. . . . A modest number of people usually sooner or later reduce the food resources within convenient range of camp. Thereafter, they may stay on only by absorbing an increase in real costs or a decline in real returns. . . . The solution, of course, is to go somewhere else. Thus the first and decisive contingency of hunting-gathering: it requires movement to maintain production on advantageous terms.
>
> But this movement . . . merely transposes to other spheres of production the same diminishing returns of which it is born. The manufacture of tools, clothing, utensils, or ornaments . . . becomes senseless when these begin to be more of a burden than a comfort. . . . The construction of substantial houses likewise becomes absurd if they must soon be abandoned.
>
> Almost the same thing can be said of the demographic constraints of hunting-gathering. The same policy of *débarassment* is in play on the level of people, describable in similar terms: diminishing returns at the margin of portability, minimum necessary equipment, elimination of duplicates, and so forth.[37]

In his hypothetical case study entitled "Two Weeks in the Life of an Early Hominid," Clive Gamble "visits" a group of twenty to fifty "early time-walkers" on the African savanna. Their lifetime range of about 120 square miles would have been divided into seven habitats with varying food supplies. "The problem that faces the core group," writes Gamble,

> is how to gather the information to make the move to the best resources as food starts to run out in their current habitat. A solution is . . . two migration routes. . . . The core group moves between safe sleeping sites and feeding grounds. Several subadults take different routes and are temporarily out of contact with the core group. . . . The decision to move to the habitat with the best feeding prospects is taken on the "look" of the subadults who have just returned from that area. . . . This would be an example of calculated migration.[38]

Other scholars have described the migrating habits of specific groups of early humans. Lewin reports that early hominid population groups would probably need to migrate at the rate of about twenty miles per generation simply to refresh the ecosystem on which they depended.[39] Richard Potts, curator of the Department of Anthropology of the National Museum of Natural History, asserts that hominids living 1.8 million years ago had a "ranging distance" of 10 to 46 kilometers (6.2 to 28.5 miles) to obtain needed supplies, whereas 100,000 years ago, *Homo sapiens* ranged up to 100 kilometers (62.1 miles), and "the first hint of trade developed."[40] In his book on the making of Stonehenge, Rodney Castleden describes the nomadic life of Middle Stone Age inhabitants of Britain:

> People lived by hunting, fowling, fishing and collecting fruit, berries and nuts. A semi-nomadic life style seems likely, with each band of people using several contrasting environments relatively close together in a more or less systematic rotation. In the Stonehenge area, they probably walked from campsite to campsite, exploiting in turn the riverbanks, marshes and water meadows on the valley floors, the scrublands of the valley sides, the closed pine and birch forests and woodland clearings up on the rolling plain, and then returned to their base camps near the river to start all over again. There are signs that in the late mesolithic people had already started cutting down trees and we can only speculate about the reason. Obviously they were not clearing land for farming because farming had not yet begun, but they may have been creating grassy woodland clearings that would attract game animals for grazing.[41]

For many years, anthropologists have tried to combine into a single paradigm two observations: that early humans were forced to range far afield to find sufficient food and that they accumulated large deposits of stone tools and animal bones in a few specific sites that have been uncovered across the ancient world, but especially in East Africa.[42] For years, the preferred explanation was that of the "home base," a paradigm that brought together a number of characteristics of early humans, some empirically confirmed and others imputed or inferred.[43] For example, it was easily demonstrated that early humans ate meat, either hunted or scavenged, and carried food and stone tools over great distances to central locations, or home bases. In addition, anthropologists inferred that these home bases were the sites of a number of important social activities, such as food sharing, male-female division of labor, long-term dependency of infants, male-female pair bonding, and enhanced communication skills.

In recent years some observers have contended that the home base hypothesis is unnecessary to explain the accumulation of bones and stone tools in East Africa and that the social characteristics of home bases (e.g., food sharing, a proto-family structure, division of labor) probably emerged only long after the sites of accumulation were created. As described by Richard Potts, based on his study of the important sites of early human activity in the Olduvai region of northern Tanzania, these sites can be seen as an early attempt to cope with the energy requirements implied by meat gathering and preparation:

Once stone tools became involved in the processing of animals or other foods . . . , a new factor was introduced to hominid foraging—how to ensure or to facilitate the presence of food and tools together at the same places. By transporting, making, and using stone artifacts as part of the foraging process, hominids incurred an extra energetic cost not involved to any appreciable extent in the foraging behavior of any other primate. However, the cost of transporting stone must be viewed against the benefit of having stones in the vicinity of foraged resources that required processing with tools.

. . . Once stone tools and the processing of animals tissues became linked, the availability of transported tools and stone raw materials governed where in the foraging range hominids also carried parts of carcasses for processing. We know that at Olduvai the two resources, tools and animal tissues, were linked. . . . The creation of concentrations of stone and bone debris was possibly an effect of bringing these two resources together in an efficient manner.[44]

By means of computer simulations, Potts and his associates examined the most rational ways to subdivide a hypothetical foraging range to maximize net energy resources. The results vary, depending on assumptions about how much more energy is required to carry stone than animal carcasses: The greater the energy requirements for stone transport, the fewer the number of sites. The simulations showed that for maximum net energy production, the foraging range would be divided into areas centering on eight to twelve sites where stones and animal carcasses would be accumulated. These sites would over time begin to take on the imputed social functions of the home base, but it was the energy consequences of meat eating and stone tools that first drove early humans to gather together.

In addition to migrating long distances in search of fresh food supplies, early humans also severely restricted their own population growth by means of a variety of techniques, probably including limiting sexual intercourse, breast-feeding, infanticide, abortion, and abandonment of the elderly. Indeed, it is thought that population mobility and population self-limitation went hand in hand in hunter-gatherer societies. Göran Burenhult puts it this way:

> In present-day or historically known mobile societies, groups are not allowed to increase in size unless there is enough for all the members of the group to eat, even during the hardest of times, and in any case, it is impossible to carry more than one child during long migrations. Long periods of breast-feeding (which automatically reduces female fertility), abortion, and infanticide all serve to regulate population levels. As a result, starvation and malnutrition are almost unknown among mobile hunter-gatherers, despite the fact that they often inhabit areas with poor food resources.[45]

If early human populations failed to regulate their population and found themselves restricted to a single site, such as Easter Island, another scenario would be to grow to the limits of the resource base and then let natural forces such as famine, starvation, disease, and violent competition for food reduce the population. A third possibility, emergence of which we recognize as the Neolithic Revolution, was to squeeze more food energy out of a stationary resource base. Once we exhaust the potential of a stage of agricultural intensification, however, the preference of humans has been for mobility: Move ourselves to new resources or move the resources to us. As we have learned how to do these things, we have set in motion cycles of increases in the size and complexity of the systems on which we depend. In this sense, the first steps taken by *Homo erectus* to spread out from their East African origins across the rest of Africa and the other continents began a journey on which we are still embarked today.

Episode Two

The Neolithic Revolution

In the beginning, humans dealt with consumption needs by moving across the landscape, leaving behind entropic costs to be absorbed by abandoned ecosystems. Mobility, combined with draconian population controls and subsistence consumption levels, served to minimize our impact on the Earth. We lived from gathering food grown in the wild and hunting animals in their natural habitat; our material possessions were limited literally to what individuals could carry. Somewhat later, we began to engage in low-intensity management of migrating animal herds (culling out the weak or diseased animals for hunting), exploitation of birds and marine life (fish, oysters), slash-and-burn (swidden) agriculture, and pastoral nomadism. Eventually, however, we learned what we must do to remain in one place and draw increased quantities of food energy from the local ecosystem—more energy, in fact, than we needed to survive. The result was a change of historic proportions: a transformation from subsistence to surplus. This change we refer to now as the Neolithic ("new stone age") Revolution.[1]

In a limited sense, the word neolithic refers simply to food production based on cultivated crops and domesticated animals but achieved without metals; that is, before the manufacture of bronze or iron tools.[2] The revolution we label neolithic involved much more than the domestication of plants and animals to produce a regular and predictable food supply, however. Also involved were changes in transportation (watercraft and land vehicles, as well as the smoothing of surfaces for roads and the use of animals for hauling and traction), manufacturing (stone implements, woven containers, pottery, cloth, cultural objects), building construction (dwellings, religious sites, warehouses), social structure (urbanization, class differentiation, functional specialization), and culture (religion, organized warfare). Julian Thomas puts it in these words:

> It is not the adoption of the odd Neolithic trait or innovation into a Mesolithic lifestyle which represents the onset of the Neolithic: it is a wholesale transfor-

mation of social relations which results from adopting an integrated cultural system. Such a system has as its purpose not merely the provision of sustenance, the biological reproduction of the community, but its social reproduction, including the maintenance of power relations, knowledge and institutions. Owning a cow, or an axe, living in a house, or burying one of one's kin in a particular way does not make a person Neolithic. It is the recognition of the symbolic potential of these elements to express a fundamental division of the universe into the wild and the tame which creates the Neolithic world.[3]

All these changes had one paramount objective: to increase the quantity of food energy that could be obtained from a given amount of land through the application of increased quantities of human and animal muscle power and technology.

The neolithic was not so much a clearly demarcated period in history as it was a long phase of gradual transition from the countless millennia of foraging, hunting, and gathering that preceded it to the rise of ancient cities and empires that followed. Different parts of the world experienced neolithic changes at different times and in no place did the neolithic way of life completely supplant the prehistoric ways of hunting and gathering, at least not immediately. For thousands of years after plants and animals were domesticated, human settlements continued to depend heavily on hunting, fishing, and chance encounters with seeds and fruits. For example, when English colonists arrived in Virginia in 1607, the people they encountered, the Powhatan, derived about 60 percent of their food energy from cultivated crops, 15 percent from gathered foods such as berries and nuts, and 25 percent from hunted foods such as deer or fish. The agricultural "revolution," then, was more of a gradual transition, which Clive Ponting describes in these words:

> A fundamental distinction between agriculture and gathering, herding and hunting should not be drawn. No radically new techniques or relations between humans and plants and animals developed in the period beginning about 10,000 years ago. Humans had been involved in obtaining subsistence from the various ecosystems of the earth for many hundreds of thousands of years. . . . Each of the methods that characterise agriculture had been adopted by one or more groups at some time in the past, though usually in isolation. What was new was the combination and intensification of techniques that began to emerge in a few areas of the world about 10,000 years ago.[4]

✢   ✢   ✢

The earliest center of the Neolithic Revolution was southwestern Asia, more precisely the thousand miles between western Iran and Greece, including parts of what today are Iraq, Syria, Lebanon, Jordan, Israel, and the Anatolian plateau of Turkey.[5] From about 8900 B.C., semisettled or semipermanent "protoneolithic" communities existed in northern Iraq, where the people depended in part on domesticated sheep for their survival. These settlements, with a typical population of 100 to 150, should not be seen as villages or protocities, since they were not occupied year-round and did not house the variety of occupations and classes we associate with an urban economy. One example of such a settlement was Jericho, which housed a protoneolithic community by 7800 B.C.[6] Between 7000 and 6000 B.C., "aceramic" (i.e., before pottery) neolithic sites were occupied in parts of Iraq and Iran; some scholars see signs of this period as early as 8000 B.C.[7] Neolithic cultures with pottery existed at Catal Hüyük in Anatolia (Turkey) by 6800 B.C. and in Iran by 6500 B.C. By 5600 B.C., neolithic settlements with pottery existed in Greek Macedonia.

The neolithic way of life had its beginnings in the foothills of the Zagros mountains and on the Anatolian plateau, where water from natural sources was adequate and crops could be grown without recourse to artificial irrigation. By about 5500 B.C., however, these original settlements gave way to much larger communities in the nearby alluvial plains on the banks of the Tigris and Euphrates Rivers. Here, crops could be grown in sufficient quantities only under irrigation, and the early stages of the neolithic were replaced by the wholly different urban way of life associated with ancient cities, which I discuss in the following episode.

By about 6000 B.C., the first stage of the Neolithic Revolution was consolidated in southwestern Asia, where small villages had become the customary way to organize populations. The crops and animals that had been domesticated here in the fertile crescent spread to become the basis for the great river civilizations of the Nile in Egypt and the Indus in southern Asia. The revolution also spread into Mediterranean Europe with little difficulty because of the similarities in climate and soil; between 6000 and 5000 B.C., Greece and the southern Balkans shifted to an agrarian economy. By 4000 B.C., agriculture was established in many areas around the Mediterranean.

It took another millennium or two for Mediterranean crops and animals to spread successfully to northwestern Europe. The neolithic way of life arrived in Britain, for example, no earlier than about 4700 B.C.[8] By that time, a different kind of neolithic transformation had already begun to evolve on the shores of the new bays and estuaries created by the flooding that accompanied the end of the last ice age. As temperatures rapidly rose to something approximating their present levels, the mile-thick ice melted and sea levels rose dramatically. Over a span of 2,000 years, almost half of western Europe was submerged. Britain and Ireland became islands, cut off from the mainland by the newly formed English Channel and Irish Sea. The rising waters created numerous bays and estuaries along the new coastline, and these new ecosystems proved to be rich sources of marine life for human consumption. Lured by the easy availability of new protein sources, Stone Age Europeans began to settle down in semisedentary communities. Instead of staying constantly on the move, they established base camps near the coast, from which they could venture forth to hunt large game when the fishing seasons were poor.[9] A somewhat similar change took place in newly created coastal areas of North America, including, for example, on the shores of Chesapeake Bay.

About 3,000 years after agriculture began in Mesopotamia, that is, about 6000 B.C., the Neolithic Revolution began independently in two other distant sites: along the Yellow River in China and in the tropical highlands of Mesoamerica (see Figure 2.1). In China, several kinds of millet were domesticated by 6000 B.C., the first villages arose in the Yellow River area by 5500 B.C., and rice was domesticated in the Yangtze area by 5000 B.C.[10] From China, the neolithic culture spread to Korea, where it gradually became consolidated over four or five millennia from 6000 B.C. to about 2000 B.C. In Japan, a foraging culture known as Jomon, which had prevailed from about 10,000 B.C., gradually gave way to a wet rice culture in the southwest shortly before the beginning of the Christian era and in the northeast a millennium later.

A somewhat similar timetable was seen in the Americas.[11] In Central America, tomatoes and squash were domesticated by about 6000 B.C., and the critical staple crop, maize, was adopted by 5000 B.C. From the Mesoamerican highlands, maize was carried north where it became the staple food in the diet of countless North American peoples, including the mound cultures of the Mississippi and Ohio River valleys. Between 100 B.C. and A.D. 400, the Hopewell civilization in the upper Ohio valley exploited grain crops of local origin fairly intensively. These groups engaged in trade with areas as far away as the Gulf coast and Wyoming and eventually they received maize from Mexico. There are signs of maize in eastern North America as early as A.D. 100, but it did not become the dominant crop in the region for another seven centuries.[12] This new food caused a break in the Hopewell civilization by disrupting existing cultural patterns and requiring much higher levels of labor. The successor Mississippian civilization, based on maize and beans, occupied the Ohio and Mississippi valleys from A.D. 900 until the arrival of Europeans early in the sixteenth century. In South America, there is evidence of the domestication of the potato and manioc along the Peruvian coast as early as 8000 to 6000 B.C., with squash and many other vegetables, beans, tobacco, and cotton appearing in the archeological record prior to 1800 B.C. Maize cultivation appeared between 1800 and 1200 B.C.

✺   ✺   ✺

"Perhaps the most remarkable happening in our prehistory as a species," write Anne Birgitte Gebauer and T. Douglas Price,

> was the almost simultaneous appearance and spread of domesticated plants and animals in many different areas of the world between about 10,000 and 5000 years ago. What is astonishing is the fact that this process . . . appears to have taken place . . . independently in a number of different areas at about the same point in time. Given the long prehistory of our species, why should the transi-

FIGURE 2.1   The oldest and most important areas of agricultural activity.

Source: Cavalli-Sforza, *The Great Human Diasporas*, Translation © 1995 Addison-Wesley Publishing Company Inc. Postscript © Luigi Luca Cavalli-Sforza. Reprinted by permission of Addison-Wesley Longman Publishing Company, Inc.

MILLET

RICE

WHEAT, BARLEY

MAIZE, POTATOES, ETC.

SORGHUM, MILLET, ETC.

tion to agriculture happen within such a brief period, within a 5000 year segment of the span of human existence?[13]

Despite more than a century of research, scholars still disagree about the reasons for the origin of agriculture.[14] Richard MacNeish has identified the two principal competing paradigms to explain this greatest of all transformations.[15] Environmentalists, scholars whose tradition has evolved today into cultural ecology, believe that the transition to agriculture was driven principally by environmental changes, such as the rise in temperature that took place at the end of the last ice age. On the other side of the debate are those whom MacNeish calls materialists, or cultural materialists, who argue that aspects of human civilization, such as rising population, played the key role in the transformation.

In the opening chapter of their collection of essays, Gebauer and Price summarize the principal theories about the beginnings of the neolithic way of life. In the 1950s, the "oasis" hypothesis proposed that agriculture began when the end of the last ice age produced a much hotter and drier climate in Mesopotamia, forcing both humans and animals to cluster around the few remaining sources of water. Agriculture emerged, then, out of a symbiotic evolution of humans, animals, and the plants needed to feed them both. By 1960, there were enough data available on climatic conditions to show that there was no such climate crisis at the time and therefore no reason why humans would have needed to concentrate around oases. Instead, archeologists argued, agriculture was a highly desirable and welcomed invention that provided food security and leisure time, and once our ancestors recognized the advantages to be gained from farming, they began to do it more or less "naturally."

In the 1960s, however, an alternative theory appeared, one based on population pressure. Farming was now seen as back-breaking toil that yielded a poorer diet and less leisure time than hunting and gathering; the only reason why humans might have embraced such a drastic change in lifestyle was because we had no choice. We were in danger of being overwhelmed by our own numbers and agriculture was a last resort to feed a rising population. One early version of this hypothesis, known as the "edge" hypothesis, held that such pressures would have been felt first in marginal areas of the fertile crescent, so agriculture would have arisen first in these marginal zones.

Another version of this paradigm appeared in 1977, when Mark Cohen, in his book *The Food Crisis in Prehistory,* argued that agriculture was the response to the inherent tendency for growth in human populations, leading to global colonization. By about 8000 B.C., asserts Cohen, with all the inhabitable (given existing technologies) areas of the Earth occupied and population continuing to grow, agriculture was the only solution to the problem of overpopulation on a global scale:

The nearly simultaneous adoption of agricultural economies throughout the world could only be accounted for by assuming that hunting and gathering populations had saturated the world approximately 10,000 years ago and had exhausted all possible (or palatable) strategies for increasing their food supply within the constraints of the hunting-gathering life-style. The only possible reaction to further growth in population, worldwide, was to begin artificial augmentation of the food supply.[16]

Many other scholars have found the population pressure paradigm a convincing explanation. Peter Rowley-Conwy contends that in northern and western Europe a sedentary life based on newly available marine life led to such a population increase that the fish and oysters were no longer adequate to sustain the expanding groups. Agriculture was their solution. In other words, the transition from hunting and gathering to farming arose not from the failures of the species, but from their successes.[17] In his study of the historical impact of diseases, William McNeill suggests that human beings resorted to agriculture only after we had hunted to extinction most of the large game animals on which we had depended for food energy for more than a million years.[18] Luigi Cavalli-Sforza's research on the genetic map of Europe shows that agriculture spread out of the Middle East to Britain, Iberia, and Scandanavia as the people themselves moved. "The spread of agriculture was accompanied by movements of farmers," he argues, because

> it is very hard to change one's way of life, and the differences between the hunter-gatherers' lifestyle and the cultivators' were, and are, profound. The hunter wants to remain a hunter-gatherer because, under the right conditions, the lifestyle offers a pleasurable, easy existence. The invention of agriculture was probably dictated by pure necessity: either over-population or climatic changes causing fauna and flora changes meant that hunting and gathering no longer granted local human communities adequate survival levels.[19]

More recently, scholars have advanced a number of social theories to explain the origins of agriculture. Arguing that the transition to farming cannot be understood solely in terms of environment and population, these scholars believe that agriculture arose out of the unequal distribution of acquisitiveness and talent that endowed certain individuals with the ability to accumulate food surpluses and transform such surpluses into other items of value, such as rare stones and metals. One of these propositions, known as the "big man" theory, holds that food production was driven by social rivalries that led contending elites to engage in "competitive feasting" and food accumulation.

An alternative paradigm was offered by David Rindos with his book *The Origins of Agriculture: An Evolutionary Perspective*, which appeared in 1984.[20] Rindos challenged the belief that the domestication of plants was the result of an intentional act by humans to alter their environment in response to some perceived problem (e.g., climate change or population pressure). Basing his approach on the ideas of evolution and natural selection first advanced by Charles Darwin, Rindos argues that human and plant species evolved together (his term is *coevolution*) in a symbiotic relationship. Indeed, Rindos defines domestication as a situation in which predator (humans) and prey (plants and animals) cooperate instead of compete. The reason for this cooperation is simple: When predator and prey cooperate, a rise in the population of one brings about a rise in the population of the other, quite the opposite of what occurs when predators and prey compete. Initially, the spread of plants by humans and other carriers would have occurred by accident, but as humans and plants adapted to one another and evolved their cooperative relationship and crop productivity grew, so did human populations, and vice versa. Rindos's approach constitutes a warning against attributing too much rationality to human agents in the long transition to farming as a way of life.

Whatever the cause, the neolithic transformation did not occur suddenly. A more probable scenario would be for hunter-gatherers to establish a base camp from which they would conduct hunting or foraging expeditions as the seasons and the conditions dictated. Rowley-Conwy describes the process this way:

> Modern hunter-gatherers live in many different ways. Many ... are mobile, living in small groups and moving from camp to camp according to the availability of food. Such people have an intimate knowledge of their environment and monitor resources closely, showing great skill in the way they plan their movements so that food is available in all seasons of the year. Other groups ... live in a base camp all year, sending out hunting and fishing parties to satellite camps in appropriate seasons. The more sedentary way of life, of course, is possible only in areas where a variety of food resources is available in the immediate vicinity, and even these groups usually have to store food to get through the bad seasons. Other present-day groups of hunter-gatherers do both, staying put in the good seasons, and moving in the bad. This is perhaps the most common pattern. ... Enough is known of the Mesolithic period in Europe to suggest a similar pattern.[21]

↬   ↬   ↬

Given the enormous variety of plants and animals available to us for food and other agricultural purposes, it is noteworthy that relatively very few species were ever domesticated and all of these had been brought into the food culture of human beings by the close of the neolithic period. Subsequent civilizations have altered and combined these basic foundation stones of our diet, but no new species have been successfully exploited for four or more millennia. "Historically," writes A. J. McMichael, "a total of about 5,000 plant species have fed the human population. Today, approximately 150 species meet most of our nutrient and caloric needs, and fewer than 30 species provide more than 90 percent of human dietary energy. Just three species, wheat, rice and maize, provide half the world's food; potatoes, barley, sweet potato and cassava account for another quarter."[22]

Plant domestication began with the cultivation of grain, an enterprise that in all probability started accidentally. In the process of collecting and transporting wild cereals or fruits, some seeds would have fallen, taken root, and sprouted as if by miracle. Jared Diamond points out that humans would have unwittingly collected seeds and carried them to their home site in their hands, their mouth, or their gut. Thus, he concludes, "Our ancestors' garbage dumps undoubtedly joined their latrines to form the first agricultural research laboratories."[23] The purposeful sowing and harvesting of grain would have followed in due course as cause and effect became clearly understood.

The great civilizations that emerged from the Neolithic Revolution were all centered on a single staple food, a concept that many of us today find unthinkable, as Sophie Coe explains:

> The carbohydrate-providing staple, often with a name that is synonymous with that for food in general, without which a meal is not a meal, has no place in our thinking. Our usual reaction when confronted with the idea of eating a single substance, every meal of every day, is to exclaim at the desolate monotony of the prospect. But this is the way that most people have lived since the Neolithic revolution made it possible. Rice in the East, wheat in Europe, and maize in much of the Americas; these were the staples. Everything else that one ate was an accompaniment, pleasant but not essential.[24]

Chronologically, wheat and barley were the first grains to be domesticated, in the Middle East, followed by millet and rice in southern and eastern Asia, maize in Mesoamerica, and the potato in the Andean highlands. Wheat and barley were grown together at all early neolithic sites in the Middle East. The grains are highly nutritious and can be easily stored, and the return in food energy is high. Experiments in Turkey showed that a family working for three weeks harvesting wild wheat with a flint-bladed sickle could gather more grain than they could possibly consume in a year. All these foods are rich in carbohydrates and when combined with beans form a near-perfect diet for a sedentary but hard-working population. The basic grain foods were supplemented by legumes (e.g., beans, peas, lentils), oil-producing plants such as olives, fruits (particularly apples and grapes), fish, other marine food (oysters), and meat from domesticated and wild animals.

It is impossible to say whether the breeding of animals in captivity came before or after plant domestication. Some scholars speculate that animals such as sheep and goats began to attach themselves to humans when they discovered that the humans possessed a regular food supply that they were willing to share. Dogs were probably the first animal to be domesticated, not so much for food (although they were occasionally eaten), but to help in hunting and herding. The earliest known date for any animal domesticated for food is 8900 B.C., for sheep. Protoneolithic peoples in the Old World kept both sheep and goats; cattle and pigs followed somewhat later.[25]

At one time or other, neolithic peoples tried to domesticate almost every large mammal species that came to their attention. Jared Diamond asserts that 10,000 years ago there were on the Earth 148 "candidates" for successful domestication, that is, terrestrial, noncarnivorous mammals weighing more than 100 pounds.[26] These species were not distributed evenly across the planet; 72 were located in Eurasia, 51 in sub-Saharan Africa, 24 in the Americas, and 1 in Australia. In the vast majority of cases, domestication failed. Only fourteen species were ever successfully domesticated, of which thirteen were in Eurasia and one in the Americas. Thus, neolithic people relied heavily on very few species (as we still do today), of which only five came to be of global significance: sheep, goats, horses, pigs, and cattle. These animals were easily domesticated because, among other characteristics, they need not necessarily compete with humans for their food supply. Quite the contrary. These animals all eat plant food that humans cannot digest, so they enabled humans to tap otherwise inaccessible food supplies. In addition, the successful domesticates had to be noncarnivorous (the energy lost in the food chain makes meat eaters unattractive sources of human food), easily bred in captivity, docile, and even tempered, and live in herds with hierarchical social structures.

One important dimension of the globalization of life forms has been the loss of biodiversity.[27] According to Stephen Budiansky, since the Neolithic Revolution we have lived in an "age of interdependent forms," that is, a world increasingly dominated by species living in symbiotic relationship with one another.[28] Following David Rindos's paradigm,[29] Budiansky, Raymond Coppinger, and others have argued that the domestication of plants and animals resulted as much from "coevolution" of species as it did from human actions—that is, animals like cows and dogs adapted *to* humans as much as they were tamed or dominated *by* humans, and the same can be said of plants like wheat or (especially) maize. One of the principal ways that animals adapted to humans was by becoming more juvenile, that is, by retaining the traits of the young of their species into adulthood. Such traits as dependence, playfulness, docility, and respect for dominant individuals ensured that cows, sheep, and dogs would become part of our world, while animals with opposite traits, such as lions and tigers, would remain our enemies.

When predators and prey live cooperatively, their populations thrive and grow. Such is the case with the plants and animals on which the human food supply is based. When predators and prey are in competition, their respective populations rise and fall in alternating cycles. Such would be the case for animals that prey on humans, such as lions or tigers, were it not for the technological and organizational superiority of humans. As it is, humans and their codependent species will inevitably win this competition and the consequence must be the extinction of those species that cannot for whatever reason adapt to become more cooperative with humans. House cats will outlive tigers, then, because the cat's adaptability to humans makes them "fitter" in an evolutionary sense.

As humans have become a global species, we have been accompanied by other life forms with which we have coevolved for food supplies, mobility (the horse), or simply companionship (the dog). Without these coevolving life forms, we could not have become global. Some of these organisms (diseases) are not themselves beneficial to us but form part of the price we pay to enjoy the company of their host species (cows being the host of smallpox; horses, of encephalitis). Thus, globalization means that mutually interdependent species are gradually outcompeting more specialized and independent species, and this leads to the latters' extinction. So, globalization of life means the loss of biodiversity and the increase in the percent of animal biomass represented by humans and our domesticated species.

Once the neolithic transition had been consolidated in its several locations, the various food supplies of domesticated plants and animals remained isolated from each other for another three to four millennia. "By about 2000 B.C.," explains Clive Ponting,

> all the major crops and animals that make up the contemporary agricultural systems of the world had been domesticated. However, for thousands of years there were separate streams of agricultural development as a result of lack of contact between Eurasia and the Americas and even between different parts of Europe and Asia. Then, in two waves, the various separate systems were brought together. From the seventh century AD Islamic traders brought many of the semi-tropical crops of south-east Asia to the Near East and the Mediterranean. Then, much later, in the sixteenth century American crops were brought to Europe (and eventually Asia) and European plants and animals were taken to the Americas and Australasia.[30]

But the domestication of plants and animals was only the most obvious component of the Neolithic Revolution. In addition, early farmers had to invent an array of technologies to manipulate their new plant and animal domesticates better, including tools to harvest crops and process food and hides, and barriers and restraints to control animal movement.[31] More important—and to return to the terminology introduced at the beginning of this book—early neolithic peoples had to invent bulk flow technologies that would enable them to move resources and waste materials from one place to another: containers in which to store the materials (pottery), structures in which to store the containers (warehouses),[32] and vehicles and vessels to move the containers (the origin of waterborne trade).

One of the most important materials to the Neolithic Revolution was flint, from which ax heads and other tools could be fashioned. Where the neolithic began to penetrate dense forests, timber clearance required effective cutting tools. In all neolithic societies, tools were needed to harvest grain, scrape hides, grind grain,[33] and so forth. In Europe, flint mining was carried out in Britain and across the continent from Portugal to Poland. Flint miners became one of the first specialized crafts supported by the food surpluses of the neolithic economy.

In neolithic times, travel was principally by water, roadways being virtually nonexistent and animal traction yet to be discovered. Most early neolithic settlements had access to rivers, which served as the arteries of the economy; some open sea travel can also be documented by archeological finds throughout the Mediterranean and on either side of the Irish Sea. Boats were constructed from a wide variety of materials, depending on what nature provided: bundles of papryus along the Nile, wooden logs on the Congo, hides stretched over frames on the Tigris and Euphrates. Dugout canoes appeared sometime after polished stone axes, about 2500 B.C. in Europe.

Land travel was particularly arduous. Sledges were the only land vehicle available to early neolithic peoples and (apart from humans) dogs were the only source of traction for them. The wheel and its associated changes did not appear until about 3000 B.C. in the Middle East and about 500 B.C. in Europe; its story properly belongs to the following episode, as does the domestication of animals for pulling wheeled vehicles. (The horse was introduced into the Near East as a draft animal about 2300 B.C. By 1600 B.C., the Assyrians had learned how to mount and ride the animal, and the horse-drawn chariot appeared in various parts of the ancient world.[34])

By about 10,000 B.C., pathways beaten first by animal hooves and then by human feet were in use to connect campsites with food and water supplies. When Europeans arrived in North America, they found an extensive network of beaten paths connecting villages and hunting sites, most just wide enough for single-file traffic. Manufactured paths, the product of deliberate human intervention to reshape the landscape, have been identified in Britain as early as 5000 B.C.

Once human beings adopted a sedentary lifestyle and began to extract increased quantities of food energy from the soil, they were confronted with the need to store some amount of surplus; from these demands flowed history's first examples of crafts and artisanry. The earliest known woven baskets, made from wheat straw, are from Catal Hüyük (6500 B.C.). All of the earliest neolithic settlements, from Egypt to East and Central Africa, contain some evidence that weaving was one of their first technological discoveries. Although mesolithic peoples knew how to use fibers or animal skins for binding or sewing, spinning and weaving were not known until the neolithic period. Leather and stone were also used to fashion containers in these early settlements. Pottery made from clay may have antedated the Neolithic Revolution. Remnants of clay pottery found at Catal Hüyük have been dated from 6800 B.C. The art of working clay is quite an intricate process that probably was discovered by accident and proceeded at first through long periods of trial and error. Before the potter's wheel was invented, about 3250

B.C., potters built up their vessels in spirals of clay, a technique still being used in the Americas when Europeans arrived.

Judging from the excavations of settlements dating from 7500 to 8000 B.C., humans began to accumulate debris almost as soon as they settled down and began to farm. At Jericho, for example, a mound of debris, called a *tell*, had risen to a height of some forty-five feet even before the first pottery appeared. As early as 6800 B.C., Jericho had a population of about 2,000 people living in homes made of mud bricks, with roofs of plastered branches and beaten mud floors. By about this same date, Catal Hüyük covered thirty-two acres and contained about 8,000 people. Homes in Catal Hüyük had living rooms with built-in furniture, hearths and ovens, and storerooms. In other climates, in northern Europe for example, dwellings were constructed of abundant oak logs by about 3000 B.C.; in Britain and Ireland villages from about 2000 B.C. were constructed from logs and locally quarried stone.[35]

      ❧   ❧   ❧

The first consequence of the Neolithic Revolution was felt in the number of humans on the Earth. The transition to agriculture had both negative and positive consequences for population growth.[36] The positive effects appear to have been principally economic, social, and cultural: Small children became more valuable because they could perform useful chores around the home and farm, women in a sedentary society could afford to have more children than they could carry in their arms, and families had the ability and incentive to plan ahead for the long-term future. The negative effects were, on the whole, biological: People in close contact with animals for the first time began to acquire diseases previously unknown in human populations, humans living in dense concentrations spread diseases more quickly and effectively, and the appearance of food surpluses stimulated intergroup violence at a level not known in hunter-gatherer societies. One possible benefit of agriculture—the ability of a well-fed population to better resist infectious diseases—seems not to have had a significant long-term impact on population levels, either because farmers in fact had a worse diet than hunter-gatherers or because the increase in food supply was more than offset by the increase in population.

In any case, the effects of the Neolithic Revolution were felt more on fertility than on mortality; both increased, but the former rose at a faster pace. The net result was to cause population to rise at unprecedented rates. Estimates of world population at the beginning of the neolithic period range from 4 to 6 million.[37] We can consider this the more or less natural carrying capacity of the planet, that is, without the use of technology to extract additional resources from the Earth. In the 30,000 years prior to the neolithic era, population had grown at the barely perceptible rate of 0.008 percent annually. By the beginning of the Christian era, some 8,000 years later, the Earth's population had reached approximately 252 million and was expanding at the

rate of 0.037 percent per year, still extremely low compared to today's figures, but four times as fast as had been the case before the discovery of agriculture.

The next result of the Neolithic Revolution was an increase in the proportion of the population dedicated to nonagricultural pursuits, which led to the
emergence of classes of people whose labor was not needed to maintain a
precarious food supply. Because the fate of a settlement's food supply was
still believed to rest in the hands of the supernatural, religious elites were
among the first of such nonagrarian classes. Their contribution to a bounti-
ful harvest was to intercede with the gods and goddesses to seek their bless-
ing for the community's labors. But religious practices implied ritual, and
rituals needed sacred places, whose construction called for a significant share
of the available labor supply. For example, Rodney Castleden has estimated
that the various stone monuments of Stonehenge, erected between 3100 and
1800 B.C., required about 2.7 million worker hours, mostly from young
teenagers. The second phase of Stonehenge, about 2150 B.C., required the
movement of some 125 four-ton megaliths by boat from Wales over a route
220 to 400 miles long, a task that would have cost about 840,000 worker
hours. The third phase, begun in 2100 B.C., required even greater effort: the
transport of seventy-five 125-ton sarsen stones a distance of twenty-five to
thirty miles overland by means of huge sleds. The total effort required for
Stonehenge III is estimated to have cost over 1.5 million worker hours. And
of course, the agriculture of the region would have had to supply these laborers with a substantial, high-calorie diet throughout the construction
process that lasted many generations.[38]

The emergence of agriculture is also connected to the beginning of cities,
but the nature of the relationship is disputed. Most scholars of the neolithic
believe that the agricultural revolution occurred first and the resulting food
surplus made possible the rise of villages, towns, and eventually the first
cities. Robert Adams, for example, writes that "the urban revolution . . .
rested ultimately on food surpluses obtained by agricultural producers
above their own requirements and somehow made available to city dwellers
engaged in other activities."[39] Jane Jacobs, on the other hand, has argued that
cities came first and their demand for additional food supplies drove the
agricultural revolution.[40] In Jacobs's view, small settlements grew up around
mineral deposits where trade in such minerals as obsidian would have been
concentrated. The first villagers, then, were people who worked these deposits and others who brokered the trade. Food supplies consisted of food
gathered in the wild and brought to the village, as well as wild animals
brought into the village confines for milk and meat. Eventually, out of their
experiences with these wild food sources, villagers would have learned
enough to grow their own food and domesticate their own animals; agricultural pursuits would have been relocated to rural areas as urban land became
more valuable for other uses. Whichever came first, it does seem clear that

both agriculture and cities needed each other in an interlocking embrace of supply and demand. Neither could have existed alone.

The problem was that, as Marshall Sahlins has pointed out, agriculture in the early neolithic period (i.e., before 5000 B.C.) was too underproductive, and agricultural resources too underutilized, to support large, densely settled populations. Taking as his model contemporary societies still in the swidden, or slash-and-burn, stage of agriculture, Sahlins found that these societies underused both land (density of settlement one-fourth to two-thirds as large as the potential), and labor (many people worked hardly at all and none worked as many hours as modern people). Sahlins theorized that early neolithic peoples were still organized in what he calls the "domestic mode of production," wherein the family was the unit of production. Key to the domestic mode was the fact that the family could handle virtually all the tasks and technologies of production autonomously, that is, without outside assistance. Production units were spread out widely across the landscape (Sahlins writes that "maximum dispersion is the settlement pattern of the state of nature") and units had little connection or commerce with one another. Finally, families had little incentive to produce a surplus greater than what they needed for their own sustenance throughout the year.

Unfortunately for the family, there were larger outside agencies that could not permit the comparative luxury of underutilization and underproduction. Beyond the family, power elites that Sahlins calls the political system came to depend on a level of surplus that the domestic mode of production could not yield: "The political economy cannot survive on that restrained use of resources which for the domestic economy is a satisfactory existence." Through various policies, the political system pressured households to increase production and to enter into the flow of commerce with cities and with each other. Before long, then, even "stone age economies" traded with one another.[41] To quote Gordon Childe:

> Complete economic self-sufficiency was nowhere attained. Everywhere intercourse between adjacent groups is attested to the archeologist by an interchange of objects. Such might result from accidental contacts between herdsmen and hunters, . . . from formal visits, from the practice of seeking a wife outside one's own village, and so on. It might lead up to a sort of irregular trade through which objects might travel great distances.
>
> . . . Such trade was not an integral part of the community's economic life; the articles it brought were in some sense luxuries, non-essentials. Yet the intercourse . . . was of vital importance to human progress; it provided channels whereby ideas from one society might reach another, whereby foreign materials might be compared, whereby, in fact, culture itself might be diffused. Indeed, "neolithic civilization" in part owes its expansion to the prior existence amongst still sparser hunting communities of a rudimentary web of intercourse.[42]

Early neolithic farmers discovered that not only did they have to transport food and other products in trade, but they themselves had to remain

mobile despite their desire to "settle down." For millennia, farming remained such a precarious enterprise that families were forced to move about
regularly to find and exploit fertile lands to replace those that their labors
had exhausted. In Britain, Castleden reports, soil was already declining in
fertility by 3100 B.C., some 1600 years after the Neolithic Revolution began
there.[43] To return to the paradigm of David Rindos, faced with a Darwinian
imperative,

> The most frequent response of any animal population to a decrease in carrying
> capacity is emigration. Emigration (rather than starvation or decline in per
> capita consumption) is especially likely if only one component of the carrying
> capacity is suddenly reduced. Part of the animal population will leave the origi-
> nal area in search of a place where the limiting resource is more abundant. Agri-
> cultural humans experiencing a decline in food supply could be expected to re-
> spond in the same way.[44]

The combination of these forces—demographic growth and pressure, urbanization, class and functional differentiation, incorporation into larger
systems, and the still-precarious nature of food production—meant that despite the Neolithic Revolution human beings still faced an expansion imperative. The increased food energy our ancestors managed to extract from the
Earth was simply not enough to enable them to rest on their accomplish-
ments.

By the time all these changes had been consolidated—about 5000 B.C.—
humans in a number of widespread sites had given up mobility in exchange
for a life tied to trying to extract additional food energy from a fixed amount
of land. But this additional energy came with quite a price tag. Each time
they introduced changes to raise the energy yield of their land, they discovered that the cost was greater than the value of the new energy. The vicious
cycle thus set in motion has already been remarked. The Neolithic Revolution—agriculture, bulk flow technologies, and the rest—did not resolve humankind's dilemma, first because the urban population grew faster than did
the agricultural productivity of the land around the cities, and second because the costs of population concentration (i.e., urbanization) placed new
demands on the environment.

Episode Three

Ancient Cities
and Trade Routes

The changes we know as the Neolithic Revolution were the spark that set off an explosion of related innovations in civilization between 500 and 3,500 years ago. Writing and mathematics were invented to maintain accurate records of property and commerce. Large draft animals had to be domesticated and harnessed to haul wheeled vehicles. Construction technologies and materials had to be invented to meet the need for temples, warehouses, and other large buildings. Navigation techniques and ship propulsion technologies were needed to allow the safe and speedy transit of open waters. And markets had to be created to connect producers with consumers and buyers with sellers.

A dual cultural revolution thus ensued. Cities arose and expanded to coordinate production and commerce, and trade routes were opened to move objects of value from where they existed naturally to the cities where people needed them. These changes were inevitable because as Fernand Braudel has observed, "A world-economy always has an urban centre of gravity, a city, as the logistic heart of its activity. News, merchandise, capital, credit, people, instructions, correspondence all flow into and out of the city."[1]

The two halves of this revolution were mutually reinforcing. Cities became the site for transaction services that linked the increasingly diverse and separated components of a complex economy. The switching, routing, and brokering of economic functions required an increasingly specialized workforce, housed in cities but fed and clothed from an agricultural surplus gleaned from an intensive working of nearby fields and waters. Trade enabled merchants to identify and exploit value gradients as these became more significant in the global distribution of resources. Until the advent of the specialized trading companies in the seventeenth and eighteenth centuries

A.D., trade across cultural boundaries required a special kind of intermediary, or "trade diaspora," comfortable in both cultures, fluent in several languages, willing to live abroad for extended periods, and housed in special residential areas of major cities.[2] These innovations made possible the production and transport of additional food energy, which in turn supported a social order in which a growing proportion of the population was relieved from the tasks of growing food to assume other social roles, such as priest, soldier, merchant, or bureaucrat.

By today's measures, most of these cities were quite small. The Aztec capital, Tenochtitlán; imperial Rome; or the capital of Han dynasty China, Xi'an, might contain several hundred thousand people, but most cities had populations counted in the thousands or tens of thousands, with territory measured in acres, not square miles. In the beginning, these cities housed a tiny elite plus the people needed to support their lifestyle and carry out their control and transaction functions. But eventually the demands of trading forced the city to expand its boundaries. Thus, the city, which came into being because of an agricultural surplus, was enabled (and forced) to grow by the creation of trade networks to bring vital resources to it from great distances.[3]

William McNeill has described the achievement of a socioeconomic base adequate to support an urban population as "a fundamental advance in human history." But, he emphasizes, it was not an advance easily or quickly achieved:

> In the third millennium BC, civilization had been unattainable upon merely rain-watered land. In the second, civilization had begun to spread beyond the confines of river flood plains; but in the regions where irrigation was impossible, it remained a tender and weakly rooted plant, dependent always upon a precarious concentration of wealth in the hands of a small number of rulers, landlords, or merchants. By contrast, in the first millennium BC, the overthrow of a particular political regime, the destruction of a given body of cultured landowners, or the interruption of an existing pattern of long-distance trade no longer implied the disappearance of urban life, and with it, the collapse of the economic specialization and social complexity needed to sustain civilization.[4]

It is surprising to see how fast ancient cities pushed against, and eventually grew beyond, the boundaries of their natural support systems. Despite small populations generally living at what we would consider bare subsistence, these ancient cities quickly expanded to the limits of their local ecosystems.[5]

Cities that confronted resource limits had three options. First, they could limit their populations or consumption levels. In a discussion of hunger in ancient civilizations, Lucile Newman et al. argue,

> On the family level, adjustment to hunger or the fear of hunger has often taken the form of intentional limitation of the number of children a family would

have. The prevalence of references by early authors to abstinence, contraception, abortion, exposure, and infanticide in times of want, suggest that these were strategies that were known and used in households for spacing between children or to limit the total number of offspring.[6]

Although self-restraint was often practiced at the level of the household, for societies generally it was seldom the preferred choice. City dwellers might be compelled to limit themselves if confronted with food shortages or disease might reduce the population by raising the mortality rate. But otherwise the comforts and benefits of urban life and civilization were too attractive and the costs of such a lifestyle too distant or ambiguous to make self-restraint an attractive choice. Another way to limit consumption was through colonization, that is, the exporting of surplus population to other lands. Of course, the success of such a strategy depended on the discovery of land nearby that was either uninhabited or inhabited by people who accepted (or could be made to accept) the new arrivals.

As another option, city dwellers could devise ways of extracting more food energy and other resources from nearby territories. This they did by exploiting local agricultural resources more intensively through irrigation, fertilization, and technologies such as the plough. In addition, they found that they could expand food output by investing increased amounts of animal power in the form of domesticated oxen or horses or of human power through slave or forced labor. In the long run, that is, over a span of several centuries, this option did not succeed. In most instances, the soil became exhausted, salinization ruined the land, and the control of so many unwilling laborers required measures of coercion with costs that eventually outweighed the benefits of increased food.[7]

Before 2400 B.C., for example, the city of Ur in Mesopotamia achieved large increases in agricultural productivity by building an irrigation network that fed the nearby fields. For a short time, the city's population grew and prospered. It was a false prosperity that could not last. In this region of Mesopotamia, the natural water table comes to within 6 feet of the surface, but by means of intensive irrigation, local farmers brought the water table up to within 18 inches. Salt was carried to the surface, killing most of the wheat crops. About 2400 B.C., wheat supplied about 16 percent of the grains produced around Ur. By 1700 B.C., wheat was entirely abandoned and the centralized control that Ur had maintained in its region had dissolved. And, Charles Redman concludes, "Many cities were abandoned or reduced to villages, and the emphasis shifted from producing as much as possible for the central rulers to just satisfying the needs of the local population."[8] It bears noting that some scholars interpret these changes in agriculture and food production as the result of climate changes rather than excessive irrigation. Arie Issar, for example, asserts that "rather than being caused by the people, the salinization may have resulted from a diminished flow of the Euphrates

and Tigris rivers. As a result, the inhabitants did not have enough water to ir-
rigate and flush the salts from their soils. A reduction in the flow of these
rivers would be a natural consequence of a warmer and drier climate."[9]

Constraints on overland transport technologies also limited cities' ability
to tap regional food supplies. Land transport via ox cart or donkey was so
slow and expensive that most ancient cities were located near open waterways to make it easier to import food and other supplies.[10] One revealing exception was the Roman town of Arles, in southern France, which tried to
supply its own food needs from local sources.[11] Near Arles was the great
mill complex of Barbégal, built about the fourth century A.D. The complex
consisted of sixteen waterwheels arranged so that water cascaded from one
wheel to the next, thus using the kinetic energy of the same water to drive all
the wheels. Water was brought to the mill via an acqueduct over a distance of
about seventeen kilometers. It is estimated that Barbégal could grind into
flour as much as 4.5 metric tons of grain a day, enough to feed a population
of about 12,500, which corresponds closely to the estimated population of
Arles in the fourth century. The mill complex Barbégal shows that the Romans possessed the technology of transporting water and harnessing its kinetic energy to supply local food needs without resort to extensive waterborne trade. That they did not do so more often was due, in the opinion of
Trevor Hodge, to their inability to utilize the pulling power of the horse.
Oxen were the animal hauler of choice for the Romans, and the harness they
had developed for oxen could not be adapted to horses without strangling
the unfortunate animals to death. Oxen were, however, painfully slow.
Overland transport, therefore, remained too expensive to justify the mass
processing of grain from regional sources that Barbégal signifies.

Ancient cities also had to ensure their inhabitants a supply of clean water,
which usually meant carrying it over some considerable distance, both before and after it was used. To support Rome at its height, a great system of
aqueducts was constructed to bring water from the surrounding hills.[12]
Every day, over 200 million gallons of water, about 1 million tons, was
brought into the city by a system of channels with a total length of about 350
kilometers. For about fifty kilometers of this length, the water flowed
through causeways raised high above the ground on arches or tiers of arches.
Other large cities throughout the Roman empire were similarly equipped.
To build such structures required a high level of engineering and design skills
as well as complex organization and control systems. Water supplies were
critical for the removal of urban waste as well. The Minoan palaces on Crete
were constructed with bathrooms placed over channels of moving water to
carry human waste away from the residential areas.[13]

Water was also essential for crop irrigation, as the example of Ur attests.
The total amount of water needed for various crops depends on many environmental and agronomic factors, but Vaclav Smil reports that typically a
crop of wheat needs a volume of water equal to about one thousand times

the mass of the harvested grain.[14] Thus, 1,500 tons of water are needed for a ton of wheat; 900 for a ton of rice; and 600 for a ton of maize. In most cases, gravity was not sufficient to move this volume of water, so a variety of lifting technologies had to be devised to lift water, including scoops, buckets, and so forth. All such technologies demanded enormous quantities of energy, either from humans or from animals such as cattle or donkeys.

If ancient cities did not limit their growth and could not meet their needs from local sources, their third option was to establish trade networks that brought distant resources to them, a major change in social order and technology. These cities had to be located on easily defended sites that provided access to food and water supplies. With few exceptions, they also had to be close to natural harbors connected to open waterways, the natural trade routes in an era when overland travel was still slow, arduous, and expensive. If by chance a great city lacked natural access to open water, its leaders had to construct satellite ports through which the city's import needs could be satisfied. For example, the city of Rome established a string of port cities along the west coast of Italy during the second and first centuries B.C. One of the most important of these, Cosa, reached its height about 100 B.C. It was the site of an amphora factory, a winery, and a fishery as well as extensive docks and a freshwater distribution system.[15] Another key port city was Ostia, located near the mouth of the Tiber River.[16] Ringed around the city's main square were the offices of merchants, traders, and shippers, each devoted to a specific cargo or offering service to a specific destination. Like other ports, Ostia also attracted establishments that offered less respectable services: bars, brothels, and a particularly low kind of restaurant known as the *popina*. From Ostia, a traveler or merchant could reach any point in the Mediterranean, from Greece and Egypt to Spain. The Mediterranean coast of Spain was a mere four days away by ship; the port of Cadiz, only seven days.

Scholars still debate the exact degree to which ancient cities depended on imported food. The case of Athens is illustrative.[17] One view is that the city's hinterland, Attica, was agriculturally poor and its population large and growing (120,000–150,000 in the early fifth century B.C., rising to 150,000–200,000 in the next century). Dependence on foreign grain thus began early and increased to the point where Athens imported up to 70 percent of its needs. A second view is that Attica was much more productive and the city's population grew more slowly, so dependence on foreign grain dates only from the fifth century B.C. and imports totaled no more than half of the city's requirements. Even scholars with this latter view concede, however, that by the fourth century B.C., Athens was permanently in need of imported grain. Imports were brought from many sources, including around the Black Sea, Egypt, Sicily, Cyprus, Syria, and Cyrene (on the coast of modern-day Libya). Despite increasing imports of food, however, recent archeological work reveals that to feed a growing urban population ancient

Greek farmers engaged in destructive land use practices that led, in the words of Curtis Runnels, to "episodes of deforestation and catastrophic soil erosion over the past 8,000 years."[18]

Because transport was still extremely costly, trade over long distances was dominated by items that had high value combined with low volume. Chief among these were luxury goods or exotic materials, the rare and expensive nature of which made them greatly desired by the tiny but growing urban elites. Gems, ivory, ostrich eggs, rare woods, spices, silk, artworks—these were the high-status goods that flowed across the early trade networks. These goods were the price the elites exacted for governing society and administering the transactions systems that connected cities to sources of supply.

We do not know for sure which came first, city growth or trade, but we do know that both developments had to happen more or less together for either to occur. Extensive trade networks seem to have emerged almost as soon as people began to live in cities. The very earliest city dwellers of Mesopotamia, about 3000 B.C., had need of imported raw materials, including metals, wood, and stone, and rudimentary contacts with distant people began to emerge even at this early date.[19] As early as the fifth century B.C., the Greeks had established trade routes eastward; the Chinese began to trade to the west during the time of the Han dynasty (206 B.C.–A.D. 220).[20] Trade between India and Babylon dates from 800 B.C. One of the earliest civilizations of northern India, the Maurya (321–185 B.C.) experienced an unprecedented expansion of both cities and trade networks during the last two centuries B.C.[21] In this chapter, we examine three trading systems of the ancient world: the maritime network in the eastern Mediterranean based on Crete; the combination of sea and caravan routes called the Silk Road that connected China with Mediterranean Europe, the Middle East, and southern Asia; and the overland trade system that connected pre-Columbian Mesoamerican cities with their agricultural hinterlands and with each other.

⊷   ⊷   ⊷

The Bronze Age culture of the Minoans existed on the island of Crete for two millennia, from about 3000 to 1000 B.C. Archeological evidence suggests that small groups of people had lived on Crete from early neolithic times. Their gradual expansion, together with some later migration to the island, probably from western Turkey, fueled the population growth recorded from about 2800 B.C.[22] At its height, the Minoan civilization was based on five small cities: Kydonia, Phaistos, Knossos, Mallia, and Zakro. At the core of each of these cities was a single large structure, interpreted by some scholars as a palace where the royal family resided and by others as a temple devoted to religious ceremonies.[23] Before the temples (or palaces) were constructed, in the Early Minoan period, Phaistos covered about 1 hectare and had a population of 300 to 450; Mallia, 2.6 hectares and 700 to 1,000 people; and Knossos, 4.8 hectares and a population of 1,300 to 1,900. After the construction of the temples, the cities grew by nearly an order of magnitude. By 1930 B.C., Knossos covered 45 hectares and had a population of 12,000 to 18,000.[24]

Whatever their nature, whether spiritual or dynastic, as these Minoan cities grew they came to depend on a fairly large hinterland for their food supply and on a regional trade network for an amazing variety of other products. According to Peter Warren, the palace or temple of Knossos, which covered 4.3 acres, needed a "natural territory" between 22.5 and 25 miles in diameter and an intensively worked agricultural region of about 2,500 acres to supply a population of several thousand people with wine, olive oil, and cereals.[25] Similarly, the palace at Phaistos covered only about 2.1 acres, but drew its food supply from an agricultural region of 70 square miles.

The rural system so essential to the survival of these cities consisted of widely spaced villages of 150 to 200 people; even smaller hamlets; and isolated single farmsteads, or villas. The people who worked these lands had available to them oxen and the plough with which to prepare the soil, bronze axes or adzes as all-purpose tools, and obsidian sickles for harvesting. Wheat, barley, and millet were the staple crops. A typical estate or villa near Knossos produced 15 to 20 metric tons of grain annually. In addition, the rich land yielded peas, sesame, hemp, flax, castor oil plants, grapes, olives, and figs. The practice of animal husbandry was extensive; cattle, sheep, goats, and pigs were all raised on the island. Bees provided honey, the island's main source of sugar. With so much food being produced in such great variety, the temples or palaces also served as storage sites or warehouses for the surplus. Most of the large central buildings included storerooms equipped with large cylindrical containers where grain and olive oil were stored between harvests. The palace at Knossos, for example, included storage rooms with a capacity estimated at 246,000 liters, enough to store the oil from 16,000 to 32,000 olive trees.

Even with this hinterland on which to draw, the Minoan people still found it essential to establish a trade network that covered the eastern and central Mediterranean up to distances of 600 to 700 miles from the island. Minoan palace-cities traded extensively as far north as Greece and Turkey; as far west as Sicily; and as far east and south as Egypt, Cyprus, and the Levant. To service this trade, Minoans could call upon a system of ports, harbors, and dry docks, most of which were located on their island's north coast, facing the Aegean. In addition, they established overseas trading sites arranged in three concentric rings: more or less permanent colonies on the islands of the southern Aegean; trading diasporas on the Greek, Turkish, and Egyptian mainland as well as on Cyprus; and purely transient connections across an outer fringe that stretched from Syria and Palestine to Sicily. Some scholars speculate that Minoan traders transited the Mediterranean and may even have traveled as far as southern Britain.

Most of the island's export trade consisted of products we would today describe as "high value added," that is, the result of the investment of considerable skilled labor. The number one Minoan export was decorative, painted, and distinctively shaped pottery, described by Rodney Castleden as "the finest pottery in the civilized world."[26] Minoan vases have been discovered throughout the Aegean and as far away as Italy, Turkey, Egypt, and Syria. Other important exports were objects of worked bronze, lead, gold, and silver; decorative ostrich eggs; woolen cloth and timber; and olive oil, which the island produced in abundance. Because many of their exports were "invisible," requiring the application of technical skill and artistry as well as information, the Minoans were, as Castleden puts it, "the Americans of the bronze age Aegean, exporting style and tone as much as products."

Because Crete supplied the bulk of the food needs of the Minoans (at least until about 1500 B.C., when population growth began to put pressure on the island's food supply), most of their imports were exotic and hard-to-find raw materials they used to manufacture luxury goods. To make bronze, tin was needed, and since Crete has no tin deposits, it had to be imported, perhaps from Italy, Spain, or even Britain. Copper and other basic raw materials were imported from Cyprus, Turkey, and the Greek mainland. Precious stones and metals came from as far away as Afghanistan and Babylon.

The discovery of a shipwreck off Ulu Burun, on the southern coast of Turkey, has revealed a wealth of details about Mediterranean commerce in the Late Bronze Age.[27] The wreck has been dated from the fourteenth century, no later than 1350 B.C. Metals were the chief cargo, including hundreds of ingots of copper and tin. Other products on board included aromatic resin used in making perfume and incense (carried in hundreds of amphora jars); food (figs, grapes, olives, almonds, and much more); ebony logs from Africa; elephant and hippopotamus ivory; ostrich eggshells and cobalt blue glass; bronze tools and weapons; balance pan weights; lead weights for fishing nets and hooks; gold and silver jewelry; and, of course, pottery. Clearly, inhabitants of the Aegean Bronze Age had moved quite far beyond the agricultural subsistence lifestyle of the first half of the neolithic period, and a far-reaching trade network was essential to support such a civilization.

↩   ↩   ↩

More than a millennium after the Aegean merchant ship went down off Ulu Burum, there began to take shape far to the east one of the most significant trade routes of the ancient period.[28] Later scholars called this collection of sea and land routes the Silk Road because Chinese silk played such a vital role in the transactions along the route.[29] These trade routes evolved from the uniting of Chinese and Graeco-Roman networks somewhat before the beginning of the Christian era. Their success was made possible by the power of the Chinese and Roman empires, the collaboration and tolerance of the nomadic peoples who lived along the routes, and the services of numerous traders and merchants who supplied intermediary services. In one form or another, the network linked China with Mediterranean Europe, the Middle East, and India for about 1,500 years.

Strictly speaking, the Silk Road was not a single "road" but an interconnected network of land and water routes (see Figure 3.1). Beginning about 300 B.C., India and China established trading connections by water with Greece and later with Rome. From India, the goods were carried by Arab traders through the Indian Ocean to the Red Sea or the Persian Gulf, then overland to the Mediterranean, and then on to European ports. By 100 B.C., Greek traders were already familiar with northwestern India, although their trade routes were all overland. Arabs still tightly controlled the sea routes between the Mediterranean and Asia.[30]

Extensive overland trade between Europe and China was made possible by the domestication of the camel. The two-humped Bactrian camel originated in Central Asia and was domesticated in Persia by about 2000 B.C. The Assyrians brought the animal to Mesopotamia by about 1000 B.C. Better suited for cold weather and mountainous terrain, the camel was used exclusively as a pack animal from the beginning. The dromedary, on the other hand, is a desert animal, better suited for hot weather and useless in rough terrain. Although the dromedary was earlier used in desert warfare, its service as a beast of burden was delayed until about the middle of the first millennium B.C.[31]

The Persians are credited with inventing the camel caravan, the institution by which trade with China was conducted, but caravan routes could not be established until the trading partners, particularly the Chinese, had consoli-

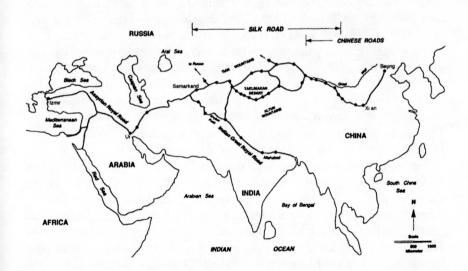

FIGURE 3.1   The Silk Road

Source: M. G. Lay, *Ways of the World,* copyright © 1992 by Maxwell Gordon Lay. Reprinted by permission of Rutgers University Press.

dated their control over the narrow strip of land (known as Chinese Turkestan) between the Himalayas, Tibet, the Taklimakan desert, and the Tian Shan mountains to the south and west and the steppes of the nomadic tribes to the north, in what is today Mongolia.

Control over this land corridor was finally established by the Han dynasty in 154 B.C.,[32] but it was from the beginning a precarious hold that depended on the cooperation of the nomadic tribes to the north. During the years of the Han dynasty, one tribe in particular, the Hsiung-nu, emerged as the principal threat, and in 139 B.C., the Han emperor sent a delegation west to make contact with the nomads.[33] The envoy and his retinue disappeared for thirteen years, ten of which he spent as captive of the Hsiung-nu. Eventually freed, the envoy made his way as far west as northern Afghanistan, to an area known as Bactria, an outpost of Greek culture since the time of Alexander the Great. Thus, this envoy, Chang Ch'ien by name, made the first enduring contact between China and Mediterranean Europe, in its own way as significant as the contact between Columbus and Western Hemisphere natives a millennium and a half later. Chang's return to China sparked great interest in the lands to the west—and to the south as well, for he brought back news of another great kingdom to the southeast of Afghanistan, a land that was "said to be hot and damp. The inhabitants ride elephants when they go into battle. The kingdom is situated on a great river." Chang had learned of India and land routes would soon connect it with China as well.

The first caravan to travel straight through to Persia (or Parthia, as it was then known) left China in 106 B.C. and development of the Silk Road was rapid from that moment on. Little of the trade was conducted directly by Chinese agents; rather, intermediaries brokered the trade at several points along the route. Half a century later, after the Romans had captured Palestine, the natural western terminus of the route, Chinese silks were being traded in Rome itself. Since the Romans had little the Chinese wanted except for gold, there emerged a trade of Mediterranean bullion for Chinese silks. The emperor Tiberius soon found it necessary to prohibit the wearing of silk because of the drain on the gold reserves of the empire.

For several centuries, there was no more significant factor than the Silk Road in promoting what would have been considered at the time a global economy and culture. The principal overland route began in Italy, Greece, Turkey, and Egypt; ran east through Tehran and Samarkand; split into two routes (north and south of the Taklimakan desert); and terminated in the Han capital of Xi'an. Other land routes connected this main road with markets in Russia and the Balkans and with India, Burma, and the rest of Southeast Asia. Sea routes connected southern China with Burma and India and then extended across the Arabian Sea, through the Red Sea and the Persian Gulf, and thence by land to the Mediterranean.

William McNeill refers to the establishment of this earliest global system as the "closing of the Eurasian ecumene," a transformation essentially completed by about A.D. 200.[34] From this point until 1500, the world system would consist of the Eurasian landmass with the northern steppes at the center and arrayed around the periphery the successive states in Europe, the Middle East, India, China, and—somewhat later—Japan. Beyond the fringes of this ecumene lay the lands that counted for little in such a system: the Western Hemisphere, Africa below the Sahara, and Australia.

Not only goods and raw materials, but ideas, knowledge, and skills (in a word, culture) were spread between Europe and Asia by the route.[35] Political ideologies, religious faiths, techniques of production, arts, and fashions were all exchanged along its length and breadth. Thanks to the Silk Road, Buddhism was taken from India to China and later to Korea and Japan, and Islam was spread from Arabia to Turkestan. The Chinese received glass, grapes and wine, wool, cotton, ivory, large horses, and papyrus. In return, West Asians and Europeans received silk; jade; tea; apricots, peaches, and pears; paper making; porcelain; jewelry; art objects; and precious spices, including pepper, cinnamon, ginger, and cloves. Products and ideas were not the only things spread by the commercial contacts of the Silk Road. Microorganisms causing measles, smallpox, diphtheria, and the plague were carried to new lands as well. William McNeill explains:

> When ... travel across the breadth of the Old World from China and India to the Mediterranean became regularly organized on a routine basis, so that thousands of individuals began to make a living by traveling to and fro, both on shipboard and by caravan, then conditions for the diffusion of infections among the separate civilizations of the Old World altered profoundly.... Within the circle of Old World civilizations, a far more nearly uniform disease pool was created as a byproduct of the opening of regular trade contacts in the first century A.D.[36]

Over the long term, commercial activity along the Silk Road rose and fell as a function of the stability of the empires at either end and the willingness of nomadic tribes along the route to let the travelers pass.[37] From 200 B.C. to A.D. 400, trade grew steadily, carried mostly by camel caravan across Asia. With the collapse of the Han and Roman empires, trade declined sharply for the two centuries between A.D. 400 and 600. After the rise of the silk industry in Byzantine territory after 600, there was a decline in the importance of the silk trade along the road. Other products were in great demand, however, and during the next 400 years to about A.D. 1000, there was a resurgence of commercial contacts along both land and sea routes, stimulated in large part by the entry of Arabs into maritime trade between East Africa, India, and the Mediterranean.

The Silk Road reached the height of its importance between 1000 and 1350, especially in the thirteenth century. From the 1240s, when the Mon-

gols first invaded Europe, European merchants visiting China and the Far
East were protected by the Mongol leaders, the great khans. Contacts between Europeans and Mongols increased for both religious purposes and to
trade for silk, porcelain, and spices. It was during this time, in 1271, that
Marco Polo left Venice to accompany his father and uncle on their famous
commercial expedition to China. In 1294, however, Kublai Khan died and
the Mongol empire, known as the Yuan dynasty, began to decline. In 1368,
the Mongols were driven from China; their successors, the Ming dynasty,
eventually plunged China into an era of isolation and European merchants
lost their privileged access to Chinese markets. The devastating effects of the
bubonic plague in the mid-fourteenth century also severely damaged trade
between Europe and the East. The fall of Constantinople to the Ottoman
Turks in 1453 sharply reduced access to the land routes across Asia and
forced European traders to seek ocean routes to the Orient. When, on May
20, 1498, the Portuguese explorer Vasco da Gama dropped anchor in the harbor of Calicut and thus opened a sea route from Europe to the riches of Asia,
the decline of the Silk Road was complete.

⊸ ⊸ ⊸

On the other side of the world, two other great civilizations also confronted
the problem of how to transport goods and cultures between settlements of
peoples. Unlike the civilizations of the Old World, however, the Maya and
the Aztecs lacked a number of things needed for bulk flow technologies: the
wheel, large draft animals, deepwater ports, and long navigable rivers. How
they compensated for these deficiencies and developed commerce offers another perspective on this human imperative.

For decades, scholars have debated the size of the indigenous population
of the Americas upon the arrival of Europeans in the late fifteenth century.
Estimates have ranged as low as 8.4 million total, with only 3 million in
Mexico, to as high as 90 to 112 million total, with Mexico between 30 and 37
million.[38] Although I cannot resolve here the issue of the total native population in 1492, I can at least confirm that in Mesoamerica and in the Andes,
cities had reached the point where they could not be supported by food supplies drawn from their immediate surroundings. Just like their Old World
counterparts, large cities in the Western Hemisphere quickly grew to their
territorial limits. Teotihuacán, in Mexico, with a population estimated at
50,000 to 100,000 about A.D. 500, and 150,000 or more by 750, depended on
resources drawn from a valley more than fifty miles long.[39] The pre-
Columbian Peruvian city of Tiahuanaco had to drain and reclaim 198,000
acres of the lakeside marshes surrounding Lake Titicaca to grow the potatoes
and other crops needed to sustain its population of 20,000 to 40,000 (400
B.C. to A.D. 1000).[40] Between A.D. 600 and 800, the Maya city of Tikal contained 10,000 to 90,000 people, with the latter figure being the most likely.
Squeezed into a little more than six square miles, Tikal had a higher population density than a modern city in Europe or the Americas. Indeed, such was

the growth of the Maya population that Michael Coe concluded that "by the end of the eight century, the Classic Maya population of the southern lowlands had probably increased beyond the carrying capacity of the land. . . . There is mounting evidence for massive deforestation and erosion throughout the Central Area. . . . In short, overpopulation and environmental degradation had advanced to a degree only matched by what is happening in many of the poorest tropical countries today."[41]

But of all the cities of the Americas, by far the grandest was Tenochtitlán, founded in A.D. 1325 by a people who called themselves the Mexica, but whom we know as the Aztecs.[42] At its height, in 1521, the city (now the site of Mexico City) held 250,000 people, out of a total regional population of over a million and a Mesoamerican empire of some 6 million.[43] It was the largest city in the Western Hemisphere and certainly one of the largest in the world at the time, larger than Venice in the fifteenth century (about 100,000) or Amsterdam in the mid-seventeenth (about 200,000).

Sitting on an island near the western edge of Lake Texcoco, Tenochtitlán faced a serious problem: how to feed its quarter-million citizens without a rich agricultural hinterland or the technologies necessary to transport food over long distances.[44] Aztec leaders solved this problem by a unique combination of transport technologies, land use innovations, economic institutions, and political control.[45]

First, I must dispel the notion that the Aztecs were poorly nourished or that they were facing famine when the Europeans arrived. Ross Hassig calculates that adult male laborers in preconquest Mexico were fed 2,800 to 3,800 calories per day from a diet that was largely maize, supplemented with beans and chilies.[46] According to Sophie Coe, the Aztecs relied on a wide variety of foodstuffs, including maize (prepared in a great variety of styles), beans, spices, fowl, fish, and cacao.[47] Some scholars have argued that the practice of cannibalism indicates that the Aztecs were so starved that they were reduced to eating their own, but Bernard Ortiz de Montellano shows that cannibalism was restricted to a very few members of the Aztec warrior elite and had a ceremonial function rather than a nutritional one. Far from being near starvation, concludes Ortiz de Montellano,

> the Aztecs actually lived in a resource-rich environment and exploited a superb variety of foods, which even in small amounts would have remedied all the shortcomings of a corn diet. It is also clear that the Basin of Mexico was not populated near the limit of its carrying capacity and that the Aztecs were neither malnourished nor suffering from protein or vitamin deficiencies. In fact, they were probably much better fed than the modern Mexican population.[48]

The first goal of Aztec food policy had to be to increase the land available for farming. This they accomplished by constructing artificial islands, called *chinampas,* in the midst of the lake system in the Valley of Mexico. These plots were created by dredging soil from the lake bottom and depositing it in walled enclosures made from wooden posts and interwoven vines and branches. When Europeans arrived at Tenochtitlán, the *chinampas* covered an estimated 9,000 to 13,000 hectares; each hectare could have produced as much as 4 tons of maize each year.

Despite these measures, the city could not have survived without food and other resources brought from some distance. Lacking any animal larger than a dog, the Aztecs used a system of human porters called *tlamemes*. These were members of a hereditary occupational group trained from childhood to engage in lifelong portage labor. Each *tlameme* could carry a load of about fifty pounds for an average distance of thirteen to eighteen miles before he was relieved. By themselves, however, the *tlamemes* would not have been sufficient to supply a city as large as Tenochtitlán. For that, the Aztecs took advantage of their access to a long series of interconnected lakes and developed their principal technology for moving heavy loads: canoes. Modern estimates place the number of canoes in the Valley of Mexico in colonial times at 100,000 to 200,000. Even as late as 1580, as many as 3,000 to 4,000 canoes brought cargo into Mexico City each day.

These technologies and social institutions were augmented by two special kinds of economic structures. Urban markets were found in nearly every settlement but were especially important in facilitating the flow of commerce in the large cities. The Spanish were astounded by the size of the market in Tenochtitlán, which daily attracted some 25,000 shoppers and vendors. In addition, there existed a hereditary class of merchants, known as *pochetcah*, who brokered the movement of commerce. Organized as a separate guild, the *pochetcah* lived in their own neighborhoods and enjoyed a status somewhat above that of the ordinary peasants. Some scholars speculate that with the *pochetcah* long-distance trade reached as far north as the Chaco Canyon area of New Mexico.

Finally, Aztec leaders depended on a system of tribute payments to mobilize resources and direct them into the markets of the capital and other large cities, augmenting the flow of commerce for economic reasons. Tribute payments were made in various forms; food was only one of several possible ways in which outlying cities and tribes expressed their loyalty to the imperial ruler. Four staple grains were used to render tribute payments: maize, beans, chia, and amaranth. According to Spanish records, the maize tribute alone amounted to 5,900 to 16,700 metric tons per year (depending on the conversion rates used for the *fanega*, a Spanish dry measure), enough to feed 40,000 to 150,000 people per year. By adding the other foods, Ortiz de Montellano concludes, it is clear that the people of Tenochtitlán could be sustained by tribute foods at a diet superior to today's standards.[49]

⊷ ⊷ ⊷

The rise of cities and their growing dependence on trade and transport forced ancient peoples to innovate bulk flow technologies with capabilities (volume, speed, etc.) and orders of magnitude greater than anything ever seen before. One such technology involved bulk food storage and transport. Greek and Roman shippers made extensive use of the amphora, a large (about 1 meter in height, with a capacity of about 26 liters) two-handled jar that transformed the trade in olive oil and wine.[50] The Aztecs had huge storage bins, called *troxes,* made of wickerwork and plastered on the inside, capable of holding 8,000 to 10,000 bushels.[51] Wheeled vehicles made their appearance early in this period, perhaps as early as 3500 B.C. in Sumer. Carts and wagons followed soon after, though the horse-drawn chariot did not appear until the second millennium B.C.[52] The more efficient use of animal traction required the innovation of better harnessing devices, particularly for horses, which are by far the superior animals for hauling. The horse collar appeared in China about the first century B.C.[53] By the ninth century A.D., it had made its way to Europe, where it was in general use within 300 years.

Finally, overland transport required manufactured roadways and improved road surfaces. The first indications of manufactured roads are the stone-paved streets in Ur that date from about 4000 B.C.[54] By 1200 B.C., a manufactured roadway connected the Elamite capital of Susa to Sardis in western Turkey via the Tigris and Euphrates valleys. An extensive road system existed in ancient China, including paved roads and bridges. India had a network of brick-paved streets with subsurface drainage, with bitumen used as mortar between bricks, as early as 2000 B.C. In contrast, in Greece in the fifth century B.C., practically the only roads of any worth were those built to ease travel to sacred places, particularly the sites of great religious festivals.[55]

The state of the art in road building among ancient civilizations was achieved by the Romans, whose road network ran from Britain and Spain across Europe to Turkey and around the north coast of Mediterranean Africa. At its height, about 200 A.D., the Roman system encompassed some 80,000 kilometers of first-class roads.[56] Moreover, travelers along these roads had at their disposal an ample supply of inns where they could spend the night as well as restaurants where they could dine, making it unnecessary to carry large food supplies with them. Regular postal service was available to Roman officials from the second century A.D. Mail service for short distances overland was fast and reliable; letters from Rome reached Naples in four to five days, on average.[57]

Despite some improvements in land transport, for centuries travel over land routes remained a hazardous, slow, and expensive experience. "For the majority of those who were obliged to move about," writes James Burke,

> journeys consisted of brief periods of security in the communities along the route, interspersed with hours or days of fear and danger in the forests. This was not primarily due to the presence of outlaws or wild animals lurking in the trackless woods, ... but because the majority of travellers had only the haziest notion of where their destination lay.
>
> There were no maps, and few roads. ... Rivers changed course. Fords deepened. Bridges fell. The safe way, indeed the only way, to travel was in groups. In the Middle Ages, a lone traveller was a rare figure. ... rumour colored the re-

ception of news even in the cities, when it arrived often after lengthy delays. In the fifteenth century it took eighteen months for the news of Joan of Arc's death to reach Constantinople. The news of that city's fall in 1453 took a month to get to Venice, twice as long to Rome, and three months to reach the rest of Europe.[58]

For millennia, then, traders would have to depend on water routes and sailing technologies to move goods and information. As noted earlier, the Aztecs depended heavily on their canoes, which were little more than dugouts, shallow-draft craft hewn from single trees, with neither sails nor rudder for maneuvering. Some of the craft were capable of transporting loads of more than a metric ton or up to sixty passengers.[59] Minoan shippers used rather small vessels with a single mast and a single square sail, steered by an oar mounted at the stern. To supplement the sail power, up to fifteen to thirty rowers worked on each side of the vessel.[60] By the beginning of the Christian era, the expensive and exotic cotton imported from India had been replaced by locally grown (and cheaper) flax as the raw material from which sailcloth could be made.[61] By A.D. 800, Arab traders in the Indian Ocean used vessels with triple masts, triangular sails, a steering oar, and outriggers for stability in difficult seas.[62]

It was also during this period that societies began to invent bulk flow technologies to speed the transport of information as well as food and manufactured goods. The increase in transactions over long distances forced ancient traders to develop ways of recording sales, tracking shipments, presenting bills for payment, and proving ownership. Minoan merchants employed scribes to record important information on clay tablets as early as 2100 B.C.[63] The art of making paper arose in China about A.D. 100 and spread via the Silk Road to India by the seventh century, to the Middle East by the eighth century, and to Europe by the thirteenth.[64]

Perhaps the most important innovation in the graphic display of information involved maps.[65] The oldest surviving map of the world, engraved on a clay tablet, was made about 2,500 years ago by the Babylonians. The earliest accurate measurement of the Earth's circumference was achieved by Eratosthenes, a Greek of Cyrenean birth, who in the third century B.C. recorded a circumferential distance within 200 miles of the distance as we know it today. Perhaps the most influential achievement of the period were the maps drawn by Claudius Ptolemy during the second century A.D. Although his maps erred by showing the Indian Ocean as landlocked, his work revolutionized the perception of the Earth by introducing grid lines as a way of preserving accurate proportions and distances. Ptolemy's maps were lost when the great Royal Library at Alexandria, Egypt, was destroyed, but their discovery and wide spread reproduction in Renaissance Italy played a key role in the Age of Discovery.

There is no doubt that trade networks like the Silk Road made possible the flourishing and spread of ancient civilizations to something approximating a global culture of the times. Nevertheless, trade as a way of solving the resource constraints of cities was, in the very long run, self-defeating. Trade requires bulk flow technology: storage and shipment containers like the amphora jar, warehouses to store them, ships to move them, harbor facilities to load and unload them, and navigation and steering devices to guide the sailors. Trade also requires coordination and control: accounting devices to register and monitor orders, shipments, and payments; communication systems; and methods of maintaining schedules and timing. Trade also implies markets where buyers and sellers come together in some critical mass sufficiently large to justify the enormous costs of commerce. These tasks all required more and more workers dedicated to smoothing the flow of commerce, and this led to larger and larger population concentrations with implications for food, energy, disease, pollution, waste disposal, transportation, and housing. Trade thus required the steady expansion of cities, and as cities grew, so also did the systems on which they had come to depend for their survival.

Episode Four

The Age of Discovery

Many people think of the global system as beginning on the morning of October 12, 1492, when Europeans first established lasting contact with Western Hemisphere peoples. From a broader perspective, however, Columbus's first voyage was simply one part (although an extremely important part) of a 400-year-long transition to a global society.

When the fifteenth century began, human beings could experience directly only a relatively small portion of the Earth and only to the extent permitted by the natural forces of wind, water, and muscle power. By the time the eighteenth century drew to a close, something approaching global systems of trade, demography, diseases, and culture had emerged,[1] and humankind was poised on the brink of the great technological leap forward that would be achieved by the harnessing of fossil fuel energy.

In 1400, Europe was a relatively minor appendage of the larger Eurasian landmass with a population of only slightly more than 50 million. By 1800, Europeans and neo-Europeans[2] exerted control over the Western Hemisphere and most of South and Southeast Asia and would soon establish a foothold in China and Africa as well. The population of the continent in 1800 was 146 million, with millions more of European ancestry living abroad.

These changes would affect the worldview of Europeans as well. In 1400, the view Europeans had of the world was only slightly changed from that of Claudius Ptolemy nearly a millennium and a half earlier. They were unaware of the existence of the Western Hemisphere or the magnitude of the Pacific Ocean. By 1800, the "mental" discovery of "America" was complete,[3] and Europeans knew almost as much about the size, shape, and location of the Earth's landmasses as we do today.

Episode 4 is primarily a story of the expansion of Europeans to Asia, Africa, and the Americas. But we cannot begin that part of the story until we have examined another great adventure, the voyages of the Chinese treasure fleet during the first third of the fifteenth century.

৵   ৵   ৵

A visitor to Earth in 1400, if asked to guess which people would lead the process of globalization about to unfold, would probably have predicted that it would be the Chinese. As Daniel Boorstin put it, however, "Fully equipped with the technology, the intelligence, and the national resources to become discoverers, the Chinese doomed themselves to be the discovered."[4]

Early in the fifteenth century, the Ming dynasty emperor Yung Lo (also referred to as the Yongle emperor, Zhu Di) determined to mount a series of naval expeditions to carry word of his grandeur abroad, to exact tribute from peoples around the Indian Ocean, and to engage in trade for exotic and highly valued products.[5] He placed in command of these expeditions a eunuch admiral who had attained much influence with the imperial court, Zheng He. The voyages, seven in all, began in 1405 and lasted until 1433. They were without question the grandest display of maritime technology ever seen anywhere in the world to that time.

The industrial design and manufacturing enterprise that produced the Chinese fleet was truly monumental. The initial order for ship construction was issued in May 1403. Between 1404 and 1407, two huge shipyards on the Yangtze River built or refitted over 1,681 vessels. The nearby provinces could not supply all the lumber needed, so vast timber reserves far inland were cut down and the logs floated downriver to the yards. At the height of the shipyards' operations, 20,000 to 30,000 people labored on the project, including carpenters, sail makers, and shipwrights. The ships were constructed in seven dry docks, each one 1,500 feet long. Dry dock construction, used in China since the tenth century, would not be introduced in Europe until the end of the fifteenth.

The treasure ships were themselves marvels of maritime technology. They were each 390 to 408 feet long and 160 to 166 feet wide, among the largest wooden vessels powered by sails ever built anywhere. (By comparison, Columbus's flagship, the *Santa Maria*, was only 85 feet long.) Afloat, they were "balanced like a scale,"[6] with stability created by their V-shaped hull, long keel, and heavy ballast. Their structural strength came from another Chinese innovation, watertight compartments. The largest of these ships carried nine masts and twelve square sails; steering was by balanced sternpost rudder. Navigation was primarily by water compass, and time was measured by burning graded incense sticks. The treasure ships were built for luxury, with cabins for imperial envoys, grand salons, and antechambers. These flagships were accompanied on each voyage by numerous other vessels, including "horse ships" carrying horses as well as cargo and repair materials, supply ships, troop transports, and (another Chinese innovation) freshwater tankers.

As naval expeditions, the Chinese voyages were mammoth undertakings. The fleets assembled 48 to 317 ships, and 27,000 to 30,000 men. (In contrast, Columbus's first voyage consisted of three ships and a crew of 87. Magellan began his trip around the world in 1519 with five vessels and 240 men, only 18 of whom survived.) The first Chinese voyage, which lasted from 1405 to 1407, was to Calicut, the important trading city on India's west coast, as was the second (1407–1409). The third (1409–1411) went to Taiwan, Malacca, Sumatra, and Ceylon; the fourth (1414–1415) reached the Arab port of Hormuz. The fifth voyage (1417–1419) was to escort home the envoys of the nineteen countries that had sent representatives to the Ming court. It covered all the ports that had been visited to that time and continued on to Aden at the entrance to the Red Sea. The fleet then sailed down the east coast of Africa to the port cities of Mogadishu and Mombasa. In 1421, a shorter sixth voyage saw Zheng He return early to China, but the rest of the fleet went on to Aden and Africa. The seventh voyage (1431–1433) took more than 100 ships and 27,500 men back to India, Aden, and Africa.

After 1433, there would be no more grand voyages by the Chinese treasure fleet. Almost as quickly as they had appeared, the treasure fleets vanished, done in by a series of imperial edicts aimed at turning China inward. By 1500, it was a capital offense to build ships of more than two masts; a 1525 edict authorized officials to destroy all oceangoing ships and arrest the merchants who sailed them; and by 1551, it was a crime to go to sea in a multimasted ship for any purpose. Early in the fifteenth century, the Ming navy was the greatest the world had ever known. A century later, it was virtually extinct.

Scholars have speculated at length about the reasons for China's turn away from its oceangoing exploration. No doubt, traditional Chinese values and Confucian virtues played a part. For centuries, Confucians had decried the role of trade and commerce in Chinese society, and merchants had been looked down upon as exploiters of the natural wealth of the country and of the people. Since the time of the Silk Road, Chinese leaders had proclaimed that they had no need for the goods of foreigners and trade was of value only to acquire gold, silver, or other rare and exotic items of great value or to exact tribute from subject peoples.

Also of importance were more immediate political and economic pressures. By the mid-fifteenth century, the Ming dynasty was engaged in more or less continuous warfare against the Mongols on its northern frontier. Support of massive armies in the north drained the country of badly needed resources and turned the rulers' attention inward, away from their coastal trade relations. The completion of the 2,000-mile-long Grand Canal in 1415 altered the system for the movement of southern grain from the Yangtze Valley to the cities of the north. Instead of transporting food north along the coast in oceangoing junks, the Chinese sent it along the canal on flat-bottomed barges, thereby changing the country's priorities in ship construction.

All of these forces came to bear on the politics of the Ming court, especially after the death of Yung Lo in 1424. For years, Confucian scholars and eunuchs had battled one another for favor with the court and the issue of overseas trade now became the focal point for their struggle. The eunuchs' traditional domain had been seafaring and trade. By striking at this sector of the national economy, the Confucians could not only restore a central value of China's traditional culture but rid themselves of troublesome opponents as well. For a time, Yung Lo's successors managed to keep these two competing groups under control, but the unexpected death of the Xuande emperor, Zhu Zhanji, in 1435, left the throne to a boy of only seven, Zhu Qizhen. The eunuchs sensed an opportunity to restore themselves to their former position of power, but they overstepped their limits and the Confucians eventually were able to seize control of the country's shipyards. With the construction of oceangoing ships thus ended, China's lead in naval technology disappeared. Three centuries later, with the Chinese defeat by the British in the opium wars, the technological superiority of Europe in naval affairs would be demonstrated decisively. As the global system evolved, then, it was under the leadership of the European states of Portugal, Spain, the Netherlands, France, and Great Britain, and not China as might have been predicted when the transition began.

✦   ✦   ✦

One of history's most intriguing coincidences was the withdrawal of China from the world stage at the moment when Europe (or, more precisely, Portugal and Spain) emerged to lay the groundwork for a global society and economy. Columbus's first voyage was more than just the beginning of one of the great transformations in human history. It was also the end of something as well: the resolution of one stage of the struggle by Europeans to expand beyond the limits of their continent, a struggle that had gone on at that time for more than 600 years. These early adventures—the Norse exploration of the North Atlantic and the Crusades—were defeated or blocked by superior technology, disease, war, and politics. As a consequence, in the mid-fifteenth century, various European peoples, in city-states like Genoa or Venice or the newly emerging territorial states like Portugal and Spain, began to look for other avenues of expansion.[7]

Around the end of the first millennium A.D., Europe's towns and manor farms began to experience a demographic expansion that would last three centuries.[8] After several thousand years of stability or at most incremental change, population growth and urbanization were beginning to take off. In A.D. 1000, Europe's population stood at about 30 million, approximately what it had been at the beginning of the Christian era. In the next two centuries, population grew by half, to 49 million, and in the next 140 years by half again, to 74 million. New towns were founded at a dramatically increased pace. In central Europe in the first decade of the twelfth century, fewer than 10 new towns were settled; in the last decade of the thirteenth century the number rose to more than 200.[9] To quote Massimo Livi-Bacci, "Settlements multiplied, new cities were founded, abandoned areas were inhabited, and cultivation expanded to progressively less fertile lands." At the beginning of the fourteenth century, however, as Livi-Bacci continues,

> there is clear evidence that this cycle of growth was losing steam: crises became more frequent, settlements ceased to expand, and here and there population stagnated. This slowdown was the result of complex causes, probably connected to an agricultural economy made less vigorous by the depletion of the best land and a halt in technological progress and subject to more frequent shortages due to unfavorable climatic conditions.[10]

Food scarcities were becoming a major obstacle to further growth and urbanization. According to Henry Hobhouse,

> In about 1300 the population of Western Europe was beginning to reach saturation point. There were local famines in most years between 1290 and 1350. Most of Europe was affected in the years 1314–17. . . . The limits of technology and husbandry had been reached in the West. There was little hope for the population except for cycles of famine, death, population growth, famine, death, and so forth. It was the classic Malthusian situation.[11]

The arrival of the Black Death in Europe in 1346–1347 arrested the growth of the continent's population for decades, at horrendous cost.[12] Between 1340 and 1400, Europe's population declined from 74 million to 52 million, but by the first decades of the fifteenth century population began to climb once again (to 67 million in 1500 and 89 million in 1600), with corresponding pressures on the land. As cities grew, European farmers tried a number of improvements to increase the productivity of the land and of the men and women who worked it: more efficient ways of tilling the soil, new farm implements, retention of a greater share of the harvested seed for later sowing, crop specialization and rotation, the use of dung and other substances to enrich the land, new crops, and improved techniques for cattle husbandry. Despite these measures, by the middle of the sixteenth century, according to Fernand Braudel, some "12 to 14 million Mediterranean inhabitants (one-fifth of the total population) were living near the starvation level."[13]

As important as they were, these improvements by themselves were not sufficient to resolve Europe's population crisis. Had it not been for several other measures designed to tap new lands, even these technological innovations would not have sufficed to feed the continent's growing numbers. The first of these measures was local: the bringing of new European land into production by clearing vast stretches of forest and through devices such as (in England) the enclosure movement.[14] Other measures required the discovery of new lands outside Europe, first to provide additional foodstuffs for European cities, and second to serve as an outlet for the continent's surplus population through emigration.[15]

Thus, as their cities grew, Europeans sought to expand to new lands and to open new trade routes. The first wave of such efforts to break out of the confines of the continent lasted from about 870, when the Norse settled Iceland, to 1453, when Constantinople fell to the forces of Islam. Between 870 and the late fifteenth century, the Norse explored the North Atlantic and established settlements from Iceland and Greenland to the northeast coast of North America.[16] These settlements failed ultimately because their small ships limited the size of the migrating populations as well as other animals; their lack of navigating technology restricted the range of their vessels; changing global climate made Greenland much less hospitable; and the relatively weak weaponry of the Norse did not enable them to overcome the natives' fierce resistance. (Alfred Crosby has suggested that one of the advantages of Scandinavians in particular and northwestern Europeans in general as global colonizers was their superior ability to digest animal milk.[17] By taking goats and cows on their voyages, they carried a portable supply of protein, something that most other peoples of the world could not do. This genetic feature gave Europeans a mobility that other peoples did not enjoy. We now know that lactose intolerance is actually the norm for human adults. Although almost all infants can digest lactose, the body's production of lactase, the enzyme needed to digest lactose, declines with age. Recent cross-national studies have revealed that people who suffer lactose intolerance make up about 70 percent of the world's population. Only 30 percent retain a lifelong ability to digest lactose, mostly northern Europeans and some Mediterranean and East African groups. In all probability, such a distribution is related to the contact of these populations with cattle many millennia ago.[18])

The second attempt at expansion by Europeans was the Crusades, which began in 1095.[19] But Europeans never really established a foothold in the Middle East. They lacked the maritime technology to transport large armies to the Middle East and keep them supplied; the native population was already dense and Europeans did not migrate there in large-enough numbers to correct this imbalance; and those who did migrate were killed in large numbers, chiefly by local diseases (e.g., typhoid), exactly the opposite of what happened later in the Western Hemisphere. By the time of the Crusades, the Middle East was already heavily urbanized and people had lived in close proximity to domesticated animals for 4,000 years. These two facts—the close crowding together of people with people and of people with animals—led to epidemics. Middle East peoples had learned to live with these, but Europeans had not yet done so.

For the history of global expansion, the decisive event of this era was the fall of Constantinople to the Ottoman Turks in 1453, which altered fundamentally the cost of trade between the Mediterranean and Asia. After the mid-fourteenth century, the fall of the Yuan dynasty in China had closed the

overland Silk Road. The maritime city-states of the Mediterranean, especially Venice, sought to keep trade flowing through a route that ran through
the eastern Mediterranean, across the Levant, and through the Red Sea or the
Persian Gulf to the Indian Ocean.[20] After 1453, this route was not so much
physically closed as rendered extremely expensive by Turkish policies of
controlling foreign access to ports in the Levant and Egypt. Venice and other
trading cities were injured by this development and each sought in its own
way to compensate for these losses. For its part, Venice struggled to maintain
its traditional routes through the eastern Mediterranean, even going so far as
to wage war with Turkey between 1463 and 1479. Other maritime powers,
especially Genoa, turned their attention westward to the Spanish city of
Seville and the capital of Portugal, Lisbon. Gradually, the combination of
Portuguese sailing prowess, Genoese trading expertise, and German financial capital shifted the focus of European trade with Asia to the western
Mediterranean. But for this alternative to be feasible, a route around Africa
to Asia had to be discovered.

Some scholars, basing their arguments on the writings of Herodotus, have
asserted that the Phoenicians succeeded in sailing around Africa about 600
B.C. Beginning in Egypt, they sailed through an ancient canal between the
Nile and the Red Sea, into and through the Indian Ocean, down the east
coast of Africa, around the southern tip of the continent into the Atlantic,
north to the Strait of Gibraltar, and across the Mediterranean back to Egypt.
The voyage apparently lasted some three years. A second expedition a century later was mounted by the Carthaginians, who headed west as the Portuguese were to do much later. The Carthaginians reached no farther than
Sierra Leone or perhaps the Gulf of Guinea before turning back in failure,
and none of these daring voyages left any mark of consequence on the Europeans' knowledge of Africa. Claudius Ptolemy's map of the world shows the
Indian Ocean to be landlocked with no water route around Africa. The truth
would not be known again until the fifteenth century.[21]

By 1453, when Constantinople fell, the Portuguese had already been engaged in their great search for an alternative route to the Orient for nearly
half a century.[22] Their capture of the city of Ceuta, which faced Spain across
the Strait of Gibraltar, in 1415, marked the beginning of a series of voyages
that crept steadily farther down the west coast of Africa. Establishing trading centers as they went, in 1416, the Portuguese reached Cape Bojador, and
in the 1420s, they occupied the Azores, the Canaries, and Madeira. The Portuguese exploited the islands' wood, dyes, sugar, and wine for export back to
Portugal, devastating the local ecosystems as a result. By 1444, they had
reached Cape Verde; by 1460, Sierra Leone; by 1471, the equator; and by
1482, the mouth of the Congo River.[23] In 1488, Bartholomeu Dias rounded
the Cape of Good Hope; in 1498, Vasco da Gama completed his epic voyage
from Lisbon to India. In the meantime, the rulers of Castile had decided to
support a proposed venture to discover a water route to the Orient by going

in the opposite direction: to the west. So powerful was his belief in the emptiness of the ocean between Europe and Japan that Christopher Columbus died without realizing that he had "discovered" a new world, and in so doing, begun a phase of globalization that lasted three centuries.

⊷ ⊷ ⊷

Many Europeans of the time, of course, saw the "discovery" of the "new" world in less grandiose terms. They were concerned, quite simply, with feeding themselves. And one of the keys to doing that lay, they thought, in the spice trade, more specifically with pepper.

The early voyages of discovery were made necessary by the crucial role played by spices in European life. As Europe's population grew, food supply became a central problem. Not only was it essential to find new sources of supply, but existing food stocks had to be treated to make them stretch farther and feed more people. Until the mid-eighteenth century, food poisoning was a frequent and serious problem, weakening a population already at risk because of urban overcrowding and infectious diseases.[24] Lacking refrigeration or other ways to preserve meat supplies, Europeans turned to spices to slow down the spoilage process or in the worst of cases cover over the taste of spoiled or rancid meat.

Pepper, as Henry Hobhouse tells us,[25] was used in ancient Greece, imported from the east via Arab trade routes through the Indian Ocean. It was also a heavily consumed commodity in imperial Rome.[26] Trade in spices was interrupted by the Muslim invasion of Europe but resumed after the Crusades. The Far East supplied most of these spices. Pepper came from the west coast of India; cinnamon and cardamom from Ceylon; cloves, nutmeg, and mace from Indonesia. These valuable products were transported along what were known as the Spice Routes, a sea network that stretched more than 9,000 miles from Japan to the Mediterranean. Arab traders carried the spices from the islands of Indonesia across the Indian Ocean to ports like Hormuz at the entrance to the Persian Gulf for transshipment overland to the Mediterranean and thence to European ports. As Anthony Disney describes it, Hormuz "was chiefly important as a nerve centre for transit trade to and from Persia, Arabia and the land route to the Eastern Mediterranean on the one hand, and India and southeast Asia on the other. Persian silks and carpets, Arab horses, European silver and manufactures, Indian textiles and pepper, Indonesian spices all passed through this thriving city."[27]

By the time these trade routes were reopened following the Crusades, population growth in Europe was putting heavy stress on food supplies, particularly meat. The problem was that, to cite Hobhouse, "the only preserved meat or fish in many areas was salted. Water to wash out this salt may not always have been available, or clean enough to perform this duty, or close enough to the cooking pot for the water to be changed frequently. . . . Pepper is a safe way of making oversalted meat or fish edible. Once used for this purpose, it became difficult to persuade the natives of Europe to return to pre-pepper cooking."[28] Indeed, population pressure had become such that by the end of the fifteenth century, writes Daniel Boorstin,

> when the Portuguese led the way to Asian seas, pepper was no longer a luxury table condiment but a staple of the European kitchen. The need for pepper was a by-product of the European system of animal husbandry. Without a satisfactory winter fodder, which would not be developed yet for several centuries, European farmers could keep over the winter only the few animals needed for draft and for reproduction. Meat from the others, which had to be killed, was generally preserved by "salting"—a process that required large quantities of pepper, in addition to salt, to inhibit the unpalatable effects of the salt itself.[29]

Prior to Columbus, then, as a consequence of the need for a palatable supply of meat for a growing European urban population, pepper ranked first in the spice trade between Europe and the Orient, ten times more valuable than any other spice in world trade. Salt, on the other hand, was obtained locally by evaporating sea water or by mining, and so was virtually ubiquitous (and heavily taxed).

The interruption of trade routes with the fall of Constantinople made the pepper trade problematic. When the Portuguese discovered the water route to the east in 1498, they sought to take advantage of their discovery by establishing a monopoly over trade in the critical spice. In 1501, the first Portuguese pepper supplies arrived in the harbor of Antwerp, an increasingly important trading city, according to Fernand Braudel, because 90 percent of pepper consumption was centered in northern Europe.[30]

The trade route between Lisbon and the Indian port of Goa was worth a fortune, but its operation came at a heavy price.[31] Pepper bought in Calicut sold in Lisbon at twelve times the Indian purchase price.[32] Even by the shortest route, the distance between the two cities was some 10,000 miles and the journey took up to eighteen months. During the sixteenth century, Portugal sent out twenty ships a year; one ship out of every ten would be wrecked along the way. Mortality was high. It was common for a third of the crew and passengers to die before reaching India. Nevertheless, at the height of the pepper trade in 1520, 6,000 tons of the critical spice were shipped from Asia to Europe via Lisbon.

Portuguese domination of the pepper trade lasted a scant three decades.[33] At first, trade routes through the Levant practically dried up. In 1504, writes Braudel, "When the Venetian galleys arrived in Alexandria in Egypt, they found not a single sack of pepper waiting for them."[34] By the 1530s, however, aided by the financial resources of Genoese banks, Venetian merchants had reestablished their hold over the Mediterranean sources of pepper and by 1533–1534, Venice was supplying 85 percent of the pepper to the French city of Lyon.[35] By the early seventeenth century, the amount of pepper shipped from Goa to Lisbon had declined to less than half the level of a century earlier. The combination of rising prices for the spice in India, falling prices in European markets, and aggressive competition from the English and the Dutch had very nearly ruined the Portuguese pepper trade. In 1628, the Portuguese created their own trading company to salvage their Indian markets, but the Portuguese India Company went bankrupt in less than a decade. By midcentury, Portugal had virtually abandoned the spice trade for which so much had been risked only 150 years earlier.[36]

Meanwhile, the Spanish determined to look elsewhere for a trade route to the east and Columbus's historic voyages were the result. When Columbus sailed west, toward what he thought was Japan, he may have believed that he was carrying out a mandate from God, and others may have joined him for gold or the glory of Castile, but in truth it was as much for pepper and other spices as for any other reason that he and his men risked their lives. The historic irony was that pepper was practically the only food product of consequence that did *not* flow back to Europe as a result of Columbus.

We can summarize the complex Columbian exchange this way:[37] The flow of people[38] and large animals was almost entirely from the Old World to the New and the flow of diseases was also primarily, but not solely, from east to west. The flow of food, on the other hand, was in both directions; but that of greatest significance was from New World to Old.

The first people to be transferred in massive numbers westward to the New World were not Europeans but Africans. To replace the decimated aboriginal Western Hemisphere populations and provide slave labor for European-owned tobacco, cotton, coffee, and sugar plantations,[39] 8 to 10.5 million Africans were shipped to the Americas, largely to tropical climes. Urs Bitterli reports that 9.8 million slaves were brought to the New World, most in the eighteenth century.[40] About 4 million were taken to the Caribbean; 3.8 million, to Brazil; and about 427,000, to North America before 1860. By 1950, their descendants numbered no fewer than 47 million.

Europeans, on the other hand, crossed the Atlantic in numbers that can be counted only in the thousands or tens of thousands until the great migration waves of the nineteenth century. According to Karl Butzer, by the end of the first century of European settlements in the Western Hemisphere (i.e., Spanish colonies to 1600, British and French to 1700), the total European population in the Western Hemisphere was only about 550,000.[41] The failure of the potato crop in Ireland began the movement in the 1840s and the numbers rose into the millions annually by the turn of the century and the advent of commercial steam-powered ocean travel. Between 1851 and 1960, over 61 million Europeans emigrated, the overwhelming majority to the Americas (chiefly the United States, Brazil, and Argentina).

The result of these population flows was, as Crosby puts it, that by the 1950s there were two Africas and two Europes, one of each on either side of the Atlantic.[42] Movement in the opposite direction, of native Western Hemisphere peoples to the Old World, was virtually nil, and those few who were sent to Europe as slaves or curiosities, such as the famed Powhatan princess, Pocahontas, died soon after completing the voyage. Indeed, less than a century after the arrival of Old World people, the original population of the Americas, measured, some think, in the tens of millions, or perhaps as many as 100 million, had been virtually destroyed by a combination of disease, brutalization, combat, and plantation labor, a loss of human life unmatched either before or since.[43]

Homo sapiens was not the only large animal to be transported to the New World. As early as Columbus's second voyage, European domesticated animals were brought to the Western Hemisphere, where they spread effortlessly as if flowing into a vacuum. The people of the Americas had evolved without large animals except the llama in the Andes and the bison on the North American plains, neither of which had been domesticated or bred selectively for use as a food supply. Cattle were introduced into the Caribbean by 1505, to Mesoamerica by 1521, and to South America by the 1530s. Horses were well established on the interior plains of both North America and Argentina by 1600 and pigs were a staple of the local diet through Virginia and the Carolinas by the early seventeenth century. With an ample banquet of plants on which to feed and a landscape largely free of natural predators, horses, cattle, sheep, and hogs spread quickly across the Americas. In some instances, these species spread more rapidly than the humans who had brought them, so that surprised explorers occasionally found the offspring of their original animals waiting for them when they reached a previously unexplored site. The introduction of oxen and donkeys as beasts of burden in Mexico transformed that country's social system by eliminating human porterage and changing market systems and altered the landscape by creating new routes of transport and communication.[44]

Organisms invisible to the naked eye also spread vigorously after Columbus. European diseases, especially influenza, smallpox, and measles, devastated an aboriginal population that was unprepared for them. (In all fairness, it was also a Spaniard, a physician named Francisco Xavier Balmis, who brought the technique of smallpox vaccination to the Spanish Empire. In all, between 1803 and 1807, more than 100,000 Latin Americans were innoculated thanks to his efforts. Tragically, during the intervening three centuries, the irreversible damage had already been done.[45]) The migration of illnesses has continued in modern times with cholera epidemics ravaging the Americas in the nineteenth century and AIDS performing the same function in the twentieth. The New World responded with a dread disease of its own: syphilis. The true origin of syphilis has been a matter of considerable controversy. Crosby assesses the evidence and decides in favor of the most widely accepted theory: that the disease is of Western Hemisphere origin and was transmitted to the Old World as fast as sailors could make their way from one port to another.[46]

Food products are the one area where the New World gave just as much as it got.[47] The flow patterns are complex, but essentially the Old World sent to the New cereals (wheat, barley, oats), fruits (oranges, lemons, apples, peaches), sugar cane, green vegetables, and rice, and got back in return beans (of many different varieties), maize (known in the United States as corn), the potato and tomato, the peanut and the pumpkin, squash, cocoa, manioc (or cassava), and the pineapple.

During the course of the sixteenth century, outbound trade from Spain to the Indies rose from 3,000–4,000 tons per year to 30,000 tons annually by the 1580s. Exports reached a peak of 45,000 tons in 1608, after which they began to decline in volume, while increasing in value. "In the sixteenth century," write Pierre and Huguette Chaunu, "and as late as about 1580–1590, [exports] consisted chiefly of grain, biscuits, wine, and [olive] oil. The huge convoys of the second half of the sixteenth century . . . brought to the Spanish settlers the three basic elements of the Mediterranean diet, the wheat, wine, and olive oil which enabled these Mediterraneans exiled in the land of maize to keep up long-established eating habits."[48] By the first decade of the next century, in contrast, Spanish exports to the New World consisted largely of manufactured goods, for Europeans began to cultivate their own foods by implanting Old World crops and animals in the Americas.

In the opposite direction, Crosby asserts, the arrival of maize and the potato in Europe were a key factor explaining that continent's population surge that accompanied the Industrial Revolution. In 1400, Europe's population was about 60 million; by 1900, after several centuries of exporting its people to the Americas, its population stood at 390 million. "In the seventeenth century," Crosby concludes,

> Europeans were able to "skip" a major [population] crisis. In the eighteenth century, they were able to launch directly into massive and unprecedented advance from a plateau of capital, knowledge, intact infrastructure, and experience built up since the 1300s, rather than to stagger through additional years of crisis and *then* begin yet more decades of struggle merely to regain what had been lost. For the first time in human history a people were able to break out of the cycle of advance and retreat, of ascent and crash, a cycle that matched every era of success with an era of dismay. We are at least partly in debt to the skills of Amerindian plant breeders for that breakout.[49]

Today, crops from the Old and New Worlds share more or less equally the burden of nourishing the world's population. William McNeill observes that in 1986 the world harvested about 1.8 billion metric tons of the four chief staple crops: about 44 percent (788 million metric tons) in New World crops (maize and potatoes) and 56 percent in Old World products (wheat and rice).[50] Moreover, all four foods are now cultivated and consumed throughout the world with little regard for origin.

After an exhaustive examination of all these transfers, Crosby concludes that the Columbian exchange was on balance a tragedy for terrestrial life forms. The exchange, he argues,

> has included man, and he has changed the Old and New Worlds sometimes inadvertently, sometimes intentionally, often brutally. It is possible that he and the plants and animals he brings with him have caused the extinction of more species of life forms in the last four hundred years than the usual processes of evolution might kill off in a million. . . . The flora and fauna of the Old and especially of the New World have been reduced and specialized by man. Specialization almost always narrows the possibilities for future changes: for the sake of present convenience, we loot the future. . . . The Columbian exchange has left us with not a richer but a more impoverished genetic pool. We, all of the life on the planet, are the less for Columbus, and the impoverishment will increase.[51]

Notwithstanding Crosby's negative assessment, the Columbian exchange brought the world significantly closer to a truly global system. By crossing the Atlantic in 1492, Columbus set in motion the flow of living things that would eventually yield a single global pool of foods, diseases, animals, and humans.

⤙   ⤙   ⤙

The period from 1400 to 1800 saw numerous advances in the land transportation networks that unified national markets, chief of which were canals and road construction. These were of great importance to the creation and growth of nation-states.[52] But for our story, the technological developments of greatest significance were those affecting long-distance travel across the oceans. Without these advances, the "seams of Pangaea" (to use Crosby's phrase)[53] could never have been crossed, at least not by large numbers of people, plants, or animals.

From 1519 to 1522, mariners under the command of first Ferdinand Magellan and then Juan Sebastian Elcano took humankind's first trip around the world, an adventure that marked a dramatic step forward in the process of globalization. The next three centuries would witness the steady expansion of Europeans (and neo-Europeans), their technologies and their seeds, and their animals and their microorganisms to virtually every part of the planet. Yet, if Magellan's crew could have returned to Earth early in the nineteenth century, they would have found little to surprise them in the way the sailors of the time navigated the world's oceans, because for about 300 years the technologies of transportation and communication remained fundamentally unchanged. Three centuries after Columbus, da Gama, and Magellan, humans still moved about the Earth within the constraints of the four forces of nature: wind, moving water, animal traction, and their own physical effort.

Global expansion via the oceans is often portrayed as an exercise in raw human courage and leadership, driven by European greed for mineral riches, Christian converts, and food. Here, however, I focus on the complex system of technologies and social institutions that came together around 1500 to make long-distance ocean travel feasible.

First, there was the matter of the kind of vessel mariners needed for voyages of discovery and exploration.[54] The huge 600-ton Venetian square-rigged ships that were the foundation of Mediterranean commerce would simply not do. For one thing, they were too large by perhaps an order of magnitude. Ships of discovery had to be designed for agility and maneuverability, and in any case, their cargo was information or feedback about what lay over the horizon, not tons of pepper, silk, or gold. Most important, the new ships had to be able to travel not only outbound, with the prevailing winds, but inbound, against the wind as well. It was not enough to sail south along the African coast; Portuguese mariners also quite naturally wanted to be able to return home. The solution to all these problems was the Portuguese caravel, modeled on the Arab dhows that had sailed off the coast of Egypt and North Africa for centuries. To sail at least partially into the wind, the Arabs had invented the slanting, triangular lateen sail, which now began to appear on European ships. To these ships was added the sternpost rudder, imported from China via the Arabs, which afforded a great improvement in ship maneuverability. Shipbuilding technology also advanced during the sixteenth and seventeenth centuries to meet the demand for more durable and seaworthy vessels. European shipbuilders pioneered in the use of iron nails to connect the external planking to the frames and bulkheads; from shipyards in India they learned the advantages of teak over oak for extended sea duty.[55] These innovations constituted a complete package of technologies for the design and construction of ships and ship guidance systems. There would be no further substantial changes in ship design until the end of the eighteenth century, when the Baltimore clipper ships were first used for regular trans-Atlantic mail service. These clipper ships were to become extremely important from the 1830s to the 1860s in the triangular trade system involving opium and tea between India, China, and Great Britain.

Then there was the question of the knowledge mariners needed in order to move across the trackless oceans and reach their intended destinations safely. Here the breakthrough came in the early fifteenth century, when a group of Florentine entrepreneurs brought home from Constantinople a treasury of classical Greek literature, including the *Geography* of Claudius Ptolemy, written during the second century A.D. To this point, to traverse open waters navigators had used portolan charts, meticulously drawn maps of coastal areas with distances between landmarks, prevailing winds, and other information colorfully represented. Ptolemy's maps presented the entire known world in a consistent and standardized way. The key was his use of latitude and longitude grid lines. In 1474, inspired by Ptolemy's grid lines and the new way of looking at the natural world that we know as perspective geometry, a young Florentine physician and son of prosperous spice merchants named Paolo del Pozzo Toscanelli tried his hand at mapping the world. Because it omitted the Western Hemisphere, his chart showed that the east-west distance between Europe and the Orient was a mere 6,500 miles across uninterrupted ocean. His map fell into the hands of Columbus, who used it to argue for the feasibility of his voyage. The other technologies that made it possible for navigators to know their location were the compass, brought from China in the twelfth century and in common use around the Mediterranean by 1400, and the astrolabe, perfected by the Arabs in the ninth century, which would be the basic astronomer's tool for the next 700 years.

Even after the arrival of Europeans in the Western Hemisphere, their vision of a world consisting of only three continents died slowly.[56] Driven by a paradigm that depicted the passage between Europe and the East as open water unbroken by large landmasses, early explorers and cartographers refused to believe that what Columbus and others had encountered was a continent separate from Asia and previously unknown to them. It was not until 1778, when the English explorer James Cook sailed along the coast from Oregon to the Bering Sea, that the world understood that North America and Asia were two separate masses of land.

All these technologies of guidance and control and of observation and measurement would have been of little value had it not been for the slowly emerging institutions to collect and preserve precious information about the oceans and teach successive generations of navigators the use of the data and tools. Here, the prototype institution was what Daniel Boorstin calls "a primitive Research and Development Laboratory,"[57] the headquarters of the Portuguese Prince Henry the Navigator, established in 1419. Prince Henry built his center near the Portuguese town of Sagres on the promontory known as Cape Saint Vincent, the southwesternmost tip of Europe. Here, he began the slow and painstaking process of gathering all new information about the known world as it became available from successive waves of explorers. He required his mariners to keep accurate logs and charts and to transcribe these details on master charts kept at Sagres, so that cartography, navigation, and shipbuilding could become cumulative sciences. Knowledgeable people came from all over the world to consult these growing repositories and to add to the storehouse with their own discoveries. Prince Henry's center was an early example of what today we would call institutionalized feedback.

Finally, none of the above would have been available or sustainable had it not been for the port cities where there could be assembled a critical mass of sailing experience and information, trade networks and brokers, docks, wharves, warehouses, financial capital, ship construction and repair, maritime expertise (especially navigation), and consumer demand. Columbus's home town, Genoa, was one such place; so were the key French ports of Dieppe and Rouen.

Two kinds of cities played a key role in the emergence of a global economy before 1800. The first included cities that were the center of economies by themselves, such as Venice, Genoa, Antwerp, and Amsterdam.[58] The second category included regional port cities that served the hinterland of large territorial states (nation-states as they were coming to be called). The prototype of this type of city was Bristol, on England's west coast, from where John Cabot set sail to search for the fabled Northwest Passage to China in May 1497.[59]

Bristol was founded at the confluence of the Frome and Avon Rivers in the early Middle Ages. The site turned out to be fortuitous. The town was protected from pirates and other sea enemies by its distance from the coast and by the tidal currents that made a water approach hazardous. Its port served as an outlet for the wool produced by the sheep of its surrounding farmlands and its location about midway between Iceland and Iberia made it a natural transshipment point for wool, codfish, wine, and olive oil. The result was a burgeoning commercial middle class, which fed the town's profits back into trade of all kinds, including spices and woolens. The town's fishermen went looking for new cod supplies as early as 1480 and, some sources contend, discovered Newfoundland, nearly twenty years before Cabot's first voyage. In any case, by the time Cabot sailed, Bristol already contained a number of mariners with experience in sailing the North Atlantic, an advantage that must have been of immense value to the English as they rushed to offset the early lead of the Spanish and Portuguese in world exploration. (Partly because of the city's port and its ready access to the sea, Bristol would become one of the centers of British metal-working industries in the seventeenth and eighteenth centuries.)

Again, we see the intimate connections between globalization and the rise of cities. Without the increase in city size, density, and specialization exemplified by ports like Bristol, the great wave of European expansion in the sixteenth and seventeenth centuries would not have been possible. Likewise, without overseas expansion toward something resembling a global economy, city growth would not have been possible either.

⊕   ⊕   ⊕

The 400-year span between the first voyage of the Chinese treasure fleet in 1405 and the first use of steam power to move a vehicle on wheels in 1804 was a crucial turning point in the process of globalization. After a vigorous initial effort at establishing a global commercial network, the Ming dynasty withdrew to focus on domestic concerns, leaving the world stage to Europeans at a time when Europe was poised on the brink of an expansion of its economy, its population, and its creativity.

That Europe was able to seize this historic opportunity was due as much as anything to its ability to exploit the new energy and other resources of the Americas, Africa, and South and Southeast Asia. Perhaps more vividly than any other episode in global history, the Age of Discovery illustrates the central importance of a periphery to which a dynamic core can dissipate its entropy. The new periphery, called into the service of European development by the caravel, the compass, and the lateen sail, provided critical supplies of food, labor, and investment capital at precisely the moment Europe needed them.

The new food and fiber supplies of the Americas and the tropics could feed, clothe, and energize Europe's growing industrial working class. Coffee from Brazil and the Caribbean, tea from China and Ceylon, and tobacco from Virginia and the Carolinas provided cheap stimulants for laborers; sugar from Jamaica and Barbados provided quick energy; and the Amerindian food staples, maize and the potato, sustained huge working-class populations with the valuable food energy of carbohydrates. Add cheap and durable clothing made from cotton from Egypt and the U.S. South and one can appreciate the importance of such crops in supporting a growing European working-class population. From 1400 to 1650, Europe's population grew from about 60 million to about 105 million, a rate of only 0.3 percent annually. From 1650 to 1900, despite the emigration of tens of millions, the continent's population grew from 105 million to 390 million, an increase of 285 million, or a rate of 1.1 percent per year, nearly four times that of the preceding period. There were surely many factors involved in this increase, including measures to improve urban sanitation and health conditions, but no one can deny the role played by crops from the new periphery in such a development.[60]

Nor can we overlook the key role played by the indigenous peoples of the new periphery in supplying the labor needed to exploit these newly opened lands. Amerindians played such a role for a short time after the arrival of Europeans. In the Andes, sufficient native labor survived so that Bolivia's enormously valuable silver deposits were worked by the Quechua, but elsewhere the natives' susceptibility to previously unknown diseases together with brutal treatment on plantations and in mines caused their near extinction by the end of the sixteenth century. African slaves were pressed into service to fill the void in the New World, with historic consequences for global demography. In India, Ceylon, and the islands of Southeast Asia, native labor was abundant to work the tea and spice plantations for local landlords and their European contractors.[61]

Finally, we must note the role of the new periphery in creating capital for investment in Europe's industrialization. From the Americas, gold and silver flowed back to Spain and Portugal and eventually into the coffers of merchants in Amsterdam and other international trading centers. American silver was transported via the Mediterranean, the Levant, and the Persian Gulf to India and China, where it financed the booming trade between Europe and Asia and thus made possible the satisfying of Europe's growing taste for Asian luxury goods.[62] The huge profits reaped by the British owners of sugar and coffee plantations in the Caribbean were returned to Great Britain where they played a vital role in the early stages of industrialization, financing manufacturing enterprises as well as launching banks and insurance companies.

In sum, from the sixteenth century on, Europeans could draw on a vast new periphery for the resources they needed to fuel their historic expansion. Although it is always difficult to draw causal linkages on such questions, it seems hard to imagine how Europe could have transformed itself from a world backwater to the engine of globalization in only three centuries without tapping into the enormous resources of this periphery. Because of what had transpired during the preceding 300 years, the energy revolution represented by coal and steam in the late eighteenth century could be mounted atop a storehouse of resources that was in the most literal sense global in scope.[63]

Episode Five

The Partnership of Steam and Coal

Until about 1800, the expansion imperative faced by human society had to be resolved within the constraints of wind, moving water, and human and animal power. Expressed in terms of energy resources, these limits dictated that human beings had to exploit the sun's energy relatively quickly after it reached the Earth. Some food energy could be stored for a short time in various levels of the food chain (e.g., in growing crops or in the flesh of cows, pigs, or fish); the waterwheel exploited the kinetic energy of falling water contained for a brief time after it had precipitated out of the atmosphere; sailing vessels exploited prevailing wind and water currents that were the recent and ephemeral products of the interplay of landforms, the planet's orientation toward the sun, and the behavior of the sun itself. The burning of biomass allowed the tapping of energy stored for a decade or two. But with no way to store the sun's energy for any significant span of time, human ability to build and operate bulk flow technologies was constrained by a limited budget of available energy.[1]

In the last half of the eighteenth century, these limitations began to yield before the efforts of experimenters, inventors, and scientists searching for ways to tap energy supplies that lay in reservoirs beneath the surface of the Earth. Fossil fuels—coal, natural gas, and petroleum—bore in their molecular structure energy that had reached the Earth many millions of years ago and continued to be stored in the remains of once-living organisms as if waiting for the moment of liberation by the Industrial Revolution (see Figure 5.1).

With these new energy supplies, the pace of globalization quickened and its scope expanded dramatically. Journeys that once took many months or even years could now be completed in weeks, days, or (eventually) hours. Lifestyle options unimagined before 1800 now became commonplace, for

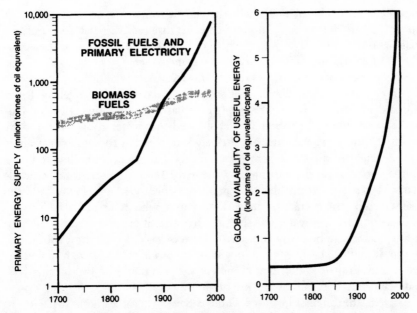

FIGURE 5.1   Global energy supply, 1700–1900, total and per capita.

Source: Vaclav Smil, *Energy in World History,* copyright © 1994 by Westview Press.

example, the availability of Argentine beef in the diet of Londoners. As we began our systematic conquest of the natural world, globalization separated into two currents. One current involved the movement of raw materials, manufactured products, people, energy, and waste byproducts of the industrial process; the second, the transmission of information, symbols, and images. In Episodes 5 and 6, technologies such as railroads, steamships, and airplanes that transported information by moving its human carriers will be considered part of the revolutionary exploitation of fossil fuels. The movement of information electronically via telephone, radio, or television will be discussed in Episode 7.

꿍   꿍   꿍

Complex technological innovations do not spring fully formed from a single great mind. Rather, they evolve over many years, if not decades, and many parents share responsibility for their birth. The steam engine was no exception.[2] In the first century A.D., Hero of Alexandria wrote how "vapours of water" could be manipulated to produce contrived effects such as making a horn blow, doors open or close, or a hollow ball turn. In the Middle Ages, the exploitation of falling water to produce energy for milling and other mechanized work laid the foundation for later experiments with steam while at the same time fostering economic and social developments that generated huge new demands for energy. In the early seventeenth century, a French landscape gardener named Salomon de Caus discovered that water could be raised above its own level with the help of heat. His discovery would eventually be of enormous value in solving the principal energy crisis of the times: how to pump water out of flooded coal mines. By the middle of the seventeenth century, the experiments of scientists from Italy (Evangelista Torricelli and Vincenzio Viviani), France (Blaise Pascal), Germany (Otto von Guericke), and England (Robert Boyle) showed that water could be raised by having it flow into a vacuum; but the height to which it rose was constrained by the weight of the air, so some device other than an air pump had to be invented for creating the vacuum. By the early 1690s, the scientific principle that was to solve this problem and make possible the steam engine had been discovered by the French scientist Denis Papin, who described his discovery in these words: "As water has the property that it is converted by fire into steam . . . and can be easily condensed again by cold, I thought it should not be too difficult to build engines in which, by means of moderate heat and the use of only a little water, that complete vacuum could be produced which had been sought in vain by the use of gunpowder."

In 1698, the English inventor Thomas Savery became the first person to build and sell a workable steam apparatus for raising water. Within decades, Savery's engines had been replaced by the superior machines of Thomas Newcomen, who built his first steam engine in 1712. After improvements by John Smeaton and others, the Newcomen engine reigned supreme for half a century, despite its inefficiencies.[3] By 1733, more than 100 engines were in service; by 1800, more than 1,500.

Reduced to its essentials, the Newcomen engine used the heat of burning coal to boil water and produce steam, which was collected in a cylinder within which a piston moved back and forth. After steam had filled the cylinder, cold water was injected into the cylinder, condensing the steam and producing a vacuum that caused the piston to descend. As it did so, it pulled down a huge beam attached to a pump that extended into the mine shaft. When the stroke of the piston was completed, the weight of the beam returned it to its original position, and the cycle was repeated.

In the winter of 1763–1764, a young Scot named James Watt was asked to repair a model of a Newcomen engine at Glasgow University. As he studied the model, Watt confronted what other engineers had considered an insoluble problem: For the sake of economy, the cylinder of the Newcomen engine had to be kept hot constantly; to maximize power, the cylinder and its contents had to be cooled instantly and at frequent, regular intervals.[4] The solution came to Watt in a flash of insight while walking in Glasgow on Easter Day, 1765: He would add a second cylinder separate from that in which the piston moved. Thus, the piston and its cylinder could be kept hot all the time, ready for the influx of steam, while the condensing cylinder, or condenser, could be kept cold. For this and other innovations, including the addition of a rotary beam to transform lateral into rotating motion, Watt is conventionally credited with being the inventor of the steam engine. In the same year as the American Declaration of Independence and the publication of Adam Smith's *Inquiry into the Nature and Causes of the Wealth of Nations,* Watt installed his first two large engines, one to pump water from a coal mine, the other at an iron foundry.

Watt's engines, produced in a business partnership with Matthew Boulton, dominated the market well into the nineteenth century. In 1775, with Watt's original patent due to expire in thirteen years, the British Parliament extended his patent protection until 1800, a measure that secured Watt's monopoly over the technology during its critical expansion phase. Given Watt's commitment to his particular model for harnessing steam power (i.e., a preference for low-pressure over high-pressure boilers), this monopoly actually retarded the application of steam to transport for a generation.

From its inception, the steam engine evolved in a partnership with coal. The function of the steam engine was to convert the solar energy stored in coal into the kinetic energy of a moving piston (and whatever was connected to it) by means of heat and the expansion and contraction of steam. Coal had been used for various purposes in British industry since the Middle Ages:[5] first by blacksmiths, armorers, and metalworkers; then by coppersmiths and gunsmiths. By the fifteenth century, coal was being burned to extract salt from seawater and soon coal was put to use in dyeing and other textile-finishing operations; felt making; malt drying; and the manufacture of brick, tile, glass, gunpowder, and chemicals. In 1709, Abraham Darby succeeded in smelting iron with coke, a byproduct of coal, a step that was to have enormous impact on the future of iron and steel manufacture.

Despite the growing importance of coal, wood continued to be a significant fuel until serious wood shortages in the sixteenth and seventeenth centuries in Britain led to rising costs for firewood, charcoal, and lumber. In response, the large-scale exploitation of coal began in Britain between 1540 and 1640. Vaclav Smil describes the consequences of this development:

> By 1650 the annual coal output [of Britain] had exceeded 2 million tonnes; the annual output reached 3 million tonnes in the early eighteenth century and more than 10 million tonnes by the century's end. . . . Once they had depleted the outcropping seams, mine operators developed deeper pits. . . . The deepest shafts surpassed 100 meters shortly after 1700, 200 meters by 1765, and 300 meters after 1830. By that time daily production was between 20 and 40 tonnes per mine, compared to just a few tonnes per mine a century earlier. With the deeper pits, mine operators encountered more water, which had to be pumped. They also had to ventilate the deeper mines and hoist the coal from deeper shafts. And, of course, they had to distribute the coal to their customers. Waterwheels, windmills, and horses powered these needs.[6]

Steam power made it possible to pump water from greater depths and to extract and lift coal from much deeper mines, thereby expanding enormously the coal reserves of Great Britain and other countries. Steam-powered railroads and sailing vessels also facilitated the long-distance distribution of coal to cities and factories, thus liberating civilization from its ancient dependence on water for power and transport. By burning coal, steam engines also stimulated demand for the fuel they made more accessible. At the same time, without coal, steam engines would have remained technologically infeasible for several centuries until the discovery of the energy potential of another fossil fuel: petroleum.

✦   ✦   ✦

The analysis of G. N. von Tunzelmann suggests that the principal impact of steam power was felt not on stationary manufacturing installations such as cotton mills but rather on mobility.[7] Most of the breakthroughs in manufacturing technology that we associate with the Industrial Revolution (e.g., the factory system to manufacture textiles) were developed to utilize other energy sources, particularly falling water. As Terry Reynolds makes clear, machines driven by the kinetic energy of waterwheels had been central features of European industry since the Middle Ages.[8] As early as the eleventh century in some places and throughout Europe by 1500, water-powered machinery milled grain, sawed lumber, finished cloth, hammered metal, turned lathes, crushed stone, rolled metal sheets, ventilated mines, hoisted heavy loads, pounded cloth into pulp to make paper, and performed many other tasks. The *Domesday Book* census taken in England in 1085 recorded the existence of some 5,624 waterwheels, which together would have produced enough electricity to supply a small town today.[9] An industrial census taken in France in 1694 identified some 95,000 mills and factories of various types, nearly all of which were powered by water.

Thus, for some decades after the Industrial Revolution began, that is, until the 1830s, coal and steam offered little in the way of cost advantages over windmills, waterwheels, horses, or the hands of women and children to carry out mill and factory work. Such was not the case with transport, however. After the introduction of high-pressure boilers in the early nineteenth century, the application of steam power to land and water transport made a critical contribution to the Industrial Revolution and to the process of globalization. The shift to high-pressure boilers was blocked for several decades by technological limitations in boiler construction and by James Watt's monopoly over the manufacture of steam engines. Until 1800, when his patent expired, Watt had successfully opposed efforts to build steam engines using high-pressure boilers out of a fear that they would explode. Low-pressure boilers, however, were too heavy and bulky and not powerful enough to provide steam locomotion, which presented insuperable obstacles to the mounting of a steam engine on a moving platform.

After 1800, these obstacles were overcome, thanks to the work of Richard Trevithick, a Cornish mining engineer who is given credit for being the first to exploit steam power for overland mobility.[10] The son of a mine manager,

Trevithick had grown up in the late eighteenth century surrounded by mining technology and thus learned early on about the use of wheeled carts rolling over tracks or rails or within iron-clad grooves to move heavy loads of coal. Freed at last from Watt's patent restrictions, Trevithick designed and patented his own high-pressure boiler in 1802; by 1804, he was using his invention to move heavy loads of raw materials and finished products around an iron works at Pennydarren, South Wales. By 1809, he was exploiting the novelty of his invention by opening a circular track and charging people a shilling to take a ride that went nowhere.

In addition to devising a way to connect a steam engine to a moving platform, Trevithick also solved the design problems blocking the construction of high-pressure steam boilers. With the advent of superior technology for contructing stronger and more reliable boilers, he was able to design and build a steam engine that added the power of steam expansion to that of steam contraction to provide a dual impetus to the piston (a process known as compounding). Once the compact high-pressure boiler was available, it was an obvious next step to mount steam engines on rail cars and ships and the age of steam transport was born. As Asa Briggs puts it, "The change to high pressure steam seemed in its own time as big as the change from the atom bomb to the hydrogen bomb in the twentieth century."[11]

For commercial rail transport to succeed, many diverse components had to be drawn together from other fields of commerce and technology. The laying of specialized tracks on which the rail cars could move was already a common practice in British coal mines and ironworks. Wooden carts called "dogs," running on wooden wheels and iron axles and guided along wooden tracks, had been used in coal mines since the sixteenth century. With the second requirement, power traction, met by Trevithick's high-pressure boilers, blacksmiths, enginewrights, and mechanics acquired the knowledge necessary to construct the locomotives. The organized movement of freight was borrowed from canal transport, which in Great Britain dated from the 1760s; regularly timed passenger traffic was adopted from stagecoach companies, which had initiated regular service in Great Britain in 1784. Canal engineers had already mastered the techniques of digging tunnels and constructing embankments, while canal companies had established the legal precedents for compulsory land puchase as well as the contractual formalities needed to assemble and manage large numbers of workers.

By 1814, George Stephenson, called by many the father of the locomotive, was running a steam-powered locomotive with flanged wheels along a track laid with cast-iron rails.[12] In 1825, the Stockton and Darlington Railway became the first public transport company to use steam locomotives, although at first only for freight. Until 1833, only horses pulled passenger trains. In trials near Liverpool in 1829, Stephenson's new locomotive, the Rocket, achieved the unheard-of speed of 28 miles per hour while pulling a car carrying thirty-six passengers. This accomplishment convinced many skeptics that a new era in land transportation had indeed arrived. By midcentury, it became possible to talk of a railway *system*, with regular passenger service and printed timetables. In 1837, there were 500 miles of track in Great Britain; by 1844, 2,000; by 1852, over 7,500. Other countries in Europe followed the British by several decades. France and Germany had each laid nearly 30,000 miles of track by the end of the century.

British engineers carried the gospel of steam locomotion abroad, including to the Americas. The first rail company in the United States, the Baltimore and Ohio Railroad, was chartered in 1827 and opened part of its line for business in 1830. The Camden and Amboy Railroad and Transportation Company was chartered in 1830 and began to offer service for most of the distance between Philadelphia and New York in 1831. This rail line, which grew eventually into the Pennsylvania Railroad, reduced the time of a trip between these two major eastern cities from two days to two hours. After 1829, U.S. investors built and operated intercity railroads using engines constructed in Great Britain. Domestic U.S. firms produced 100 locomotives in 1840 and 1,000 in 1880. In the 1850s, railway mileage tripled in the United States. The first transcontinental line was completed in 1869, and in the 1880s, more miles of track were laid than in all previous years combined. By 1920, U.S. mileage exceeded that of Europe and constituted one-third of the world's total. The railroad united the nation and created a national market, gave its people a heretofore inconceivable mobility and sense of connectedness, created great cities like Chicago, and embedded itself forever in the folklore of the country. Moreover, the railroad was a stimulus to other advances in what James Beniger calls the "control revolution."[13] In a story to be explored more thoroughly in Episode 7, Part 1, the expansion of rail service across the United States brought forth communications inventions like the telegraph and administrative changes like uniform time zones. In the 1850s and 1860s, other countries followed the lead of the Americans and the British, including Canada, Argentina, Australia, and India. Rail lines crossed Canada by 1885, conquered the Andes by the turn of the century, and linked Moscow with Vladivostok in 1902.

Applied to land transport, the steam engine fostered the expansion and consolidation of the modern nation-state and of national markets in two directions at once. Within the nation, rural areas and farmlands once isolated from the city were now connected by the newly laid rails, stimulating the exchange of products and the movement of people and culture within a vastly increased national market system. In his study of the modernization of rural France after 1870, Eugen Weber observes that,

> roads and rails brought men into the market, permitted them to drink wine or
> sell it profitably, or to develop crops that could not be marketed before, and to
> give up growing others that could now be bought more cheaply. They also
> brought ruin to local enterprises no longer protected by earlier isolation, to out-

dated occupational groups like the riverboatmen, and to producers of mediocre local goods or crops fated to be outmatched by specialized ones. They set people on the move—because those people could get away more easily or because they had to get away, because things were going better or worse, because opportunities beckoned somewhere else and could now, for the first time, be seized. The move was not only in space, but in time and mind as well: roads and rails introduced new foods into the diet, new materials in the building of the house, new objects in its interior, new tools in the fields about it, new things to do on holidays, and new kinds of clothes to wear.[14]

The steam locomotive that made it possible for the nation-state to expand inward to connect previously isolated regions and to link farms with growing cities was also responsible for the consolidation of the European colonial system, particularly in Africa and South Asia. By reducing the costs of long-distance transport and commerce, the railroad made possible the long-term maintenance of imperialism.

After more than three centuries of attempts by European states to penetrate India, observes Daniel Headrick, their influence was still weak, confined mainly to the coastal cities of the subcontinent.[15] Then the railroad arrived. The British effort to build India's railroad system was the largest single construction project of the colonial era (at one point, some 42,000 Indian laborers were involved) and produced the largest international capital flow of the nineteenth century (some £95 million between 1845 and 1875). Construction began in 1852; the main trunk lines were completed by 1869; and by 1902, British India (today, India, Pakistan, Bangladesh, and Burma) had nearly 26,000 miles of railroads, the fourth longest rail network in the world (after the United States, Canada, and Russia). In the 1830s, inland transport in India cost an estimated $0.12 per short-ton mile. By 1874, the cost had dropped to $0.02; by 1900, to $0.008!

European colonialists in nineteenth-century Africa complained of even worse barriers to internal transport than the British encountered in India: Canoes on rivers were too small and slow, the tsetse fly blocked the introduction of European beasts of burden, and human porterage was inefficient and hence expensive. Speakers at an 1876 conference on railroad construction asserted that a single train could do the work of more than 13,000 human bearers. As in India, the colonial states (chiefly Great Britain, France, and Germany) built railroad trunk and feeder lines primarily to facilitate the flow of African raw materials (e.g., palm oil, copper, cotton) to European consumers. The first railroad in Africa was the Alexandria-Cairo line built in the 1850s. The big push came in the 1870s and 1880s after the discovery of diamonds and gold in South Africa. By 1914, Africa had acquired the pattern of railroads that exists today, that is, concentrated primarily in Egypt and Algeria in the north and in South Africa, Southwest Africa, and the Belgian Congo below the Sahara.

Beyond the physical impact of infrastructure, the steam-powered railroad reinforced the belief of Europeans in their superiority over their African and Asian subjects. Europeans were both intrigued and delighted by the awe and even fear exhibited by Africans and Asians as they encountered for the first time the power of the railroad locomotive. By conquering the physical forces of space and time, the railroad came to symbolize the moral as well as the material superiority of the European over the native, and European colonists saw in steam technology the key to raising the moral standards of their "primitive" charges. As one British colonial official in West Africa in the 1860s put it, "There is no civilizer like the railway."[16] The railroads would show the non-Western peoples the power of technology and industrial production and in so doing put an end to superstition, fatalism, religious myths, tribal isolation, and other barriers to the material advance of African and Asian peoples. That such changes would redound to the great material benefit of the Europeans seemed to them wholly appropriate.

✧ ✧ ✧

Although the British were the pioneers in rail transport, it was in the United States where steam power was first used to move vessels across water. There were numerous precursors to the steamship, some going back several centuries. The French scientist Papin had proposed using steam to drive paddle wheels as early as 1690 and throughout the eighteenth century inventors struggled unsuccessfully to find a way to mount the Newcomen engine on watercraft. Americans began to experiment with paddle wheel craft as early as 1763; James Rumsey demonstrated a steamboat on the Potomac River to George Washington in 1786. Robert Fulton usually gets the credit for building the first successful steamboat, a side-wheel design he demonstrated on the Seine in 1803. By 1807, his famous boat the *Clermont* was offering trips on the Hudson River between New York and Albany. By 1811, the first steamboat had been launched on the Ohio River, opening up the western frontier via the Ohio and the Mississippi.

The process of globalization was greatly accelerated by the use of steam to cross the oceans. At first, passengers and ship owners were nervous about crossing the oceans using steam alone. The first crossing of the Atlantic, in 1819 by the *Savannah* from Georgia to England and then on to Saint Petersburg, was carried out primarily under sail. Steam was used only during the initial leg of the journey, as the ship's coal supply had been exhausted by the time it reached Ireland. The Savannah-to-Liverpool segment of the trip took 27 days. Likewise, the first ship to make the trip west, from Great Britain to Chile in 1821, was also a sailing vessel with steam power added. It was not until 1838 that a ship powered by steam alone, the *Sirius*, crossed the Atlantic. By the 1840s, regular steamship service was established between New York and London. The first steam-powered trip to Asia came in 1825, when the *Enterprise* made the voyage from Europe to Calcutta in 103 days. Regular service to Asia was established in 1842.

It would be difficult to exaggerate the importance of the steamship to globalization. Although the sailing vessel struggled to compete with steam for mercantile shipping, by the 1870s and 1880s steam vessels had demonstrated their superiority over sail. The steamship made it possible for millions of Europeans to emigrate west, principally to the United States, during the last half of the nineteenth century. In their golden age before World War I, steam-powered cruise ships inaugurated the practice of global tourism and people of ordinary means could begin to envision "getting away from it all" as a real possibility.

The movement of the world's food supply, especially meat, was also reshaped by the steamship. In 1869, Henry Howard delivered a load of frozen beef by steamship from Texas to New Orleans. In 1873, two Britons, Thomas Mort and James Harrison, immigrated to Australia to open a meat refrigeration plant for preparing shipments back to London. Both eventually went bankrupt after several shipments spoiled because of failure of the on-board systems. But the plants in Australia were still in working order and in only a few years the problems with the ships' systems had been solved as well. In February 1880, the first frozen meat from Australia was unloaded at the London docks. Queen Victoria dined on some lamb from the shipment and was much impressed. By the 1880s and 1890s, great profits were being made by shipping meat and fruit long distances to the rapidly growing cities of Europe.

If anything, the steamship was of even greater significance than the railroad in Europe's overseas expansion.[17] In the mid-1820s, the British discovered the usefulness of river steamers in warfare during the brief war between the British East India Company and Burma. Although these early steamers were used principally to tow warships upriver, during the next two decades a number of steamships were designed specifically with fighting in mind. The first use of such vessels occurred in China in the first opium war (1840–1842). Led by the heavily armed iron-clad *Nemesis,* the British fleet defeated a much larger Chinese force on the Pearl River below Canton in 1841. A number of additional British steamships were committed to the two opium wars with China as well as another conflict in Burma. In addition to changing the face of colonial warfare, the steamship also was a part of the revolution in communications and transportation technologies that linked Europe with India and the rest of Asia during the last half of the nineteenth century. These new bulk flow systems included iron-hull ships, screw propellers, the opening in 1869 of the Suez Canal to reduce transit time between Great Britain and India, and the laying of a network of submarine cables for sending telegraph messages around the world.

↭   ↭   ↭

For the story of globalization, one of the most important consequences of the tapping of fossil fuel lay in what Ernest Schusky calls the "Neocaloric Revolution" in agriculture. In this context, farming can be seen as an exercise in managing energy flow, that is, farmers sought to extract more energy out of the ground in the form of food than they had to invest *in* the ground through their own labors and from other sources.

For millennia, farmers extracted food energy from the ground with only their own muscles and the assistance of cattle, oxen, and horses; they could transport food to consumers only with draft animals, canal barges, and sailing vessels. Anthropologists have determined that contemporary hunter-gatherer societies reap a return of 10 to 20 calories of food energy for each calorie they invest in foraging for food. On the negative side, however, these societies typically invest 90 to 95 percent of human energy in looking for food. The ability to exploit the stored energy in fossil fuels meant that industrial societies could feed themselves with an investment of as little as 15 percent of their available human energy. "Despite this drop in percentage," writes Schusky,

> overall energy use in food production reaches revolutionary new heights. . . . The modern grain farmer using an array of machinery, fertilizers, and pesticides expends about eight calories for every one calorie that is produced. In an energy-short world such "production" makes no sense, but in a world where fossil energy is cheap and seemingly unlimited it is highly profitable. Of course, the direct use of fossil energy on the farm is only the beginning of the food system. Even more calories are expended in the transportation, storage, and processing of food, and most estimates agree that once food reaches a modern kitchen, another eight fossil calories are expended to prepare one calorie for eating.[18]

The Neocaloric Revolution progressed through two phases. During the first phase, coal and steam enabled the movement of food across greater distances via steamship and railroad and thus made possible the exploitation of more distant lands for food consumption in Europe, a process that was an integral part of colonialism. Steam power was also widely used in factories and mills to process food and fiber for individual consumption. For many decades, however, numerous obstacles prevented the full application of steam to the tasks of farming itself and the horse remained an economically competitive alternative source of energy through most of the nineteenth century. The second phase was marked by the more intensive exploitation of land by the application of gasoline-powered equipment to actual food production (see Figure 5.2).

The migration of huge numbers of rural folk to the cities was a central feature of the Industrial Revolution. For those who remained on the farms, steam power increased their productivity enormously and thus made possible the rapid growth of cities. The first farm to use steam power was in North Wales in 1798. By the 1850s, steam pumps were in use to drain wetlands and lift water for irrigation, but the problems of designing the accessory technologies for high-pressure boilers were to delay the full application of the steam engine to farming until about 1870. By that time, chain drives

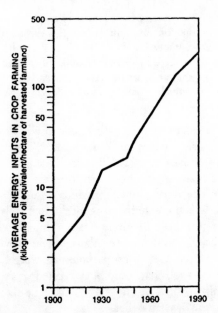

FIGURE 5.2   Energy inputs in crop farming, 1900–1990.

Source: Vaclav Smil, *Energy in World History,* copyright © 1994 by Westview Press.

and gear assemblies had been invented that made it possible to connect steam power to machines for specialized farm tasks like threshing, cultivating, plowing, ginning cotton, crushing sugar cane, and digging drainage ditches. In 1889, an American, Daniel Best, introduced a "steam harvesting outfit" consisting of a traction engine with a combined harvester attached. The device was said to be able to harvest up to 100 acres a day (although it could operate only over flat land). Without steam power, the farms of Europe and North America could not have kept pace with population growth and urbanization between 1870 and World War I.

Notwithstanding the importance of steam power in the actual working of the land itself, where steam really made a difference in the world food network was in transport. The railroad and the steamship extended the food supply system of a great city many times over, resulting in dramatic improvements in food quality, variety, and reliability of supply. In addition, as A. J. McMichael puts it,

this new abundance and security of food caused major public health gains by eradicating stavation and nutritional deficiencies. It also foreshadowed a new type of diet with a much changed nutrient composition. . . . The per capita con-

sumption of fat and sugar increased ten-fold to twenty-fold in England over the
past 250 years, while the consumption of complex carbohydrates and dietary
fibre has declined substantially. . . . While the affluent diet has increased life ex-
pectancy . . . , it has also caused increases in a range of chronic . . . diseases: heart
disease, stroke, diabetes, various cancers, dental caries, gall stones, chronic
bowel disorders and various bone and joint disorders.[19]

In 1816 and 1817, most of Europe experienced what John Post calls "the
last great subsistence crisis in the Western world."[20] The crisis began, according to Post, with an unusual increase in volcanic activity between 1811 and
1818, including the massive Tomboro eruption on the island of Sumbawa
(Indonesia) in 1815. These eruptions threw into the atmosphere huge quantities of ash and soil, which created stratospheric dust veils that encircled the
Earth. Surface temperatures dropped across the Northern Hemisphere
through the critical spring and summer planting and growing seasons in Europe and North America. Cereal crops failed or were harvested at record
low levels, much of the food that could be harvested was spoiled by molds or
blight, and draft animals died of hunger or had to be slaughtered to replace
the missing grain in the peasants' diet.

Across Europe, the result was social upheaval of massive proportions.
Death rates, which had been steadily declining for two generations, now
shot up again, and marriage and birth rates dropped, producing declining
populations in the midst of what was otherwise a period of demographic expansion (1750–1850). Since agriculture was still the most important sector in
the economies of Europe, the disaster spread until it affected nearly every
working person. Beggars and vagrants appeared in historic numbers and ma-
rauding mobs of food scavengers roamed across the country. Public health
measures failed and the plague and other infectious diseases reached epi-
demic proportions.

Many factors contributed to starting the food crisis and to aggravating and
maintaining it once it began, but transport limitations and rigidities certainly
played a key role in preventing governments from replacing Europe's lost
food with imported staples.[21] Europe's leaders desperately searched the
world's grain stocks for relief: Russia, the Baltic, the Middle East, North
America. In each case, new food supplies could be transported only by sailing vessels and Europe thus lay completely at the mercy of the prevailing
winds. The French government placed its first orders for foreign grain supplies in November 1816, but the first shipments did not arrive in French
ports until summer of the next year. The government of Prussia acted more
quickly, seeking grain from the Baltic in the spring of 1816. Because of a virtual absence of an east wind across the Baltic in March, April, and May of
that year, however, grain deliveries were delayed for months, causing bread
prices to rise to record highs. A government scandal ensued as critics sought
to discover whose incompetence had led to such a disaster.

The famine of 1816–1817 would be the last time, however, that Europe as a whole would experience such a crisis in feeding its population. With the advent of steam transport, Europe could now tap distant food supplies and move staple crops quickly to urban markets. The latter two-thirds of the nineteenth century saw a fundamental reordering of the global food system. In the 1840s, for example, Great Britain imported 5 percent of its food supply. In 1846, the restrictive Corn Laws were repealed and by the end of the century the country imported 80 percent of its grain for human consumption, 40 percent of its meat, and 72 percent of its dairy products.[22] In the 1830s, the city of London satisfied most of its food needs from British sources or at the most distant, from the Baltic. By 1910, the city was importing its basic food supplies from the United States, Canada, Argentina, Australia, and New Zealand, the latter some 11,000 miles away.

Between 1880 and 1920, the humble fish-and-chips shop became the mainstay of the diet of the British working class. And the growing popularity of fried fish and potatoes was tied directly to the steam-powered fishing trawler and the railroad. The steam cargo ship and the fishing trawler extended the British food network to Icelandic waters and even to Canada for new supplies of white fish such as haddock. Potatoes could be brought from Germany, Belgium, and the Netherlands when local crops fell short of meeting demand. And the oil in which both fish and chips were prepared came from Egyptian and U.S. cottonseed as well as Argentinian beef drippings. Finally, the railroad transformed Great Britain's internal food supply network. The country's exploding industrial cities were supplied from a few large port cities, leaving many of the old farming and fishing villages bypassed and abandoned.[23]

Between 1860 and 1920, a billion acres of new land were brought into food production, mostly in the United States and Russia. Without these new sources of food, Europeans would have starved. And it was the railroad and steamship that made such expansion possible (see Figure 5.3). In 1838, the steamship *Great Western*, slightly larger than 1,000 tons, crossed the Atlantic in just under 400 hours, only marginally better than a vessel under sail. By 1890, the *Lucania*, at about 15,000 tons, accomplished the same trip in about 125 hours.[24] The effect was to turn virtually the entire planet into a potential source of food for Europe's cities.

One such city, Manchester, England, illustrates the impact of steam power on the feeding of an industrial city in the early nineteenth century.[25] Steam power came early to Manchester and was critical to the city's commercial success, as Angus Sinclair relates:

The ancient city of Manchester, the headquarters of the Lancashire textile industries, had long been famous for the enterprise and public spirit of its citizens. This important mart of manufacturing was distant about 30 miles from Liverpool, the nearest seaport, and Manchester's trade languished through the delays

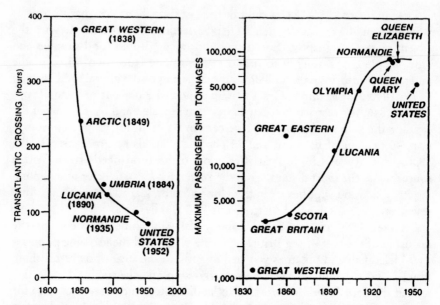

FIGURE 5.3   Transatlantic crossing times, 1800–1960, and maximum passenger ship tonnages, 1830–1950.

Source: Vaclav Smil, *Energy in World History,* copyright © 1994 by Westview Press.

and difficulties encountered in transporting goods to and from the port of shipment. Sometimes it took longer to transport a cargo of cotton from Liverpool to Manchester than it did to bring it across the Atlantic in a sailing ship. About [1825] a few leading merchants of Liverpool and Manchester organized a company to construct a railway from Liverpool to Manchester. Permission to build the line had to be obtained from Parliament and stupendous opposition was offered. After a long and vigorous fight the promoters of the enterprise were successful and the railway was constructed [1828].[26]

A competition was held in late 1829 to determine whose locomotive would be selected to launch the new railway, a trial won by George Stephenson's Rocket. Rail service between Liverpool and Manchester was begun on September 15, 1830, amid much publicity. It was a huge success from the beginning and the railway became the model against which all subsequent rail service in Great Britain would be measured.[27]

And just in time, too, for the population of Manchester increased sharply through the nineteenth century. Depending on the definition one chooses of the city's limits, Manchester's population (which in 1773 had been only about 29,000) grew from about 90,000 in 1801 to between 250,000 and 500,000 by 1871.[28] The aggregate demand of the city for food was driven by these increases in population coupled with steadily rising family incomes.

The relative economic comfort of Manchester's population made possible a diet that exceeds today's recommendations in most categories: a per capita daily caloric intake of about 2,600 and levels of protein, iron, and vitamin C well beyond what an adult needs to maintain a satisfactory level of nutrition.[29]

The effects of steam power on Manchester's food supply were not felt overnight. Until the early 1840s, the city continued to draw most of its food from traditional nearby sources. But slowly after 1830, Manchester's merchants began to tap more distant markets and in the period 1850 to 1870 the city's food network became truly global.

Livestock began to be imported from Ireland soon after regular steamship service was established between the two islands; in 1852, for example, more than 420,000 cows, sheep, and pigs were brought from Ireland through Liverpool.[30] By the 1880s, the advent of refrigeration made feasible the long-distance transport of dead meat and U.S. bacon and ham was imported through Liverpool at the rate of 9,000 tons each year. The transport of milk by railway began in 1844; by the 1860s the use of roads and canals to bring milk to the city had virtually ceased. Imports of butter from Ireland nearly doubled between the 1820s and 1850; cheese was imported from the United States after the 1860s. When in the 1840s rail services began to be used to transport fruit and vegetables to Manchester, the effect was to transform completely the traditional networks on which the city had relied and to increase the importance of other regions of Great Britain as sources of food for the city. Cultivation and consumption of the potato were also encouraged as well. After the mid-1840s, rail transport of iced fish also introduced major changes in Manchester's diet. The city now became connected to fishing ports on Great Britain's east coast from which the cod fleet sailed to fish the North Sea.

The effects of the globalization of Manchester's food supply were not necessarily felt in the overall caloric intake of the city's population; perhaps those needs could have continued to be met from local and regional sources for some time during the nineteenth century. Without question, however, the global spread of Manchester's trade networks via the railroad and steamship made possible three major changes in the city's diet: Supply was made more reliable, quality was improved, and a wide variety of food items were now available throughout most of the year instead of only on a seasonal basis. Perhaps most significant, however, was the impact of steam on the price of food in Manchester. As Roger Scola concludes:

> So far as fluctuations in food prices are concerned, it is possible to envisage two sharply contrasting situations: one in which most of the food requirements are produced locally and, as such, are prone for natural reasons to years of plenty and years of dearth; and another, characteristic of the present day, in which the majority of people—unless in the farming business—are blissfully unaware of,

say, the state of harvests over the last five years. . . . During the period
1770–1870 Manchester, with its ever-widening range of potential sources of
supply, and enhanced scope for choice, was moving away from the first of these
abstract models towards the second.[31]

⊷   ⊷   ⊷

The shift in energy sources represented by the fossil fuel revolution was a
crucial step in bringing the global system into existence. Although the three
centuries after 1492 laid the foundation, coal and the steam engine made
globalization feasible by providing the energy supplies necessary to operate
bulk flow technologies with the speed, range, and capacity that global systems required. In the process, the partnership of coal and steam raised global
change to a new level of complexity and speed. The pace and scope of global
change increased to the point where individuals could note marked transformations in the span of one lifetime. With the exploitation of the enormous
power of fossil fuel, bulk flow technologies—like technology in general—
began to exhibit positive, or self-reinforcing, feedback loops. One example,
to be explored in more detail in Episode 7, involved the symbiotic development of steamships and trans-Atlantic transport and communications.

The irony of steam power was that steam technology led in the nineteenth
century to the study of heat and heat loss, a field that eventually became
known as thermodynamics. As we saw in the Introduction, this research led
Rudolf Clausius to coin the term entropy as a measure of energy loss or
decay in a system and to propose the second law of thermodynamics, that
entropy increases in the universe to a maximum. These discoveries showed
that humankind's efforts to squeeze more productivity out of nature were
doomed to failure in the very long term. In the immediate context of the Industrial Revolution, however, this reality was (and still is) masked by dissipative structures. Some dissipation of entropic costs involved the creation
and maintenance of far-flung empires that were linked together by railroads
and steamships. Other structures were achieved by knitting expansive countries—such as the United States and Canada—into unified nation-states and
markets, a process made possible by the railroad and the river steamer. Finally, the application of steam technology to farming opened new lands to
the plow and raised the productivity of old lands. In these ways, the steam
engine of Savery, Newcomen, Watt, and Trevithick postponed the day of
reckoning for the costs of industrialization by fostering a new round of
global expansion even as it undermined the intellectual assumptions that had
made industrial civilization possible in the first place.

Episode Six

Petroleum and the Internal Combustion Engine

Early in the twentieth century, steam gave way (grudgingly and not without a fight) to the internal combustion engine as the driving force behind globalization. Heat was still the source of energy, but with internal combustion high temperatures were achieved not by an external source (steam from an external boiler) but directly by burning a mixture of fuel and air. Cooling was achieved not by dousing the cylinder with cold water but by expelling the burned gas and replacing it with a new supply of the air-fuel mixture. This device offered many advantages over steam, chief of which were a much lower engine weight and much higher fuel efficiency. The internal combustion engine was not without its drawbacks, however, because it also generated considerable waste products (air pollution) and it drew on a fuel supply (petroleum) that was at the time—and still is today—much more limited than coal. Thus, the eventual triumph of internal combustion over steam was far from inevitable. Episode 6 involves the applications of the internal combustion engine that most affected the process of globalization: the automobile (and related technologies like the truck) and the airplane.

↭   ↭   ↭

It is difficult to appreciate the magnitude of the contribution of the internal combustion engine to the energy supply of the industrialized world. In 1979, according to John Fenn,

> the aggregate work-performing capacity of all prime movers in [the United States] ... was about 3×10^{10} horsepower. ... Included are all machines in electric-generating plants, vehicles, homes, factories, mines, boats, airplanes, and farms that use fuel, wind, or water as an energy source. ... Of this impressive total horsepower only about 2.5 percent was devoted to generating electricity. About 90 percent was under the hoods of rubber-tired vehicles! If we assume that at any one time about 5 percent of those vehicles are on the road and that

103

they are operating at about half their rated output, we find that there is as much power being continuously dissipated on the highways as is being produced in all the electric-generating plants put together.[1]

The automobile was the complex product of an array of technologies and materials from widely separate origins that were brought together during the last quarter of the nineteenth century and the first two decades of the twentieth. The most important of these was the engine that would power it.

Internal combustion as a source of power was discovered by the Dutch scholar Christian Huygens in 1673.[2] His engine, based on ideas drawn from Leonardo da Vinci, Jean de Hautefeuille, Otto von Guericke, and Evangelista Torricelli, used exploding gunpowder as the source of heat. When his device proved impractical, his assistant, Denis Papin, turned to steam as a possible energy source, a path that led us to Episode 5. The obstacle to internal combustion lay in developing a fuel that could be calibrated precisely and mixed easily with air. In other words, the fuel had to be available in liquid form.

Liquid fuel was first used in an internal combution engine in 1841.[3] The engine, developed by the Italian Luigi de Cristoforis, used naphtha as fuel. A Belgian named Etienne Lenoir developed the first useful internal combustion engine, with coal gas as fuel, in 1859, and another model using benzene in 1862. In 1862, a French engineer named Alphonse Beau de Rochas proposed the four-stroke cycle that became the model for the automobile engine: *intake* of the air-fuel mixture into the cylinder, *compression* of the mixture, ignition of the mixture producing a *power* stroke, and *exhaust* of the spent fuel. Beau de Rochas never actually built such a device, however; that honor belongs to a German named Nikolaus Otto, who built the first engine prototype in 1876. For this reason, the engine is still known as the Otto engine. The Otto engine began to be manufactured in the United States in 1878 and with only minor modifications is still found in almost every passenger automobile manufactured in the world today.

For a variety of reasons, including the loss of his exclusive patent rights in 1886, Otto was not influential in later years in the application of the internal combustion engine to transport. Gottlieb Daimler, who had worked for Otto in the 1870s, is credited with developing the first gasoline-powered engine powerful enough to run an automobile (in 1885); another German, Karl Benz, built the first vehicle powered by such an engine, in 1886.

In 1893, a quarter of a century after Otto developed his four-stroke engine, Rudolf Diesel patented the alternative design that bears his name. The diesel engine differs from the Otto engine chiefly in how the fuel-air mixture is ignited, a difference that produces more work per unit of fuel consumed, but which also tends to be noisier and smellier. Diesel engines power a relatively small percentage of automobiles; their real impact has been on heavier vehicles: trucks and railroads. The first diesel-powered railroad locomotive appeared in 1921 and despite furious opposition from steam advocates (chiefly in the operating unions) the diesel had replaced almost all steam locomotives by the mid-1950s.[4]

It was fortunate that the gasoline-powered automobile appeared when it did, since the chief source of traction in the growing cities of the United States and Europe—the horse—had reached its limits of efficiency and practicality. By the end of the nineteenth century, Great Britain had one horse for every ten people; in the United States the ratio was one horse for every four. Each horse consumed and then discharged about 6 tons of food each year, about as much as eight humans. Two hectares of land were needed to feed each animal and then there was the problem of how to dispose of the mountains of horse excreta and dead carcasses. In New York City in 1900, horses created *each day* 1,100 tons of manure, 270,000 liters of urine, and 20 carcasses. In cities like New York and London, the stench and flies were overwhelming, as were the noise of horses' hooves on the stone pavements and the congestion caused by their frequent accidents. Horse transport had also become quite expensive. Measured in terms of a worker's wages, a horse in 1900 cost about three times what a car costs today; a long-distance trip by horse coach cost about fifty times what an equivalent trip by bus would cost today. In sum, to cite M. G. Lay, "there were many signs that the horse was reaching practical capacity and that the cities and the countryside were both reaching the limit of their ability to support any further increases in the horse population. Transport clearly needed a technical breakthrough."[5]

At the turn of the twentieth century, it was far from settled that gasoline-powered internal combustion engines would be the preferred energy source for the automobile.[6] In 1900, U.S. firms manufactured more than 1,600 cars powered by steam, 1,575 that ran on electric batteries, and just 936 powered by internal combustion. By 1917, however, of the 3.5 million registered automobiles in the United States, fewer than 50,000 were electrics and the "steamer" had virtually vanished. The triumph of gasoline over steam and electricity was due to a combination of factors. Some were technological: Steam engines were not (in today's parlance) "user friendly" because they required constant attention from a knowledgeable operator and electric cars could never solve the problem of battery weight per unit of energy produced. In addition, gasoline cars were substantially improved by better transmissions, four-cylinder engines that reduced the noise and shaking of the early models, and electric starters that replaced the dirty and dangerous hand crank. On the other hand, some of the factors working in favor of the internal combustion engine were clearly cultural, ideological, or emotional: Electric cars were initially marketed for sale to women, a feature that made them unappealing to many men, and steamers were seen as toys or sporting vehicles for the idle rich. Gasoline-driven cars, on the other hand, were advertised as cheap, flexible, and easy-to-use machines that offered long-distance endurance as well as local convenience for the average motorist.

Other materials and technologies converged during this period to make the automobile feasible for popular transportation. Bicycle manufacturing lent a number of important technologies that the automobile adopted: steel tubing, ball bearings, chain drives, differential gearing, and tension-spoked wheels. New metal alloys made possible bodies, frames, and engines that were stronger, more durable, and more comfortable. Road construction techniques, particularly in laying long stretches of pavement, made traveling surfaces more enjoyable and less dangerous.

Another pivotal innovation was the pneumatic tire, patented in 1889 by a Scot named John Dunlop (after an earlier patent by another Scot, Robert Thompson, had lapsed). Not only did the new tire produce a smoother ride at speeds in excess of 20 miles per hour, but a vehicle equipped with pneumatic tires was only one-tenth as damaging to the road surface as were vehicles with steel wheels. The pneumatic tire became widely available for automobiles after 1900. Its effect was to encourage motorists to drive at higher speeds, which produced a new set of abrasive forces on the pavement, as well as new hazards from accidents.

But it was the discovery and development of petroleum supplies that held the key to mass ownership and operation of the automobile.[7] The symbiotic connection between the internal conbustion engine and petroleum closely resembles the partnership between steam and coal.

By the mid-nineteenth century, the burgeoning cities of the United States had come to rely heavily on whale oil for lighting. So great was the demand that Greenland's whales had been hunted virtually to extinction and the cost of whaling expeditions to the Arctic was raising the price of whale oil. Companies in the business of making and marketing illuminants began to search for alternative sources of raw materials. Their quest led them to a place in Pennsylvania known as Oil Creek.

In late August 1859, Edwin Drake and Billy Smith completed drilling the first commercial oil well in the United States, near the isolated lumbering community of Titusville in northwest Pennsylvania.[8] Although the yield of the well, only 10 barrels a day, seems modest by today's standards, the discovery set off a feverish oil boom and by late 1860 there were seventy-four wells in the area, pumping collectively more than 1,000 barrels daily. The only problem was that at first no one seemed to know what to do with such a large quantity of oil. For the next forty years, finding oil was relatively easy; figuring out what it was good for and how to increase its commercial value proved to be more difficult.

For many years prior to 1859, people had used petroleum as the base for a popular home remedy, sold as "American oil" or "Seneca oil" and touted as the solution for rheumatism, burns, scalds, cuts, and other ailments. To move beyond this small market required convincing industrial users of the values of petroleum. One obvious market, for industrial lubricants, resisted petroleum because of its impurities and foul odor. Eventually, petroleum became commercially successful by invading and winning over the market for home illuminants.

In those days, homes and offices were illuminated chiefly by whale oil or by a coal oil derivative marketed under the brand name Kerosene. Since Kerosene was already a popular product, petroleum distillers sought to wedge their way into the market by introducing a petroleum-based home illuminant under the generic name kerosene. By coincidence, the coal oil companies' patent on the name covered only the manufacturing process using coal, so it proved relatively simple to introduce a petroleum-based product similar in chemical properties but with a generic name. By the end of the Civil War, kerosene had become the commonly accepted name for all such illuminants. Kerosene remained the largest-selling petroleum product until 1911, when the growing popularity of the automobile created a great demand for gasoline.

In 1901, when the gusher Spindletop well was brought in near Beaumont, Texas, gasoline was still a nuisance by-product of crude oil. What companies like Standard Oil wanted from petroleum was kerosene for lamps (beginning to lose ground to natural gas and electricity for lighting), naphtha, lubricants, and paraffin. Gasoline was usually dumped into nearby rivers or lakes or burned as a useless and annoying by-product of the refining process. The internal combustion engine and the automobile changed all that by providing the demand for the creation of a global energy system based on petroleum. Between 1909 and 1913, a chemist working for Standard Oil, William Burton, developed the process for thermal cracking of raw petroleum, an invention that doubled the yield of gasoline from crude oil. By 1924, Burton's invention had been replaced by the even more efficient continuous cracking process. The discovery of the huge East Texas oil fields in 1930 assured the rapidly increasing motoring public that its automobiles and trucks would never lack for fuel.

The definitive event in the history of the automobile was Henry Ford's opening of the assembly line at his Highland Park, Michigan, plant in 1912–1913.[9] Ford had grown up on a farm in Michigan where he came to hate the farmers' dependence on horses for mobility and traction to pull wagons and plows. In his youth, he dreamed of creating a vehicle that would free farm families from the drudgery and expense of caring for horses. The problem was that automobile assembly was an extremely expensive process. Cars were assembled as unique products, one at a time, by teams of workers who moved through the plant from one stationary assembly site to another. The expense of such an assembly technique meant that automobile ownership was restricted to a tiny elite and was completely beyond the budget of the average worker.

As a young man working in an electric power station in Detroit, Ford had acquired a vision of a manufacturing technique wherein cars flowed through the factory just as electricity flowed through power lines. After more than a decade of study and experimentation, in August 1912, the first Ford car was assembled by moving conveyances. A process that formerly required 12½ hours had been cut to 5 hours and 50 minutes. By the end of the year, assembly time had dropped to 2½ hours; by 1925, a finished car was rolling off the line every half hour. The price dropped accordingly: In 1909, Ford's basic car sold for $900; five years later it was selling for $440. Ford's assembly line techniques appeared just in time to supply vehicles to the armies of Great Britain, France, and the United States in World War I. After the war, in the mid-1920s, Ford opened his huge River Rouge plant, at the time the state of the art in integrated automobile assembly. In later years, Ford himself would falter and his company would lose market share as other companies and other countries reigned supreme in the world automobile industry. But no one can deny Henry Ford's pivotal role in globalization, not only for making cars available to nearly everyone but for introducing the system of mass production and mass consumption that we know as "Fordism."[10]

❧   ❧   ❧

The motor vehicle powered by the internal combustion engine advanced globalization in many ways. The automobile gave drivers greatly enhanced personal mobility. Trucks brought goods to urban and suburban markets from far-off sources and moved a city's solid waste to distant sinks. Cars and trucks together stimulated the emergence of a global energy supply system that includes oil tankers, pipelines, and decentralized distribution facilities, creating thereby the preconditions for global environmental hazards such as the *Exxon Valdez* oil spill. Finally, the car became the first truly global manufactured product.

"Faster than ever before," wrote Eugene Linden in *Time* magazine in 1993, "the human world is becoming an urban world. Near the end of this decade, mankind will pass a demographic milestone: for the first time in history, more people will live in and around cities than in rural areas."[11] The process of urbanization that began with small villages in Turkey and Mesopotamia 8,000 years ago will, by the year 2000, produce twenty-one "megacities" with populations of 10 million or more. Tokyo and São Paulo will head the list, each with more than 20 million inhabitants. Such a change in the human condition would not have been possible without the application of the gasoline-powered vehicle to the complex problems of bulk flow to move people, goods, energy, and waste in huge volumes, over great distances, and with a degree of flexibility and personal choice that would have been inconceivable without cars and trucks.

The combination of personal automobiles and huge expanses of roadways, service facilities, and parking spaces has made possible the daily movement of millions of workers from home to work site within the urban area, more or less on demand (i.e., they can go where and when they wish, not dependent on the schedule of a mass conveyance). In the late 1980s, each commuter traveled by private automobile on average more than 30 miles per day in the United States and more than 14 miles per day in Germany and Great Britain.[12] The United States led the world with more than 560 cars per every 1000 persons; in Germany the number was more than 440; and in Great Britain, about 325. Commuting patterns have become increasingly complex, with work sites spreading far beyond the confines of the old central city, so that today the number of Americans who commute suburb to suburb are more than double the number who travel the traditional route from suburb to downtown.[13] Moreover, we use our unprecedented personal mobility for much more than simply getting to work. Data from the 1990 U.S. census reveal that only about 36 percent of driving miles were for work or business; the remainder were for shopping, personal business, recreation, or "running errands."

The German author Wolfgang Sachs has observed that the automobile came into prominence in Europe just as people were becoming disenchanted with the age of mass transport. The values of this age were embodied in the railway, which

> moved masses of people from one place to another, organized according to the unyielding logic of a centrally directed apparatus into multiplicitous, daily-recurring movement: locomotives, tracks, and schedules.... The automobile ... presented the possibility of escape, for it ... [represented] ... the attraction of travel guided by nothing but individual pleasure and mood.... Again and again traffic analysts have plunged into intricate investigations of why so many people prefer a car to the bus, streetcar, or subway, only to arrive at the obvious: in order to be independent in time and space, and also socially, by being able to choose one's own means of transport.... Unlike the railway, the automobile can be acquired privately and is therefore always at the owner's disposal. Because it is not bound to the tracks, ... it can be driven almost anywhere. Because one person steers it, it need not be shared with others; similarly, it can satisfy any particular desire of the driver in terms of speed.

As Sachs recognizes, however, the great paradox is that the automobile (like other privatizing technologies) achieves such a level of individual freedom only by embedding us in complex global systems that remain largely invisible to us:

> One discovers a new form of dependence behind the independence gained. Ultimately, all of these "independence machines" depend on streets and power lines, pipelines and radio waves, which in turn bind the individual with multiple ties to industries, power plants, drilling rigs, and broadcast stations. Supply networks and production apparatuses must be called into being to supply us with another increment of freedom in our private lives.[14]

Urban bulk flow technologies carry much more than people. The typical metropolitan area is a vast machine that receives enormous supplies of matter, energy, and information; processes and distributes these supplies; and sends them out again as goods, services, or waste.[15] The typical suburban supermarket offers shoppers more than 40,000 individual food products, all of which were moved through a complex global food network so immense that the typical mouthful of U.S. food travels over 1,000 miles from farm to table. California, for example, is the most important source of fresh fruits and vegetables for consumers in the Washington, D.C., metropolitan area. A food system that supplies the U.S. east coast with carrots grown in California's Imperial Valley would not be possible without truck transport and the interstate highway system. Of course, what comes in must go out again, frequently as waste; each day, for example, the city of Tokyo generates 22,000 tons of trash. Each New Yorker creates six pounds of trash per day, and each pound of it must be transported to an incinerator or landfill by truck.

The automobile and truck are only one part of a vast transportation system that involves roadways, service facilities, and an energy supply system that stretches around the world. Automobility required a road surface that could be easily laid and maintained, that was waterproof, and that provided adequate traction. By the time the automobile appeared on the scene, the technology of roadway construction had already evolved based on two substances whose existence had been known for thousands of years: asphalt and cement.[16]

Asphalt, a mixture of bitumen and porous limestone, was worked as early as the beginning of the Christian era, but was not applied as a road surface until late in the eighteenth century. Although the terms *asphalt* and *bitumen* are frequently used interchangeably, strictly speaking bitumen is the petroleum-based substance used as a binder to hold the components of asphalt together. As used initially in the nineteenth century, bitumen was a relatively minor part of the mixture, due partly to its scarcity. As the internal combustion engine increased the demand for gasoline, however, more and more bitumen became available from the petroleum distillation process and bitumen gradually became the most important part of asphalt road paving. The big advantage offered by asphalt or bitumen paving derives from the ease and speed with which it can be applied. Thus, fossil fuel became a key ingredient of the roadway over which the automobile traveled as well as the source of its energy.

Cement was known even earlier than bitumen. There exist roads built partly with concrete (cement and stones mixed) on Crete as early as 2600 B.C. and with cement in India about 1000 B.C. The modern concrete industry dates from 1824, when a British bricklayer named Joseph Aspdin obtained a patent for Portland cement, the bonding agent in today's concrete. The first reinforced concrete bridge in the United States was built in 1889, the first concrete street in 1891. Concrete is today second only to water as the world's most heavily consumed substance.[17] World production of concrete reaches about 6 billion tons annually, or about 1 ton for each person.

Of course, concrete is used in the industrial world for much more than roadways, including bridges, buildings, dams, and other infrastructure.

Asphalt and concrete made possible the construction of an enormous network of highways throughout the industrialized world by which cities and markets were integrated internally as well as connected with one another.[18] The first such roadway was the Long Island Motor Parkway built in New York in 1906 originally as a race course but opened to the public in 1908. By the 1930s, most of the major cities in the United States were linked by a road system that was usable under all weather conditions (rural roads were quite another story). In Germany, the world's first controlled-access, two-lane roadway was opened in 1921; the first stages of that country's autobahn roadway system were completed in 1932. The first stage of Italy's autostrada, between Milan and Lake Como, was opened in 1924. After World War II, with the rapid decentralization of U.S. cities and the consequent pressure on the road system, President Dwight Eisenhower initiated the planning that led to the interstate highway system. By late 1990, this system comprised nearly 43,000 miles of multilane, limited-access, high-speed roadway, referred to by one author as "the largest network of engineered structures on the earth."[19]

To supply the world's fleet of cars and trucks, a global oil network moves the precious fuel from where nature deposited it to where industrial society needs it. In the early 1990s, the world's proven oil reserves amounted to slightly more than 900 billion barrels, a supply sufficient for about forty years at current rates of consumption. Nearly two-thirds of this supply is located in the Middle East, more than a quarter in Saudi Arabia alone. North America, in contrast, possesses only about 4 percent of the world's reserves, and Western Europe about 7 percent (enough in both instances for about a decade at current rates of consumption). The world's oil rigs are pumping this petroleum out of the ground at the rate of about 65 to 70 million barrels per day. To move this petroleum from under the ground to the fuel tank of an automobile requires a global bulk flow system consisting of oil rigs and pumps, pipelines (more than 227,000 miles in the world), oil tankers (800 per day are needed just to supply the United States), barges, tanker trucks, tanker rail cars, refineries, storage facilities, and wholesale and retail distributors. In all, more than 8,200 million barrels of crude oil flow in international trade in a year.[20]

Finally, the automobile itself has become one of the leading examples of a global product: a product assembled at many different sites around the world out of components manufactured at other sites and designed for global tastes and consumer preferences.[21]

By the late 1980s, there were more than 514 million motor vehicles of all kinds in the world, more than one-third of them (183 million) in the United States alone (see Figure 6.1).[22] The world's stock of vehicles was growing by

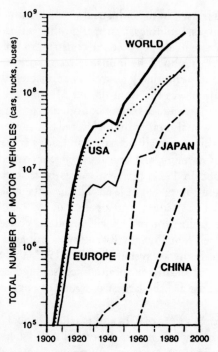

FIGURE 6.1   Motor vehicle supply, 1900–
1990, world and selected countries or regions.

Source: Vaclav Smil, *Energy in World History,*
copyright © 1994 by Westview Press.

45 to 50 million units annually, of which about 40 million were passenger
cars. The global recession and oil crises of the 1970s caused markets to
weaken in the early 1980s. But world automobile production surged ahead
in the late 1980s and 1990s as gasoline prices declined, oil supplies stabilized,
and the idea of mass automobile ownership spread to the potentially huge
and untapped markets of the developing world (Brazil and Mexico today,
India and China tomorrow). About 4 to 5 million workers are employed
worldwide in the manufacture of automobiles, with perhaps another 15 million employed indirectly through sales, service, and manufacture of materials and components.

The world's automobiles are manufactured by a relatively small number of
firms, headquartered in an even smaller number of countries. In the early
1990s, the world's top twelve manufacturers accounted for about 36 million
cars, about 90 percent of the total. These twelve included three U.S. firms
(General Motors, Ford, and Chrysler), five Japanese (Toyota, Nissan,
Honda, Mitsubishi, and Mazda), two French (Peugeot-Citroen and Re-
nault), and one each in Germany (Volkswagen) and Italy (Fiat).[23]

It would be a mistake to see these figures as evidence of national concentration of car manufacture, since the actual production and assembly of automobiles and components now takes place literally around the world, wherever the logic of labor and transport costs dictates. The global car production system that emerged in the 1980s and 1990s was a response to rising pressure from Japanese firms in the world car market. In the 1970s, Japanese firms, aided by rising fuel prices, government supports, a productive and cooperative labor force, and a commitment to what Kurt Hoffman and Raphael Kaplinsky call "systemofacture," surged into a commanding position in world auto markets.[24] There were three responses from carmakers in the United States and Western Europe. One reaction was to raise trade barriers, such as "voluntary" export quotas the Japanese imposed on themselves, which simply encouraged firms like Honda and Nissan to establish plants abroad where they could sell to U.S. and European markets "inside" the barriers. The second reaction was to move many of their component plants "offshore" to low-cost producers such as the *maquiladora* assembly plants in northern Mexico near the U.S. border. The third reaction was to enter into a large number of joint ventures that led to the emergence of a complex web of global connections among and between automobile companies. These changes in turn were made possible by technological advances in transport (containerization) and communications (fax machines, satellite telecommunications) that dramatically reduced the costs of global bulk flow.

꙳   ꙳   ꙳

As the lateen sail made possible the conquest of wind and tides, and the steam engine the conquest of land and ocean barriers, the airplane emerged in the first decade of the twentieth century to permit human beings to cross the last obstacle to globalization: the air.

At the turn of the century, scientists, engineers, and inventors in the United States and Europe were working feverishly to become the first to build a machine for controlled, powered flight.[25] Much of their attention was directed at the Saint Louis Fair of 1904, where prizes amounting to $200,000 were offered for the best aeronautical designs. In France, experiments focused on balloons as the way of gaining altitude; in the United States, aeronautical experts like Octave Chanute and Samuel Pierpont Langley concentrated on heavier-than-air craft. Early experiments involved either models or full-size gliders, since the piloting of aircraft under power was considered too risky as well as unnecessary. The principal problems lay in controlling and steering the primitive biplanes; experimenters were confident that once they had solved the problems of wing design and control, the addition of a power source would be relatively easy.

From their bicycle shop in Dayton, Ohio, Wilbur and Orville Wright joined in the race to innovate the first powered flying machine. Lacking much of a formal education, they placed their faith in frequent and continuous experimentation; careful observation and measurement; and the use of full-scale gliders, which they themselves piloted (instead of models or gliders flown by others). Their successful bicycle business taught them how to work with metal and machine tools and they read constantly about the experiments of others in the aeronautical field, so they were able to use the latest discoveries from related areas. To give stability to their wing design, they borrowed the principle of the truss from bridge construction. They studied information about the behavior of propeller screws on steamships for ideas about how to design their propellers. The idea for the skids on which their airplane rested came from the simple sled. And when they finally moved toward powered flight, their engine was a simplified automobile gasoline engine that they designed and built themselves.

In autumn 1900, with their bicycle business more or less closed for the winter, the Wright brothers set off for the sand dunes of the North Carolina coast for their first experiments with gliders. Their first season of trials taught them a number of valuable lessons, but the next year, 1901, they suffered a series of accidents and reversals that made them seriously consider abandoning the quest altogether. But they persisted and the tests in 1902 went much better, so much so that they set about to add an engine to their glider for the next year's experiments. Thus, they came to another pivotal moment in globalization: The morning of December 17, 1903, when, in the teeth of a freezing 25-mile-per-hour wind, Orville Wright became the first human being to experience controlled, powered flight. The first flight lasted all of 12 seconds. There would be three more flights that morning, the last for 59 seconds (and covering 852 feet).

The age of air travel was still some years in the future. Because of the Wrights' reluctance to exploit the publicity value of their achievement, there were no outside observers at their test site and they routinely denied interviews to the reporters seeking to know more about what they had done. The world paid little attention to this first flight and there would be little done to expand on this achievement for several years.

World War I would change all that. For the first time, warfare involved aircraft that could be maneuvered more or less at the will of the operator. Aerial bombardment and combat between airplanes made their appearance and a new generation of aircraft and pilots emerged from the war as heroes to spark an interest in commercial aviation. Radio technology made possible reliable communication between ground and air. Airmail service was established between London and Paris in 1919 and between New York and San Francisco in 1921 (with a flying time of 33 hours). Commercial air service began between London and India in 1929, a trans-Pacific route was launched between the United States and the Philippines in 1935, and trans-Atlantic airmail service started in 1939. Despite the creation of large corporate enterprises to build and operate the new airlines, this was still an age of lone heroes. The solo flight of Charles Lindbergh across the Atlantic in 1927 (in 33

1/2 hours) and of Wiley Post around the world in 1933 (in 7 days, 18 hours) drew the world's attention to air travel. What Magellan and Elcano had done in years and the steamship had done in months could now be done in a week or less thanks to the internal combustion engine.

It would be difficult to exaggerate the globalizing effects of the airplane in the period after World War II. Thanks to improvements in aircraft design, especially in the power-to-weight ratio of airplane engines, the cost of air travel fell sharply after 1945.

Between the Wright brothers' first flight and the 1950s, the piston engine was the airplane's sole source of power. In the 1930s, however, experimenters in Great Britain and Germany began working on a revolutionary new engine design, the gas turbine. After the war, engine developments were rapid. The first commercial passenger jet, the Comet, introduced in 1952, was a failure, but in 1958, Boeing introduced the Boeing 707 and jet air travel became a commercial possibility. In 1969, the wide-bodied Boeing 747 was introduced and it has maintained its primacy on long passenger flights ever since. Aircraft cruising speeds have increased exponentially, from about 90 miles (144 km) per hour in 1920 to 1,500 miles (2,400 km) per hour, or twice the speed of sound (the Concorde), in the 1970s (see Figure 6.2). Maximum ranges have likewise increased, from 360 miles (576 km) in 1920 to more than 8,000 miles (12,800 km) in the case of the Boeing 747. As a result of lowered fuel consumption per passenger mile, the cost of air travel declined steadily. In

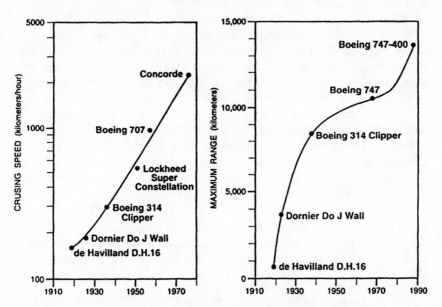

FIGURE 6.2   Aircraft cruising speeds and maximum ranges, 1910–1990.

Source: Vaclav Smil, *Energy in World History,* copyright © 1994 by Westview Press.

1990, the average air transport cost per passenger mile was only one-sixth what it was in 1930 (measured in 1990 dollars). Deregulation of airline routes and prices in the United States sparked a further drop in prices. Vaclav Smil summed up these advances this way:

> The speed and range of these planes, the proliferation of airlines and flights, and the nearly universal linking of reservation systems has made it possible to travel among virtually all major cities of the planet in a single day. Naturally, cargo deliveries can duplicate this feat. . . . These achievements opened up new business opportunities as well as mass long-distance tourism to major cities and to subtropical and tropical beaches. They also opened up new possibilities for unprecedented migrant and refugee movements, for widespread drug smuggling, and for international terrorism involving aircraft hijacking.[26]

We so take for granted today the ease and speed with which we travel by air that we forget how novel is the bulk flow of people in this way.[27] It is worth recalling that the word "travel" is derived from *travail*, meaning "work" or "torment," which itself is derived from the Latin *tripalium*, which was an instrument of torture. Roman elites invented the idea of vacation or holiday travel around the first century B.C., but the practice remained beyond the reach of all but a fortunate few for nearly the next two millennia.[28] Not until the 1960s could working-class Europeans regularly vacation farther from home than a train could travel in a day. As late as 1972, fewer than half of all Americans had ever flown in their life.

Today, travel for pleasure, or tourism, accounts for two-thirds to three-fourths of all world travel by volume. In the late 1950s, world tourism involved perhaps 50 million travelers a year. Three decades later, the number approached 350 million. Of course, pleasure travelers are not the only people who have felt the impact of the revolution in air transport. The number of world emigrants (i.e., refugees, asylees, immigrants, and others who cross national borders more or less permanently) reached 80 million in 1992,[29] a number unprecedented considering the relative absence of global warfare. In addition to about 1.25 billion passengers, the world's airlines carry each year about 22 million tons of freight, representing almost a quarter of the value of the world's manufactured exports.[30] The world's largest package delivery company, UPS, handles more than a million packages by air each day, serves 610 airports, and has more than 300,000 employees, 119,500 vehicles, 220 aircraft, and revenue reaching nearly $18 billion annually.[31]

Ironically, the industry that made possible the high-speed global flow of goods and people via the airways has not itself become a global enterprise. A 1995 article in *The Economist* put it this way:

> The world's aviation industry is, as always, in a mess. International aviation is governed by a mixture of nationalism, mercantilism and wishful thinking. In America, airlines go in and out of bankruptcy with bewildering rapidity. In Eu-

rope there is an endless flow of public subsidy. Even Asia's aviators are hidebound by restrictions and national turf battles.

The very industry that has shrunk the world physically is itself one of the least "global." There is no global market, no global allocation of capital, no global competition between airlines; indeed, set beside other industries such as cars, personal computers or hotels, there are no truly global companies.[32]

The costs of developing new technologies in the aviation field are so huge that only a few U.S. firms remain of the more than a dozen that emerged as pioneers in aircraft manufacture after World War II.[33] To launch a new aircraft model requires investments of $2 to $4 billion, cash flow is negative for five years or more, and profits do not appear for up to fourteen years. New engine models cost at least $1 billion to develop and require sales of about 2,000 units over ten years to break even. For these reasons, today only three giant firms manufacture over 90 percent of the world's aircraft: Boeing and McDonnell-Douglas in the United States, and the European consortium Airbus Industrie.

Somewhat the same picture appears when we consider the world's airline operating companies. After a decade of ups and downs in the 1980s, the world's airlines ran operating losses of nearly $8 billion in 1990 and about $5 billion in 1991. At about the same time, some of the great firms in the airline industry collapsed: Braniff in 1990 and Pan Am and Eastern in 1991. Others, such as TWA, have seen their market share cut in half and their profits turn to losses, in some years in the hundreds of millions of dollars. The fate of these huge corporate enterprises is a powerful reminder that the process of globalization has both its winners and its losers.

Episode Seven

Part One: Prelude to the Information Age

Almost as soon as trade began, exchange networks were used to move information as well as matter and energy. Bronze Age Minoans exported their tastes and lifestyle to other peoples of the eastern Mediterranean; Buddhism followed trade caravans along the Silk Road to China. The Portuguese caravel of the fifteenth century was as much a feedback device as anything else. Steamships, railroads, trucks, and airplanes all moved us closer to a global information system by facilitating the bulk flow of physical messengers: people and containers carrying or accompanying the messages.

In the nineteenth century, we acquired the ability to transmit information via waves of electric pulses, first over a physical medium (copper wire), and then through the air. By the mid-twentieth century, these matured technologies had brought us to the brink of the Information Age. Our ability to move information virtually in real time around the world has become an essential ingredient of a global economy and culture.

The key to an information-based society lay in the application of bulk flow technologies to information, an achievement that proved to be extremely difficult and expensive. Early information technologies such as writing and paper were critically important for the storage of information, but they still relied on the physical movement of the message or the messenger to transmit that information and thus remained constrained by the historic limits to the movement of matter and energy generally (i.e., wind, water, and muscle). Although some modest progress in the bulk movement of information over long distances was recorded before the nineteenth century (e.g., a network of towers and visual signals in France in the eighteenth century), "for the greater part of human history," observes Arthur Clarke, news from far parts of the world must have been rather like the information that astronomers glean about distant stars—something that happened a long time ago, and about which there is nothing that can be done. . . . When Queen Victoria came to the throne in 1837, she had no swifter means of sending messages to the far parts of her empire than had Julius Caesar—or, for that matter, Moses. . . . The galloping horse and the sailing ship remained the swiftest means of transport, as they had for five thousand years.[1]

The information revolution of the late twentieth century did not require the discovery of very many, if any, really novel technologies. Beginning with the harnessing of electricity in the nineteenth century, industrial society launched a wave of experimentation, invention, and innovation that became a flood in the second half of the twentieth. By the time the Information Age dawned, about 1960, most of its fundamental technologies were already in place. I focus first on technologies that were already in existence before 1960: electricity and artificial illumination, the telegraph and telephone, radio and television, and the transistor and computers. I briefly mention others that had yet to be applied commercially although the scientific principles on which they were based were already understood: space exploration, xerography, lasers, fiber optics, cable television, and digital encoding. Thus, the Information Age was founded not so much on new technologies as on the novel convergence and combination of already-existing technologies as well as their widespread application, diffusion, commercialization, and institutionalization.

꘎   ꘎   ꘎

The technology from which the information revolution was launched was the commercial generation and distribution of electricity over great distances and in a form that could be used in offices and homes.[2] Scientists of the seventeenth and eighteenth centuries had established some of the important principles of static electricity (i.e., electric charges), but it was not until the dawn of the nineteenth century that Alessandro Volta of Italy showed how moving electricity (electric current) could be generated by bringing two different metals into contact in a solution. Volta's first battery, unveiled in 1800, greatly facilitated experimentation by providing a steady and continuous source of electricity. In 1820, the Danish physicist Hans Oersted demonstrated that electric current had the power to deflect a magnetic needle, a discovery that launched the study of electromagnetism. Shortly after, the French scientist A. M. Ampère established the relationship between the strength of a magnetic field and that of the electric current that produces it. In 1831, Great Britain's Michael Faraday used electromagnetism to produce mechanical motion for the first time.

Steady improvement in batteries through the mid-nineteenth century was of critical importance, especially to the telegraph, and by the 1880s, batteries were being used to light railway carriages and propel automobiles. But for electric current to be of maximum utility at the level of homes and businesses, some way had to be invented to generate and distribute much larger amounts of electricity on demand (i.e., as it was needed) and at a voltage level low enough to provide room illumination. (Arc lights were being used to light city streets by midcentury, but they used voltage too high to be feasible for interior illumination.) By the early 1830s, the principle was already known that current could be produced by rotating a coil of copper wire (called the armature) inside a fixed magnet. In 1857, it was demonstrated in England that a steam engine could be used to turn the coil, and by the 1870s, the dynamo using steam to produce electricity was in wide use. At the same time, there were experiments in using falling water to turn the armature; in 1886, the world's first large-scale hydroelectric plant was begun at Niagara Falls.

The industrial world now possessed the technology to produce huge quantities of electric current on demand, but there remained the very significant problem of distribution. The earliest generators produced alternating current (AC), but many people regarded electricity in this form as too dangerous for use in homes or by average consumers—the inventor of the electric chair used AC to deliver a lethal dose to execute a prisoner (done for the first time in 1890)—and direct current (DC) was the preferred form in which to deliver the current to homes. To convert AC to DC, a device called a commutator was invented, but it was troublesome and inconvenient, and in any event DC presented great obstacles to long-distance transmission. To move electric current over great distances, it had to be done in high voltages and then transformed ("stepped down") at or near the point where it was to be used. For technical reasons, DC could be generated at high voltages only with great difficulty.

In the United States, the controversy between AC and DC took the form of what Dirk Hanson calls "the current war," an intense personal struggle between Thomas Edison, who championed direct current, and George Westinghouse, who advocated AC.[3] In this struggle, each man had his ego as well as his corporate interests at stake. Edison was first into the market, generating and delivering electricity from his Pearl Street plant in New York City in 1882. In 1893, Westinghouse began delivering alternating current for household use from his Niagara Falls plant and before long DC had essentially disappeared from the market. There remained a number of challenging engineering problems to be solved, including the design and manufacture of underground cables and methods of stringing high-voltage lines on aboveground poles. But by the turn of the century, most of these problems had been solved and the delivery of electricity to homes, offices, and factories was an established fact (see Figure 7.1).

The first device to utilize electricity to transmit information was the telegraph.[4] "In its day," writes Maury Klein,

the telegraph was no less a miracle than any of its modern offspring. It dazzled and bewildered people ... with feats that seemed magical if not unnatural....

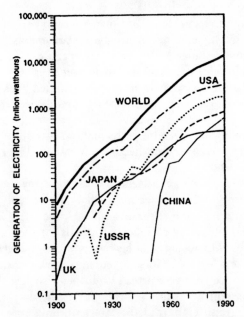

FIGURE 7.1 Generation of electricity, 1900–
1990, world and selected countries.

Source: Vaclav Smil, *Energy in World History,*
copyright © 1994 by Westview Press.

The telegraph was an innovation without precedent, born at a time when few grasped even remotely what electric current was, let alone what it might do. As the first form of modern communication, it burst upon the sensibilities of a people proud of progress but still new to technical leaps of such magnitude.... For the first time messages could routinely travel great distances faster than man or beast could carry them.[5]

Samuel F. B. Morse was not the first person to conceive of sending messages via electric current. The idea seems to have gone back as far as 1753; in the late eighteenth and early nineteenth century there were a number of efforts to send information by means of sparks, electrochemical effects, and other media. None of these offered any prospect for success until the achievements of the 1820s and 1830s: Oersted's discovery of the magnetic properties of electricity, Faraday's discovery of how to produce mechanical motion by electromagnetism, and major improvements in batteries.

It was a chance dinner conversation about these experiments aboard an ocean liner in 1832 that first caught the attention of Morse, who was returning from Europe after three years of painting, traveling, and studying. When told that Benjamin Franklin had passed an electric current over several miles of wire without perceptible delay, Morse replied, "If this be so, and the presence of electricity can be made visible in any desired part of the circuit, I see no reason why intelligence might not be instantaneously transmitted by electricity to any distance." Before the voyage concluded, Morse had sketched out his idea for the telegraph, including an early version of his code of dots and dashes. This latter invention, as modified by Morse's associate, Alfred Vail, we now recognize as one of the first devices that exploited the binary ("on-off" or "positive-negative") characteristic of electromagnetism as a way of encoding and decoding information. A century later, the binary nature of electric current would become an essential ingredient in digital technology.

In the mid-1830s, Morse experienced a series of reversals in his chosen profession, painting, and in his secondary field, politics, all of which served to focus his attention on the telegraph. In 1837, the U.S. Congress directed the secretary of the treasury to solicit proposals for such a device; by September of that year Morse had built his first working model for the competition. To create the telegraph, Morse invented no new technologies; his great advantage in the race lay in his artist's ability to visualize the way multiple disconnected components could be brought together in a complex working system. His telegraph embraced the latest findings in electromagnetism along with the graphic arts, batteries, and of course his code. Morse first demonstrated his invention in Washington in February 1838 and was awarded the contract. But Congress delayed giving him the money—some $30,000—until March 1843. He immediately began construction of the line between Washington and Baltimore and on May 24, 1844, transmitted the famous message, "What hath God wrought?"

The relationship between the two great movers of the nineteenth century, the telegraph and the steam engine, was close and direct. Without the railroad and the steamship, the wires and cables that were to carry the new "telegrams" could have been installed only at much higher cost and over a much longer span of time and perhaps the laying of submarine cable would have been physically impossible. In return, the telegraph made possible the long-distance control and coordination of the huge and complex enterprises that built and operated the world's railroads and steamships.

From the time of their introduction, the railroad and the telegraph were partners in the building of the United States. Morse's demonstration line between Washington and Baltimore ran along the right-of-way of the Baltimore and Ohio Railroad, the company giving him permission to use their land if it could be done "without injury to the road and without embarrassment to the operations of the company." As the railroads increased the number and length of their lines and the frequency and size of the individual trains, coordination and control became severe problems.[6] A particular hazard lay in trains running in opposite directions at high speeds (30 miles per hour) on the same piece of track. In 1841, a head-on collision of two passenger trains in Massachusetts killed two and injured seventeen, leading to calls for increased control over trains. The telegraph was to provide the communication technology so vital to meet these needs. The railroads in turn provided the demand for telegraphy as well as the land over which the lines could be strung. The telegraph was first used by a railroad official to control train movement in 1851 and became a commonplace technology in railroad management by the mid-1850s. By 1861, telegraph lines crossed the continent.

The stretching of telegraph cables along the ocean floor proved to be a much greater challenge and much more expensive than stringing them on poles across dry land.[7] Again, steam power proved essential to the enterprise. The first attempt, carried out in summer 1858, involved two steamships, one each from Great Britain and the United States laying its respective half of the cable, meeting in the Atlantic midway between Ireland and Newfoundland, where the cable was spliced. Commercial transmissions began on August 17, but ceased abruptly on September 1, for reasons that no one ever discovered. This first failure cost investors £350,000. In 1865, backers tried again, this time using the magnificent British steamship, the *Great Eastern,* 700 feet long and displacing 32,000 tons. Again failure was the result, this time within a few hundred miles of the Newfoundland coast. Finally, in 1866, the first success-ful trans-Atlantic telegraph cable was laid, again by the *Great Eastern,* fol-lowed just a few months later by a second, which was achieved by finding and repairing the cable lost the preceding year.

In the history of globalization, the telegraph belongs in the same category with the camel caravan, the caravel, the oil pipeline, and the steamship. Thanks to Morse and the determined financiers who supported the enor-mous initial capital investments required to construct the cable networks, by 1862 the world's telegraph system covered approximately 150,000 miles, in-cluding 48,000 in the United States. By 1872, when the mayors of Adelaide, Australia, and London exchanged messages, almost all the principal cities of the world were connected by cable. By the turn of the century, information could be sent to virtually any large population center at the speed of electric-ity. In 1903, President Theodore Roosevelt sent the first telegraph message around the world. It took just 12 minutes.

The telegraph also stimulated the advance of other information media, in-cluding newspapers. The telegraph made it possible to gather information globally and relay it to major cities to be reported in the next day's newspa-per. In 1848, six newspapers in New York jointly financed construction of a telegraph line to Boston, principally to transmit information about ships from Europe that docked in Boston before continuing on to New York. In 1856, this consortium took on the name of the New York Associated Press and began selling a wire information service that eventually became simply the Associated Press.[8]

⊷   ⊷   ⊷

It was one thing to send digitally encoded messages along copper wire by means of electric pulses; it was quite another to transmit the sound of the human voice along the same medium.[9] Human speech is carried through the air in pressure waves that vary continuously over a very wide range, from a low of 50 cycles per second to a high of about 5,000. In addition, each individual human voice is made up of a unique and incredibly complex combination of frequencies, which we detect and decode to understand and recognize each other as we converse. Any method of speech communication must carry a wide band of frequencies from one spot to another without distortion. Fortunately, it is not necessary to carry the entire range for a voice to be recognized. A more narrow range of 200 to 2,000 cycles suffices.

By the 1870s, inventors in many countries were trying to achieve the electrical transmission of speech. The historic honor of solving the problem belongs, of course, to Alexander Graham Bell, but only by several hours. Had Bell delayed even a day in delivering his design to the U.S. Patent Office, Elisha Gray would be the name every schoolchild remembers as the inventor of the telephone and Bell would be only a footnote in history.

Bell discovered the central principle of telephony in June 1875, patented it in March 1876, and demonstrated it to the world at the centennial exposition in Philadelphia that June. Considering what it had to do, the instrument was extremely simple. It consisted of an iron diaphragm placed within the field of a horseshoe magnet. The pressure waves of speech caused the diaphragm to vibrate, generating corresponding fluctuations of electric current, which were transmitted along the line to an identical device, which converted the fluctuations back into sound.

Inventing the instrument itself was only the first step. The wire network necessary to transmit the electric pulses was already in place, thanks to the telegraph, which had been in operation for some three decades. But central switching offices had to be constructed so that multiple calls could be connected and routed through a single wire to each customer. Without telephone exchanges, each user would have had to be connected with all the others on the system by a direct wire, a requirement that would have overloaded the technology in short order. (The idea of a central switching or routing facility is an important component of any bulk flow technology, such as, e.g., today's air cargo services like UPS or Federal Express.) The first central telephone exchange opened in New Haven, Connecticut, in January 1878.

A second problem was how to manufacture equipment fast enough to keep pace with demand. Bell's company, the American Bell Telephone Company, met this challenge by buying controlling interest in the largest electrical manufacturing company in the United States, Western Electric of Chicago. Finally, Bell had to fight and win a series of more than 600 court battles over patent rights to the new device, mostly with Elisha Gray's company, Western Union. The turning point in this battle occurred in 1879, when Bell and Western Union settled out of court, agreeing essentially to stay out of each other's business. The agreement gave Bell a monopoly over the telephone business in the United States, a monopoly that theoretically would expire when the patents ran out in the 1890s. By that time, however, American Bell and its successor, American Telephone and Telegraph (AT&T), had become the single most powerful provider of telephone service in the United States. By 1913, all surviving competitors had been largely vanquished or bought up, making Bell virtually the sole provider of telephone service to the United States.

When the telephone first appeared, people had difficulty imagining how it could be used. After all, the telegraph was already available to send messages at the speed of electricity. Why would anyone want to transmit voices at the same speed? The telephone seemed too complicated for average people to use without a great deal of training. It was not, in today's terms, user friendly. (The same would be said, decades later, about the computer.) It did not take long, however, for the device to spread exponentially across the United States and eventually the world. In 1878, there were 10,000 telephones in the United States, a number that increased to 100,000 by 1886, to 1 million by 1901, to 6 million by 1907 (of which 3 million were part of the Bell system), to nearly 8 million by 1919, and to more than 13 million by 1920. Local calls increased from 237,000 in 1880, to 7.6 million in 1900, to 50.2 million in 1920. AT&T grew apace. Book value of plant and equipment in the Bell system grew from $15.7 million in 1880, to $181 million in 1900, to $1.4 billion in 1920.

Connecting the world by telephone proved to be orders of magnitude more difficult than spreading lines within a single country. For two reasons, both having to do with the characteristics of submarine cables, the oceans were a much greater barrier to transmitting the human voice than to sending the electric pulses of the telegraph. First, telephone signals inevitably fade out (or "attenuate") as they pass through a submarine cable; and second, different frequencies travel through the cable at different speeds. For these reasons, when human speech first crossed the Atlantic, between Arlington, Virginia, and Paris in October 1915, it was carried by the recently discovered technology of wireless telegraphy, or what we more commonly call radio. For more than forty years, global telephony would depend on radio for its transmission medium. The first commercial radio-telephone service between New York and London was launched in 1927; the first telephone conversation around the world took place in 1935.

Beginning in the 1920s, the technology of long-distance telephone transmission through cable was improved in three ways. Coaxial cables were developed to carry multiple messages simultaneously. The vacuum tube, invented in 1906–1907, made possible signal repeater stations that could amplify the signal sufficiently to carry it thirty miles or so. And terminal equipment was designed to handle the thousands of messages being sent and received at either end. Although delayed by World War II, development of a long-distance submarine telephone cable resumed in the late 1940s. In 1950, a cable was laid between Key West, Florida, and Havana, Cuba. When it proved successful, AT&T and the British post office agreed to attempt a trans-Atlantic cable, which was successfully installed in 1956. Soon after, however, cable technology was overtaken by one of the leading bulk flow devices of the Information Age: communications satellites.

⊹   ⊹   ⊹

In 1873, the British mathematical physicist James Clerk Maxwell published his classic *Treatise on Electricity and Magnetism*, in which he argued that when an electric current oscillates in a conductor it emits waves that travel through space at the speed of light.[10] In fact, he concluded, these waves differ from light only by possessing longer wavelengths. A decade later, the German physicist Heinrich Hertz was the first to generate and detect such waves. In 1895, Ernest Rutherford transmitted messages via these waves over a distance of three-quarters of a mile near Cambridge, England. One year later, the great Italian scientist, Guglielmo Marconi, immigrated to England, where he conducted his most famous experiments in wireless telegraphy, as the new medium was called.

On December 12, 1901, Marconi made history by sending the first wireless telegraphy message across the Atlantic, from Cornwall to Newfoundland. The achievement left many physicists dumbfounded, for if radio waves behaved like light, they should not bend around the curve of the Earth but shoot off into space a few miles from their transmitter. The next year, the British physicist Oliver Heaviside proposed the answer to this puzzle: The radio waves were being reflected back to the Earth by a layer in the upper atmosphere. It was not until 1924 that the existence of this layer, the ionosphere, was confirmed.

Meanwhile, in 1904, John Ambrose Fleming invented the diode valve, the ancestor of the vacuum tube, which turned radio waves into audible signals. In 1906, Lee De Forest made one of the truly historic discoveries of the century, the triode amplifier, which made it possible to amplify these signals. De Forest's tube, which he called the audion, transformed the science of electricity into the industry of electronics. It ranks alongside the transistor and the integrated circuit in bringing us to the Information Age. By 1912, De Forest had shown how the vacuum tube could generate the continuous waves necessary to broadcast radio signals, but with his own company near financial collapse he sold his patent to AT&T, which saw in the triode amplifier the secret to long-distance telephony. World War I stimulated electronics research and development, including the first crude radar devices; submarine detection; electronic signaling; and the science of encoding and decoding messages, cryptography.

Until World War I, most people thought of wireless technology as a way of sending sound waves from one point to another, that is, wireless telephony. The decade after the war saw the arrival of radio as a commercially viable medium. In 1919, under pressure from the administration of President Woodrow Wilson, the Radio Corporation of America (RCA) was founded by a consortium that included General Electric, AT&T, and Westinghouse.[11] The goal of the new corporation was to sell radiotelegraph services, thereby keeping Marconi's British firm out of the U.S. market in this vital technology. In 1920, pursuing an idea advanced by the company's commercial manager, David Sarnoff, RCA began to explore the feasibility of broadcasting radio to a general audience.

Sarnoff was not alone. In 1920, a Westinghouse executive named Henry Davis learned of attempts by a Westinghouse engineer to broadcast wireless transmissions from his garage in East Pittsburgh, and Davis encouraged his company to enter the broadcasting field commercially. On November 2, 1920, the country's first commercial radio station, KDKA in Pittsburgh, broadcast the results of the Harding-Cox presidential election and a new information transmission medium was born.[12] By the end of 1922, 576 commercial stations were broadcasting across the country. In 1922, RCA began selling crystal radio sets; in 1923, it launched its own network of radio stations; and in 1926, the National Broadcasting Company (NBC) was formed as a subsidiary of RCA. Sarnoff became RCA's chairman in 1930 and remained until his death in 1971 one of the most influential leaders in the radio and television industries. In 1922, 100,000 radio receiver sets were sold, and by 1925, 5.5 million sets were in use. By 1930, half of all U.S. homes had radio, a proportion that increased to 90 percent by 1950.

World War II transformed the radio industry. Spurred by demands for military hardware, by 1945, industry employment climbed from 110,000 to 560,000 and sales rose from $240 million to $4.5 billion. The government, leading universities, independent research laboratories, and corporations joined in a massive research effort that focused on two-way radio communication, radar, antisubmarine warfare, radio jamming, and electronic calculating machines. The war gave the new electronics industry the military foundation that sustained it for the next four decades.

War-related changes in the radio industry had two important consequences for globalization. The first involved using radio and radar to improve the safety and efficiency of air travel. After the war, two-way radios became common in airplanes and instrument landing systems supplemented radio beacons in helping pilots know their position relative to the glide path. Radar was installed at airports for the first time in 1948, in New York, Washington, and Chicago.

The second impact was even more momentous: the invention of the transistor.[13] Before the war, two scientists at Bell Laboratories, Walter Brattain and William Shockley, had begun research to replace the vacuum tube with a solid-state semiconductor device. During the war, the military became interested in semiconductors as radar detectors and more than thirty laboratories had investigated germanium and silicon to determine how these substances could be used to make semiconductors. After the war, Bell Laboratories returned to this research. Brattain and Shockley were joined by John Bardeen and together they discovered the transistor effect in 1947, for which they received the Nobel Prize. The discovery was patented and officially announced to the world in 1948. The transistor was at first restricted to military applications, but the first transistor radio appeared in 1954, radically altering the entire radio "culture" by making the device something that could be carried in a pocket or in the palm of one's hand. By 1960, Americans were buying more than 20 million radios each year, one-third of them imported from Japan.

Of greatest significance to the story of globalization, however, is the role of the transistor as the precursor to the integrated circuit. Transistors were a great improvement over vacuum tubes in all kinds of electronic devices. They were smaller, lighter, cooler, more reliable, and used less power. But as the numbers of transistors used in computers increased to thousands, it became difficult to wire them all together. The solution lay in fabricating a device with many transistors already wired into a single piece of silicon: an integrated circuit.

֍   ֍   ֍

In the 1920s, the radio industry fostered the invention and development of another high-impact technology of the Information Age: television.[14] Credit for inventing television is shared by two people: an American, Philo Farnsworth, and a Russian immigrant to the United States, Vladimir Zworykin. Farnsworth's patents were obtained about 1930, but even though his system was technologically sound it proved to be a commercial failure. Zworykin, on the other hand, had the good fortune to be hired by David Sarnoff at RCA in 1930. Zworykin had worked for Westinghouse after coming to the United States in 1919; he demonstrated his first television camera, which he called the iconoscope, for Westinghouse engineers in 1924. When Westinghouse failed to show interest in the project, Zworykin moved to RCA, where Sarnoff was willing to invest heavily in the untried technology.

RCA began testing television in 1935 and made experimental broadcasts in 1936. In 1939, the company used the New York world's fair to demonstrate television publicly for the first time. In April, President Franklin Roosevelt's speech opening the fair was broadcast to the few people in the New York area who owned television receivers. At the RCA pavilion, visitors to the fair could watch live broadcasts and even see themselves on the screen of the new medium.

RCA was preparing to launch the new technology when the outbreak of World War II forced the electronics industry to concentrate on radar and other war projects. Television sets went on sale for the first time in summer 1946, but only 8,000 were sold that year. Most people got their first look at the new invention by gathering in front of store windows and listening to the sound via outside speakers.

It did not take long, however, for television to saturate the U.S. market. Households with television sets rose from 1 million in 1949, to 5 million in 1950, to 10 million in 1951, to 45 million (90 percent of all homes) in 1960. Television broadcasting stations increased from 100 in 1950 to 500 in 1960.

The rapid spread of television was helped by several factors. The war had imposed such a restraint on consumption that there was enormous pent-up demand that eagerly absorbed this new entertainment medium. The baby boom, which began in 1946, increased dramatically the number of families with young children and television was sold as a way for families to enjoy entertainment together and at home. Moreover, television could use existing infrastructure and did not require the invention of new technologies to distribute its signal. Thanks to the Rural Electrification Administration of the Roosevelt administration, virtually every home in the United States had electricity in 1950, something that was not the case in 1930. Television could be transmitted through the air and owners could install a set in their home simply by plugging it into an electric outlet and adjusting the antenna. "Software" was also easily available. For the first several decades, the most popular television programs were simply radio programs transplanted to the new medium.

In the 1950s, however, television demonstrated its impact on U.S. (and eventually global) culture in ways that radio and film could not match. On November 18, 1951, Edward R. Murrow's premier broadcast of *See It Now* featured a split-screen view of the Brooklyn Bridge and San Francisco's Golden Gate Bridge, prompting Murrow to observe, "We are impressed by a medium through which a man sitting in his living room has been able for the first time to look at two oceans at once."[15] Not coincidentally, 1951 was the year that *I Love Lucy* became the first true hit television program in the United States.

In 1952, television covered live the national presidential nominating conventions (making Walter Cronkite a national figure), and in 1954, coverage of the Army-McCarthy hearings demonstrated television's power to bring major events live into the living room. Sports events, game shows, and feature films also were introduced to television in the 1950s. Cable television (formally known as community antenna television, or CATV) service was established in 1948, and by 1965, there were 1,570 such systems in operation. The first transcontinental television broadcast occurred in 1951. In 1956, a U.S. firm, Ampex, made the key breakthrough (a rapidly rotating recording and playback head) that made video recording possible. Color television sets went on sale for the first time in 1956, but sales were disappointing until broadcasting in color became commonplace in the mid-1960s.

As a global medium, television belongs more properly in our discussion of the second part of Episode 7. The important advances that have linked the world via television, such as user-friendly video recording and playback, satellite broadcasting, mass usage of cable, interactive television, and many more, were all still in the future.

‹⊕   ‹⊕   ‹⊕

The notion of a machine to perform complex calculations has fascinated people since the ancient Greeks. The first adding machine was invented in 1617 by John Napier (the inventor of logarithms) and the slide rule appeared in 1621. Numerous scientists and inventors tried their hand at creating other such machines; Blaise Pascal, for example, invented a device for performing calculations in 1642. Credit for having devised the first machine for calculating mathematical tables is usually given to the English scientist Charles Babbage, who began designing a mathematical calculator in 1822. Babbage tired of this project and began designing an even more elaborate machine, which he called the analytical engine, in 1833. This device would have been programmable using punched cards and would have had the ability to perform calculations in a sequence that the machine itself selected. Babbage worked on the design for this machine until his death in 1871, but it was never built. In concept, however, it was the forerunner of the modern computer.

The hardware on which early computers were based was all available by the late nineteenth century. The idea of using a keyboard to encode messages originated with the typewriter, invented in 1829 and perfected in 1873 by Christopher Sholes into the machine we know today.[16] The first application of this principle beyond the typewriter was the linotype, invented in 1884, which revolutionized the setting of type for newspapers. The use of punched cards to store and sort information was invented by Herman Hollerith (the founder of International Business Machines [IBM]) in the 1880s and first used by the U.S. census bureau to record data in the 1890 census. Hollerith, it is said, got the idea for his system from the punched cards invented by a French silk weaver, Joseph Marie Jacquard, in 1800 to control the looms that wove complex patterns in cloth.

The rapid development of these and other technologies between the late nineteenth and the mid-twentieth century was forced by several fundamental changes in U.S. and global culture:[17] the exponential growth in world population as well as the speed and volume of global population movements, the expansion of industrial production and trade, and the increasing complexity of warfare and weapons systems. These and related changes brought about unprecedented increases in the volume of data to be gathered, stored, and analyzed, and this "analytical imperative" was heightened by the pressure of fast-moving events that made speed essential. For example, after Hollerith invented the punched card as a way of storing enormous volumes of data, life insurance companies began using these machines to compile mortality data, railroads used them to analyze their operations, the U.S. army used them to inventory medical records in World War I, and the Social Security Administration used them to store records on recipients and even to write checks after 1937.

Just storing huge amounts of information was not enough, however. Scientists and engineers began in the 1920s and 1930s to look for ways to solve the complex equations that were necessary to manage industrial society. In 1927, an electrical engineer at the Massachusetts Institute of Technology (MIT), Vannevar Bush, invented a huge mechanical calculator, which he called the differential analyzer, to solve equations needed to run electrical power systems. In the late 1930s, the Harvard physicist Howard Aiken directed IBM in the construction of the Harvard Mark I, a calculating machine that was 51 feet long and 8 feet high and contained 750,000 parts. Although the Mark I used punched cards and paper tape, it was still a mechanical device that relied on the movement of physical components rather than electrons to do its work. Nevertheless, when it went into service it was state of the art for calculating machines and the U.S. navy pressed it into service right away to calculate ballistics tables.

The calculation requirements of World War II drove the development of the forerunner of today's computers.[18] One wartime project that stimulated computer development stemmed from the Allies' need to break German codes. Computers were invented in both Great Britain and the United States to achieve this, but they remained classified after the war and had relatively little impact on computer development in the 1950s. A much more significant development began in 1943, when the U.S. army funded a proposal by engineers at the University of Pennsylvania, John Mauchly and J. P. Eckert, to create a machine that could calculate ballistics tables for artillery. The result was the Electrical Numerical Integrator and Computer (ENIAC), the first device that worked not by mechanical action but by the switching on and off of vacuum tubes. ENIAC measured 30 by 50 feet, weighed 30 tons, used 18,000 vacuum tubes, and consumed 174,000 watts of power. It was said that when the operators turned it on, the lights in Philadelphia dimmed momentarily. Based on his experience as part of the ENIAC project, in June 1945, the Princeton University mathematician John Von Neumann sketched out his vision of a computer with stored programs, memory, and electronic logic circuits modeled on the human brain. In describing the logic and structure of the next generation of computers, Von Neumann's memo would become one of the most influential documents of the information revolution.[19]

In the 1950s, computers changed from a small collection of unique one-of-a-kind devices to commercial products that were manufactured in large lots and had multiple, programmable functions.[20] The first of these was UNIVAC (the name stood for Universal Automatic Computer), built by the firm that Eckert and Mauchly formed after the war. The first UNIVAC was delivered to the census bureau in 1951 and became widely known when it was used to predict the outcome of the 1952 presidential election. In 1953, IBM brought out its model 650, the first computer to be sold in volumes large enough to necessitate production on an assembly line. Gradually, demand for computers began to inch upward. In 1955, commercial users bought about 150 computers. The IBM 650 sold more than 1,500 units between 1953 and 1968.

Computers in the 1950s were still seen as having little to do with the lives of ordinary people. Based on vacuum tube technology (UNIVAC contained 5,000 tubes), they were huge and slow machines, expensive to own and operate, unreliable, and voracious consumers of electricity. Few firms or government agencies could afford to own or lease them, few people knew how to operate them, and fewer still could conceive of how computers could affect their lives, except in the negative sense. Computers were as much feared as anything. Large computers were seen as invading our privacy, fostering "Big Brother" intrusion into our lives, and giving large institutions too much centralized control over ordinary people. The transition to the Information Age would require a new paradigm of the role of computers in society and that new paradigm required in turn a new technology to replace the vacuum tube.

⊷   ⊷   ⊷

The century and a half leading up the Information Age saw the institutionalization of the information industry. For millennia, with the exceptions of unique entities like the great library at Alexandria or Prince Henry's school for mariners in Portugal, the creation and diffusion of information had rested in the hands of single individuals. In the 1840s, institutions began to emerge whose primary goal was to create, store, and transmit information. Since these institutions were responding to the profit incentives that lay in selling information products and services, we identify this period as one in which information became commodified. Some of these institutions, such as the Pony Express, disappeared soon after their creation, overtaken by superior technologies. Many survived and remain today key actors in the information revolution.

Several forces converged in the mid-nineteenth century to bring about this important change. The arrival of something approaching mass literacy meant that there was now a commercially significant demand for news and other kinds of information. In response, in 1841, the *New York Tribune* was established as the country's first mass-distribution newspaper. In 1883, the first mass-distribution magazines, *Life* and *Ladies Home Journal,* began publication. In 1892, Joseph Pulitzer's *New York World* had a daily circulation of 374,000. By 1900, the *Daily Mail* of London was selling a million copies a day. The huge costs of building and installing information infrastructure, such as submarine telegraph cables, made it impossible for single individuals to provide these services. Capital markets and stock companies met these needs at minimal personal risk to the investors and the patent system guaranteed them a monopoly over the invention—and substantial profits should it prove to be a success.[21]

As the Industrial Revolution matured, technologies became much more complex and huge institutions were needed to create, operate, and manage them.[22] Devices such as the telephone did not stand alone but required vast arrays of accessory technologies and social institutions to function and to be useful. The electric light required power generators, transmission lines, transformers, and many other pieces of equipment; the telephone needed connecting lines, central switching facilities, repair personnel, and so forth. In 1883, Edison formed his own corporation, Edison Electric Light Company, which (against Edison's wishes) merged with a rival firm, Thomson-Houston, in 1892 to form the General Electric Company. At about the same time, 1885, AT&T was chartered in New York as the firm responsible for connecting via long-distance service all the local telephone companies that were proliferating throughout the country.

The advent of what Lewis Mumford called the "neotechnic" period[23] required the self-generating momentum of the invention process itself. The very process of invention and discovery had to become institutionalized. The solution lay in the new research and development laboratories, of which Thomas Edison provided the prototype, his famous industrial research lab at Menlo Park. Edison built his lab in the New Jersey countryside in 1876, promising a "minor invention every ten days and a big thing every six months or so." Perhaps the most important of these research institutions was Bell Laboratories, formed by AT&T and General Electric in 1925. Through the 1980s, Bell Labs had obtained some 10,000 patents and was continuing at the rate of one a day. By the 1950s, research and development firms and universities were collecting together into regional conglomerates of high-technology inventions, of which California's Silicon Valley was the prototype.[24]

With all these developments, the flow of information now became an issue of public policy and government regulation (with attendant institutions) became inevitable. In 1912, the U.S. Congress passed the first of several measures to give the Department of Commerce responsibility for regulating radio broadcasting. The Radio Act of 1927 created the Federal Radio Commission to issue station licenses, allocate frequencies, and so forth. The Communications Act of 1934 broadened this mandate by creating the Federal Communications Commission (FCC) to be the chief regulatory agency for the broadcasting industry generally, including television. This legislation also transformed AT&T from a de facto telephone monopoly into one that was legal and regulated.

Thus, by the close of the 1950s, there had emerged a full set of institutions to carry out the mission of promoting—and profiting from—the application of bulk flow technologies to information. Despite the enormous size and financial weight of these institutions, in the end it would be something quite tiny that would produce a new paradigm for the Information Age. The device that would unleash all this pent-up institutional power and lead directly to the globalization of information was small enough to fit in a person's hand. It was the integrated circuit.

Part Two:
The Information Age

In 1906, Nikola Tesla, one of the pioneers in electricity research, brought to a close one of the greatest experiments seen up to that time in the generation and long-distance distribution of electric current and radio signals.[1] Two decades earlier, in 1884, Tesla (born in Croatia to Serbian parents) had arrived in the United States armed with a vision of a planet wired into this new source of power. With the backing of one of the wealthiest men in the United States, J. Pierpoint Morgan, Tesla set out to create a prototype of his new society based on the electric grid. The place he chose was a real estate development on New York's Long Island called Wardenclyffe (also spelled Wardencliff). When Morgan and other backers tired of the project and withdrew support, Tesla had to admit failure. Before he was finished, however, he sketched out what he had intended to accomplish in a pamphlet titled "The Wardenclyffe Vision":

> The *World System* . . . makes possible not only the instantaneous and precise wireless transmission of any kind of signals, messages or characters, to all parts of the world, but also the interconnection of the existing telegraph, telephone, and other signal stations. . . . By its means . . . a telephone subscriber here may call up any other subscriber on the Globe. An inexpensive receiver, not bigger than a watch, will enable him to listen anywhere, on land or sea, to a speech delivered, or music played in some other place, however distant. . . . This great scientific advance . . . annihilates distance and makes that perfect conductor, the Earth, available for all the innumerable purposes which human ingenuity has found for a line wire . . . at distances to which there are no limits other than those imposed by the physical dimensions of the Globe.
>
> The first World System power plant can be put into operation in nine months. . . . This power plant . . . is designed to serve . . . as many technical achievements as are possible without undue expense. Among these the following may be mentioned:
>
> 1. Interconnection of the existing telegraph exchanges of offices all over the world.
> 2. Establishment of a secret and non-interferable government telegraph service.
> 3. Interconnection of all the present telephone exchanges or offices all over the Globe.

4. Universal distribution of general news, by telegraph or telephone, in connection with the Press.
5. Establishment of a World System of intelligence transmission for exclusive private use.
6. Interconnection and operation of all stock tickers of the world.
7. Establishment of a World System of musical distribution, etc.
8. Universal registration of time by cheap clocks indicating the time with astronomical precision and requiring no attention whatever.
9. Facsimile transmission of typed or handwritten characters, letters, checks, etc.
10. Establishment of a universal marine service enabling navigators of all ships to steer perfectly without compass, to determine the exact location, hour and speed, to prevent collisions and disasters, etc.
11. Inauguration of a system of world printing on land and sea.
12. Reproduction anywhere in the world of photographic pictures and all kinds of drawings or records.[2]

In visualizing an information-based global system, Tesla was ahead of his time, but not by much. In only one lifetime, most of "The Wardenclyffe Vision" was not only technologically possible but actually in operation and being commercially exploited. In Part 2 of Episode 7, we explore how Tesla's "World System" became a reality.

🙰   🙰   🙰

Looking back with the advantage of hindsight, we know that our world began its momentous transformation quietly, almost invisibly, during the last two years of the 1950s.[3] After World War II, the focus of electronics research returned to semiconductors, materials like germanium and silicon that when properly prepared (i.e., "doped" by adding small quantities of impurities) transmitted electric current better than insulators such as glass but not as well as copper or silver. The invention in 1947 of the transistor by Bell Labs engineers Walter Brattain, William Shockley, and John Bardeen was based on semiconductor technology.[4] The invention of the transistor coincided with and reinforced the emergence of the stored-program digital computer. The transistor made it possible to free the computer from the limits imposed by the vacuum tube; in return the computer and other electronics provided the demand for the transistor. The secret of this synergy lay in the nature of digital information, how it differs from analog information, and the consequences of this difference for electronics.[5]

The sensory organs of humans have evolved to detect, record, and make sense of analog information, that is, information transmitted by electromagnetic waves that vary continuously, without separation, over time. The sounds we hear and the colors we see all make their way through space in an analog format. The analog mode is ideal for moving information by diffusion, for example, by means of unmediated human speech. The seamless and nuanced quality of analog information seems to us to depict reality more accurately by portraying variations in color and sound along an infinite range of gradations. Thus, we use analog to record the passage of time, to register the movement of images across our field of vision, or to engage in face-to-face conversation with another person.

The problem with analog information arises when we try to move it by bulk flow. It is difficult, as Samuel Morse and Alexander Graham Bell discovered, to move analog information fast, in large quantities, or over great distances. It can be done, but only to a very limited degree. Most significant, each kind of information requires its own dedicated medium for transmission. As long as information remained analog, separate media were required for images, sounds, and numbers.

The solution to applying bulk flow technologies to information lay in transforming analog information to a digital format. Unlike analog, digital information is carried by electric pulses that are discrete (i.e., separated rather than continuous) and binary (i.e., existing in one of only two states, such as on or off, plus or minus, positive or negative). Although analog information can convey a much greater range of variation, such as an infinite number of shades of color, digital information has the huge advantage that it can be packaged, transmitted, and unpacked just like solid objects, a quality that permits its being moved by bulk flow technologies. Digitized information can be handled in much larger volumes than analog, sent over greater distances, at much faster rates, and for much lower cost. In addition—and this is of supreme importance for globalization—by digitizing different kinds of information, we can send them via the same medium at the same time. In the context of the global flow of information, these advantages more than compensate for the loss in texture we experience by not using analog.

Binary, or two-element, codes are not new. The ancient Greeks devised a message system using fires or torches covered and uncovered, and Francis Bacon invented such a system to represent the alphabet in 1605. A Russian nobleman named Pavel Schilling invented a binary alphabet code in 1832, and a German, Karl Steinheil, devised the world's first electromagnetic telegraph using a binary code of dots in 1836. As we have seen, Samuel Morse adopted such a system for his telegraph in 1838. The transistor could have been seen in 1947, then, as simply the latest and most sophisticated application of binary information transmission.

As Robert Noyce describes, the transistor and the digital computer evolved in a synergistic relationship.[6] An analog information system, such as a radio built around the vacuum tube, cannot handle large numbers of electronic circuits. Analog devices require the amplification of the input signal several times before it can be detected, and such amplification (called cascading) quickly reaches the practical limits of voltage levels for the components. With digital systems, however, this cascading has no effect on voltage levels since all the components together are in only one of two possible states—either on or off. Thus, although analog devices cannot handle large numbers of small electronic circuits, a digital device not only *can* handle large numbers of circuits but actually *requires* them.

The problem with the transistor lay in the realization in the 1950s that the wiring of such devices in large numbers was becoming extraordinarily complex. Computer technology and architecture could not proceed beyond large mainframe machines without solving the complexity question. In addition, engineers were trying to use transistors in devices such as missiles and satellites, where size, weight, and power were severely constrained.

The solution came to be known as the "monolithic idea": if the component parts of a device such as a computer could be made out of a single material, such as silicon, then these components—resistors, capacitors, and transistors—could all be placed on a single block of that material. And if all the parts of an electronic device could be integrated on a single piece of silicon, then connections could be laid down within the silicon chip itself, eliminating the need for complex wiring.

On July 24, 1958, the breakthrough occurred. In a Dallas laboratory, the Texas Instruments engineer Jack Kilby sketched out his version of the monolithic idea: how to make an integrated circuit out of silicon. Six months later, on January 23, 1959, in Silicon Valley, California, one of the founders of Fairchild Semiconductor, Robert Noyce, outlined *his* scheme for making a similar device. The two are now regarded as the coinventors of the technology that led to the microchip, the microprocessor, the personal computer, digital information, and satellite communications—in short, the Information Age.

✦   ✦   ✦

The Information Age did not spring fully formed from the dust of the old industrial era. Rather, it emerged gradually, in three more or less distinct phases, each defined by the bulk flow technology available to transmit information.

The first phase extended from 1958 when the integrated circuit was invented to about 1970 when the forerunner of the microprocessor appeared.[7] During these years, computers were huge, expensive, noninteractive machines that used enormous amounts of electric power, generated great amounts of heat, and were difficult to program. Very few institutions could afford computers; very few had the information requirements that justified their cost. The management of computers was entrusted to a tiny, highly educated elite. The machines and their operators were kept secluded from the rest of the organization and access to the equipment was strictly controlled.[8] Thus, the first decade or so of the Information Age saw mostly a continuation of the trends and values from the industrial era: institution growth, centralization, concentration, and change that was still for the most part linear and controlled. Most important, the globalizing implications of these changes were still only dimly perceived.

Early in the 1960s, transistors began to replace vacuum tubes in computers and the computer began to loom larger in U.S. life.[9] In 1964, the IBM System/360 series went on sale, the first mass-produced computer for general-purpose computing. Time sharing, an idea that relied on complex software to switch a computer's central processing quickly and seamlessly among users, was invented at MIT in the late 1950s. In the 1960s, time sharing made it possible for computers to be used like public utilities, much as telephone subscribers were connected to large central switching facilities. Almost as soon as the integrated circuit appeared, manufacturers began to produce minicomputers that were small and cheap enough that a single person could use one economically. The Digital Equipment Company (DEC) brought out the first commercially successful minicomputer, the PDP-8, in 1965 and sold about 50,000 units. It sucessor, the PDP-11, appeared in 1968 and sold half a million units.

As computer power and speed increased and the cost of electronically processed information declined, businesses and government offices found many new uses for the machines. The U.S. defense department used computers to manage its sophisticated data-processing effort in Vietnam. Civilian government agencies, including the census bureau, the Federal Bureau of Investigation, and the Internal Revenue Service, began to create data banks on individual citizens. Private firms used computers to set up networks and databases to track people's credit history, which led soon to the use of credit cards for consumer purchases. Mail-order firms used computers to expand and maintain their customer lists. In the 1960s, airlines began to computerize their reservation system; by 1968, the SABRE reservation system was handling 100,000 calls per day. In late 1958, banks across the country began to switch to an electronic recording method of accounting (ERMA) to process checks; by 1967, ERMA was being used to handle almost all the checks (in the tens of billions) written in the United States each year.

As a consequence of these developments, in the 1960s computers became one of the leading U.S. industries. In 1955, the value of installed computer equipment in the United States was about $250 million. By 1960, that figure had quadrupled to $1 billion; by 1965, it had risen to $6 billion. In 1951, there were 10 computers in the entire country; by 1970, there were about 75,000.

A number of extremely important advances in global communications were also registered during the 1950s and 1960s. In the late 1950s, the technology of copper cable construction and installation improved to make possible the laying of important submarine telephone cables across the Atlantic and Pacific Oceans.[10] One such technology, Time-Assignment Speech Interpolation (TASI), took advantage of the silence in one transmission to send voice signals from another over the same cable by switching rapidly back and forth among conversations. Transistors were incorporated in submarine cable design in 1970. In 1957, TAT-1 (for Transatlantic Telephone) carried 36 circuits across the Atlantic. By 1970, TAT-5 carried 845 channels between Europe and the United States. By 1970, 1,275 voice channels crossed the Atlantic, and 378 crossed the Pacific.

During the 1960s, communications satellites, once the vision of science fiction writers like Arthur Clarke, became an integral part of the global information net.[11] In this development, cold war competition between the Soviet Union and the United States was of critical importance, principally for the stimulus it provided for the exploration of space. Following the Soviet launch of the *Sputnik* satellite in 1957, the United States made the conquest of space a high priority. In 1958, the United States established the National Aeronautics and Space Administration (NASA) and launched its own satellite, *Explorer I*. In 1961, the United States set itself a goal of building a global communications system; the next year, the U.S. Congress passed the Communications Satellite Act, which created a private firm, the Communications Satellite Corporation (COMSAT), to lead the commercial exploitation of space. That same year, 1962, *Telstar* was placed in orbit by AT&T.

To be useful for truly global communications, a satellite must be placed in a geosynchronous orbit about 22,300 miles above the Earth. Here, its orbital period exactly matches the rotation of the planet so that it remains over the same spot. Such an orbit was achieved for the first time in 1964 when NASA launched *Syncom*. The first commercial communications satellite in geosynchronous orbit was *Early Bird* (also known as *Intelsat I*), launched by Intelsat, the international satellite communications consortium, in 1965.

The impact of global satellite communications cannot be exaggerated. For example, John F. Kennedy's funeral in 1963 was the first event in history seen around the world in real time. In June 1965, commercial transmission of television pictures across the Atlantic began. Through the decade, filmed transmissions from the battlefield made the conflict in Vietnam the first "living-room war." In 1969, Neil Armstrong's moon landing was the first event in history witnessed by 1 billion people as it occurred. By the end of the decade, communications satellites covered the Atlantic, Pacific, and Indian Oceans, serving essentially the entire world.

Almost immediately after communications satellites were launched and proved their commercial worth, they were challenged by another technology: information transmission by light. Photons, it was discovered, are a more efficient carrier of information than electrons. The key to this advance lay in finding both a way to concentrate the beam of light sufficiently to transmit it over great distances without attentuation and a medium of sufficient purity and transparency to carry the beam. The solutions to these problems are today well known: lasers and fiber optics. The idea for the laser occurred to its discoverer, Charles Townes, in 1951, but it was not until 1960 that scientists working independently at Hughes Aircraft Company and Bell Labs actually constructed such a device.[12] In 1975, the laser was joined with optical fiber to produce the first generation of light wave communications systems.[13]

✎   ✎   ✎

The second phase of the Information Age, which corresponds roughly to the decade of the 1970s, can be seen now as a transition between the last days of the fading industrial era and the beginnings of a truly global economy and culture.

If a single point of origin for this second phase could be identified, it would probably be the Intel Corporation in California's Silicon Valley.[14] Intel was formed in 1968 by Robert Noyce and Gordon Moore to develop large-scale integration (LSI) electronic circuits. In 1970, Intel introduced its first large-scale random access computer chip, the 1103, which stored more than 1,000 bits of binary data. At about this same time, a team of Intel engineers led by Ted Hoff began to design a chip that could hold all of the component parts of a computer in one integrated unit. This new device would be more than just an extremely small integrated circuit. Hoff's idea was to build a general-purpose programmable circuit and write software to fit any job of which computers were capable. The device would be called the microprocessor.

In 1971, the firm introduced the model 4004 microprocessor, announced as "a new era of integrated electronics: a micro-programmable computer on a chip."[15] This invention was followed in 1972 by the model 8008 and in 1974 by the model 8080, each more powerful than its predecessor. Through the 1970s, Intel continued to expand the reach of tiny electronic circuits. In 1976, Intel engineers succeeded in putting 20,000 transistors on a single chip and the computer began its transition from an exotic and somewhat mysterious machine operated by professionals to a piece of everyday life that nearly anyone could own and operate.

The microprocessor made its presence felt in two ways. First, it could be used as a computer's central processing unit. In 1972, a scientist at the Xerox Corporation, Alan Kay, designed the first computer intended for a single individual. He coined the label "personal computer" (PC) for such a machine. Xerox built a few of Kay's model but chose not to market it. The first personal computer to be marketed was the Altair, unveiled in early 1975. Although more powerful than any computer previously available to individuals, the Altair was a failure because it lacked software and a support system of repair facilities, spare parts, and so forth. These obstacles were overcome in 1976 when Steve Jobs and Steve Wozniak brought out the Apple I, the machine that introduced the personal computer to general markets. The Apple I was followed the next year by the Apple II, as well as by competing machines from Commodore and Radio Shack. In 1981, IBM introduced its own version of the personal computer, signaling that the computer had become an object for mass consumption. From 1972 to 1982, the number of computer firms in the United States tripled, increasing from 518 to 1,566; employment in the industry rose from 144,000 to 340,000. The effect was to put exponentially increased computing power into the hands of countless thousands of low-level workers stationed far from the center of large organizations, as well as several tens of millions of individuals in their homes.

The microprocessor also transformed our daily life by taking over the control functions of a wide range of industrial and consumer products. Entertainment was one such area. In 1972, Nolan Bushnell founded the Atari Corporation and launched its first product: the microprocessor-controlled video game Pong. Pong was followed by Space Invaders in 1978, Asteroids in 1979, and Pac-Man in 1980. Atari was joined in the market by Activision and Nintendo, among many others.[16] The automobile was one of the first important machines to be controlled by embedded microprocessors. The 1977 Oldsmobile Toronado featured the first engine controlled by microprocessors and promised a savings of 10 percent on fuel consumption. Antilocking brakes controlled by microprocessors were soon introduced, followed by digital instruments, adjustable suspension, and many other features. The retail sector of the economy was also transformed by the introduction of the Universal Product Code, the now near-universal scannable bar codes, in 1973.[17] Introduced to grocery stores in 1978, bar codes were operating in one-third of all food markets by 1984. These codes made it possible for manufacturers to track inventory in real time from the store where the product was bought (referred to as "point of sale") and to respond quickly to changes in consumer demand. Computers were also used to track packages as they moved through a transport system, an innovation that opened the way to the commercial air cargo business.

The technologies for connecting personal computers and other electronic devices also saw major improvements during the second phase. In 1976, the Canadian firm Northern Telecom introduced Digital World, the world's first integrated information network. This information system was made possible by digitizing analog information for transmission via telephone lines. Compared with other information technologies, the telephone had spread relatively slowly, but by 1970, 90 percent of homes in the United States had a telephone. The transformation of the nation's phone system from analog to digital technology took longer than expected, however. In 1986, a decade after Northern Telecom's announcement, fewer than one quarter of the lines in the United States had been converted to digital service.

Communications satellites were also a key part of the transition to a global information network. In the mid-1970s, COMSAT introduced a new communications system that improved connections with ships at sea, thereby contributing to an increase in oceanborne cargo. *INTELSAT IV-A*, placed in orbit in 1975, carried 6,000 telephone circuits, more than all the previous INTELSAT satellites combined; *INTELSAT V* in 1979 doubled that number again, with 12,000 circuits. In 1975, Home Box Office (HBO) began transmitting movies by satellite; in 1980, COMSAT introduced direct-broadcast satellite technology to transmit television programs directly to home viewers.

By the end of the 1960s, television seemed to have saturated its market. Virtually every household had at least one set, and many had two or three, including color. Almost 700 broadcasting stations covered the entire country. Nevertheless, the technologies of the 1970s—cable, satellites, and video recorders—would bring about what Steven Lubar calls the "second television revolution,"[18] a transformation of the role of television in daily life as well as in the way people experienced the world.

Cable television, or community antenna television (CATV), had been available as early as 1948, but for nearly twenty years its use was restricted to distant areas where conventional signals could not reach. In 1966, the Federal Communications Commission had placed a freeze on new cable systems to protect broadcasters. In 1972, when the freeze was lifted, interest in cable increased, and after 1975, cable systems grew quickly, partly because of the availability of satellite programming. Cable offered not only better reception, but more variety: C-SPAN provided public affairs programming, and ESPN offered 24-hour sports events, both beginning in 1979. Cable News Network (CNN) was founded as the world's first global, round-the-clock, all-news network in 1980 and the Weather Channel began to provide 24-hour weather information in 1982. By 1980, 18 million U.S. homes were wired for cable television.

✧ ✧ ✧

From the early 1980s, we have been in phase three of the Information Age, characterized by an information network based on technologies that are small, highly interactive, extremely cheap (per unit of information processed), with low energy requirements and extremely flexible and responsive programmability. These new information technologies—along with the associated communications revolutions in wire (cable television, fiber optics), wireless (satellites), and consumer electronics (VCRs)—have fundamentally altered our way of experiencing the world.

After IBM entered the personal computer field in 1981, the market for these machines grew rapidly. About 35,000 IBM PCs were sold in 1981 and over a million in the next two years. Apple Computer's Macintosh, on the market in 1984, made the personal computer user friendly by replacing the command system based on key strokes and words with a mouse and graphics (called "icons"). Successive generations of microprocessors, with their power expanding seemingly without limit, made the new computers capable of performing tasks previously unimagined. Spreadsheets became valuable tools for managing complex businesses in the 1980s and the union of computers and communications offered personal computer users a portal into electronic networks that were both local and global. Although many observers argued that the personal computer had been oversold and that the dream of a "wired world" of interconnected machines still lay in some distant future, the market disagreed. In 1981, there were about 2 million personal computers in use in the United States; by 1982, 5.5 million; by 1992, 65 million. With the possible exception of television, no other piece of information technology spread so far so fast. In 1984, IBM closed its last computer punch card facility, symbolizing the end of noninteractive computers.

During the 1980s, changes in the telephone system were introduced that hastened the advent of a truly global telecommunications network.[19] Since 1913, AT&T had operated as a regulated monopoly over the nation's telephones, including both their manufacture and local and long-distance service. A 1956 antitrust consent decree had reaffirmed this status, but in return AT&T had agreed not to enter the computer business. (At the time, few people foresaw the eventual merger of the two technologies in a single information device.) This sharp division in information technologies began to erode in 1968 when the FCC ruled that AT&T had to allow another manufacturer's equipment to be connected to its system. In 1974, the U.S. Department of Justice filed an antitrust suit against AT&T that eventually led in 1982 to the giant firm's divestiture of its local telephone operating systems (known as "Baby Bells") and the introduction of competition for long-distance service from such new firms as Sprint and MCI. This new system began operations in 1984, the same year that AT&T announced its new goal of universal information service, a pledge to transmit any kind of information *from* any place *to* any place on Earth instantaneously.

To meet this commitment, AT&T and other telecommunications firms had access to a rapidly expanding system of global communications satellites. As of 1984, some 120 satellites had been placed in orbit, 90 of which were still operating.[20] The 1981 launch of the space shuttle *Columbia,* transmitted live around the world by COMSAT, was a key event because it offered for the first time the possibility of sending a crew into space to repair or retrieve a damaged or malfunctioning satellite. COMSAT introduced global videoconferencing in 1982; NBC was the first broadcasting company to use commercial satellites for nationwide distribution of network television in 1983; and in 1985, CNN began to broadcast news live and continuously from the United States to Europe. In 1991, the Gulf War became the first war witnessed worldwide in real time, thanks to the broadcasting efforts of CNN correspondents.[21]

Beginning in the 1980s, it became increasingly difficult to discern the dividing line between computers and communications devices. Computers communicated with each other, while telephones were used to transmit data and images as well as sounds. The development that best symbolized this trend was the Internet.[22]

The Internet is a global network of interconnected computer systems and individual computer users. The "Net," as it is called, evolved from ARPANET, a computer network set up in 1969 by the Advanced Research Projects Agency of the Department of Defense to connect scientists at four universities. Its purpose was to enable computer users to access computers at other universities, thereby reducing waste and needless redundancies in information and research. Scientists quickly discovered that they could communicate not only with computers but with each other by establishing electronic "bulletin boards." By 1980, ARPANET connected 400 different computer systems and more than 10,000 people had access to it.

The success of ARPANET stimulated the growth of thousands of other similar networks, including national databases like Nexis and Lexis and national bulletin boards like CompuServe and Prodigy. In 1987, there were 4,000 such bulletin boards; by 1992, the number had grown to 44,000. By the late 1980s, ARPANET had evolved into the Internet, a system subsidized by the National Science Foundation but essentially free to most individual users.

John Burgess of the *Washington Post* has described the Internet as "a confederation of about 12,000 small networks of linked computers:"

> These member networks agree to exchange . . . electronic packets of digital information. The Internet does not have its own private set of communications wires. Instead, it uses whatever is available. An ordinary phone line is likely to carry data out of the home. The links between the 12,000 small networks are typically big-bore circuits leased from a telecommunications company—the data might travel over fiber optic strands or satellites. The network is growing fast in part because it has banished the great demon of computer technology—incompatible standards that make one machine unable to talk to another.[23]

Free of the roadblock of incompatible standards, the Internet has grown exponentially since the late 1980s. In 1988, about 80,000 host computers were connected to the Net. By 1993, this number had grown to 1.5 million, and by 1995, to 4.8 million.[24] Individual users of the Internet were estimated in the mid-1990s at about 25 to 30 million, but the exact number is impossible to calculate. About 70 percent of these users were in North America, 22 percent in Europe, and 7 percent in Asia.

∾   ∾   ∾

The revolution in the bulk flow of information by means of digital technologies has in one way or another transformed the life of most of the inhabitants of our planet.[25] In highly industrialized societies such as the United States, Japan, and Western Europe, the degree of change in life, work, and culture rivals that of the Industrial Revolution and has taken place in less than one-third the time. Modes of production and consumption, and thus all economic relationships, have been fundamentally reshaped into what Manuel Castells calls the "informational mode of development," a form of economic activity in which information is both the input (or raw material) and the output (finished product).[26]

The consequences of the Information Age reach into every dimension of our lives. Connecting systems in transportation and communications function with great speed, so changes are transmitted extremely rapidly throughout the system. The most significant factors of production, especially information, capital, and technology, can be moved easily, quickly, and cheaply. Changes are exponential and rapid, so there is little time to adjust to a changing environment. Changes are highly interconnected and potentially, if not actually, global in scope. System relationships are complex, nonlinear, largely unknown, and largely beyond our observation and understanding. The consequences of major decisions and changes cannot be accurately predicted; failures of large systems increase with a corresponding rise in social and environmental costs.[27] The emergence of the global manufacturing system and the collapse of state socialism as a viable alternative for organizing industrial production have introduced radically new elements into the structure of the global system. Devices such as interactive media, video recording, and virtual reality challenge our conventional understanding of what "reality" is and what it means to "know" or "understand" that reality.[28]

Notwithstanding these profound changes in U.S. life and in the world generally, I wish to emphasize here how the Information Age has affected the process of globalization. The information revolution has greatly increased the number of people who experience the world as a single place, but more important, it has transformed the dimensions, indeed the very nature, of that experience. For one thing, we now routinely experience the world *in real time,* that is, as events happen, not delayed for days, months, or years. Second, we experience the world *on demand,* that is, when we want it instead of when someone else decides we should. Third, we experience the world in an *interactive mode,* that is, we can send as well as receive information, telling the world what we think about what we are experiencing and how we would like to change it. Finally, and most significant, for many people global awareness has become *invisible,* meaning that we so take it for granted that we no longer regard such experiences as unusual or out of the ordinary. Global awareness has for many people reached what the philosopher Michael Polanyi calls the "tacit dimension," where one has learned or internalized something so well that one ceases to be aware of it.[29]

So many factors have contributed to this transformation in the global experience that we must be selective in our listing. First and foremost have been technological advances that have increased exponentially the power of the global information network. According to Vaclav Smil, "Between 1946 and 1990 the fastest computer speeds rose from 5000 to 5.5 billion operations per second, an increase of seven orders of magnitude representing twenty successive doublings. . . . Between 1959 and 1990 miniaturization techniques increased the density of transistor circuits on a silicon chip from 1 to more than 1 million."[30] In 1993, Intel Corporation launched the Pentium chip, which contained 3.1 million transistors, and less than two years later, in early 1995, announced its successor, the P6, with 5.1 million circuits on a chip that measures 0.7 inch on a side. These increases in speed and reductions in size are two important reasons why the relative cost of computing has declined so dramatically. Measured in terms of comparable computation tasks, a 1990s supercomputer costs less than 1/1000 of what it cost to operate the IBM 360 in the early 1960s (see Figure 7.2).[31]

Equally important, advances in technology have made it possible to treat information as if it was composed of discrete material substances that can be subdivided for shipment purposes. The key here is what is known as packet switching.[32] After the transformation of analog information to digital, the clusters of binary digits can be broken up into packets, or chunks of data attached to headers that contain routing information identifying the source and destination computers. Enroute to its destination, the packets may be merged with others from different sources and headed for different addresses. Small routing computers ensure that each packet gets to the correct destination and is recombined in correct order to form a coherent message. The result is that many different messages can be carried at once over the same channel. For voice circuits such as cellular telephones, four to twenty conversations can be transmitted simultaneously via the same channel. By digital signal compression, a cable television system capable of bringing 100 or so channels to home viewers can increase its capacity to 500 channels. Thus, packet switching is to the Information Age what the amphora jar was to the Bronze Age.

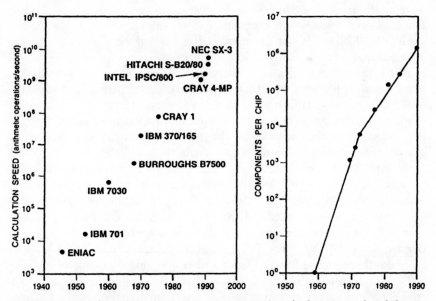

FIGURE 7.2 Advances in computers, 1946–1990, in calculating speed and density of components per chip.

Source: Vaclav Smil, *Energy in World History,* copyright © 1994 by Westview Press.

A second important factor is the mass ownership of Information Age technologies.[33] In the United States, for every 100 people, there are more than 200 radios, 80 television sets, 50 telephone lines, and 28 personal computers. More than half of all U.S. households are wired for cable television. By 1995, 16 percent of all U.S. homes had more than one telephone line in order to accommodate computer modems and fax machines.[34] For every 100 persons in Japan, the comparable numbers are 86 radios, 59 television sets, 42 telephone lines, and 8 personal computers; only 13 percent of Japanese households are wired for cable. The personal computer was introduced only in 1981; yet by 1993, there were nearly 180 million of them in the world, along with about 600 million telephones and more than 1 billion television sets.

The mass ownership of information technologies suggests that information has become an object prepared and marketed for mass consumption. An April 1995 article in *American Demographics* reports that the average U.S. household spends $966 annually on information, more than on clothing and only slightly less than on food consumed away from home.[35] About $434 of this was spent on "pure information" such as newspapers, books, basic cable television, and online computer services. The cost of telephone access to information added another $233 to the expenditures and home entertainment (pay-per-view television, video rentals and purchases) accounted for $299. No one knows precisely the value of the global information system, but the American Electronics Association estimates that the 1994 global market for information technology hardware, software, and services was $643 billion. The European Information Technology Observatory estimates that the figure was $891 billion.[36] *The Economist* estimates that the global telecommunications market alone is worth $500 billion.[37]

Third, the technologies for connecting information devices with each other have proliferated in number and increased in power and capacity. Modems that transform analog information to digital and back again enable us to connect the personal computer in our home to a global network of cables and satellites and interact with that network at the rate of thousands of bits of information per second. *Telstar (Intelsat I)* had the capacity for 240 voice circuits or one black-and-white television channel; *Intelsat VI*, launched in 1985, carried 35,000 voice channels and two color television channels simultaneously. From 1972 to 1995, 214 commercial communications satellites, valued collectively at more than $15 billion, were placed in orbit. The combination of lasers and fiber optics evolved to its fifth generation by the mid-1990s, when Bell Labs and a Japanese firm, KDD, planned to deploy beneath the Pacific Ocean a fiber optic cable capable of carrying 500,000 telephone calls simultaneously. By 1991, some 80 percent of U.S. telephone lines had been converted from analog to digital service.

Finally, many observers have pointed to the increased number of information workers as a mark of "postindustrial" status for a country. A consideration in Part 3 of the rise of the information sector in highly industrial countries will take us back to some of the central themes in this book.

Part Three:
Cities and Global Systems
in the Information Age

As we near the end of this episode in our global journey, I want to return to one of my central themes—the connections between cities and global systems—and put the information revolution in the context of humankind's long struggle to overcome the costs of entropy. I see the information revolution as an attempt (largely successful, so far) to dissipate the costs of growth and complexity in two ways: first, by connecting cities and other institutions to lengthening lines of supply, thereby making the global manufacturing system feasible; and second, by rationalizing internal control and decisionmaking within complex organizations, thereby making possible the control of global institutions. Ever since the Neolithic Revolution led to the gathering together of human populations in towns, villages, and cities, urban settlements have played a critical role in managing and coordinating bulk flow systems. Ostia was a key to Rome's lifeline as Bristol was for England's and Amsterdam for Holland's. Liverpool and Chicago were essential to the functioning of steam-based systems as Detroit and Houston were for systems based on petroleum. And the Information Age has its key cities as well: Silicon Valley and Boston's Highway 128 corridor, among others.[1]

The focal point of this part of Episode 7 is what Manuel Castells calls the "informational city,"[2] the new urban structure that emerged after 1960 to manage the information flows and other transactions necessary to make the global economy work. In the late twentieth century, cities around the world faced a growth imperative as sites of both production and consumption. As production sites, cities such as London, New York, and Tokyo housed the headquarters for global firms, the centers of control and coordination.[3] These cities were the synapses in an increasingly complex global network of computers, telecommunications, and air travel. Cities that could not supply these infrastructure requirements quickly were left behind in the global economy. As consumption sites, these cities were also connected to a global system of production of goods and services that included manufactured items made all over the world (the "global manufacturing system"[4]) and a labor force drawn from the developing world to supply labor-intensive routine personal services.[5] In this way, informational cities in the advanced industrial societies in Europe, Japan, and North America were connected to the labor of the developing world, especially in Mexico, Central America and the Caribbean, North Africa and the Middle East, and South and Southeast Asia.

The only way informational cities could perform these dual roles was by raising the information bulk flow capabilities of key institutions, including firms, governments, and the media of communications, so they could engage in real-time transactions to keep themselves connected to the rapidly changing global econoculture. But the globalizing of information, manufacturing, and culture generally has led to a new kind of city, described in a growing literature as "edge cities," "urban villages," "new cities," "global cities," and even "virtual cities." These cities serve as the work sites and habitats for the new information workers, whom Robert Reich has labeled "symbolic analysts."[6] But these people would not be able to live their preferred lifestyle and work effectively were it not for a labor force of immigrants from developing countries whose passage to, and presence in, these cities has been facilitated by the information revolution.

Thus, this new kind of city requires connections to global information technologies—which make possible the work of symbolic analysts (as coordinators of the systems) and of service workers (many of whom have emigrated from developing countries)—as well as connections to manufacturing enterprises located around the world in sites made possible by low-cost Third World labor (e.g., the *maquiladora* industries of northern Mexico).

✧   ✧   ✧

Since 1960, a new world has taken shape, a world of truly global scope, more densely populated, with many more important actors (and more different *kinds* of actors), linked together by more complex and more interdependent networks of transactions, and characterized throughout by greatly accelerated rates of change. The global system in the 1990s is a complex, interconnected set of institutions engaged in economic, political, environmental, and cultural transactions on a global scale. Such transactions have increased dramatically in their volume and variety, the distance they cover, and the speed with which they occur.

By the 1990s, three forces had converged to undermine the old industrial paradigm: the global spread of manufacturing to virtually every corner of the world; the global spread of information technology and the communications media; and the decline of state socialism as a viable option to organize nation-states, heralding a convergence of the world's economies toward some variant of the capitalist model. The result has been the emergence of a truly global economy and culture. This global "econoculture" revolves around networks of production and consumption transactions that are global in scope and in which the line between economy and culture is blurred to the point of disappearance.

There are three components of the global econoculture. The oft-used term *global economy* means that most of the products we consume have been assembled by a global workforce at sites around the world from component parts that have themselves come from other distant locations.[7] Virtually all segments of the manufacturing system—capital, labor, energy, technology, component parts, finished products, waste materials—now flow relatively freely around the world, unobstructed by technology, tariff barriers, cultural differences, transport costs, or markets. To return to a term from the Introduction, the global economy represents the latest step in the erosion of the world's gradients.

A global culture has taken shape as well. The agent of this transformation is the culture industry, a group of commercial enterprises dedicated to the creation, transmission, distribution, and sale of cultural objects.[8] Its principal sectors include media (entertainment, film, recorded music, news), fashion, sports, celebrities, and the arts. It also includes objects with principal functions other than cultural but which constitute important carriers of cultural values. Food, automobiles, and clothing are among the most important of these.

A third dimension of the global econoculture involves the growing threat of worldwide environmental and health crises. The rapid movement of people, products, and news around the world means that we now confront the globalization of crises and hazards. "Normal" accidents[9] and system failures like Chernobyl, Bhopal, Three Mile Island, and the *Exxon Valdez* are no longer confined to a particular site, but potentially affect us all. The same is true of environmental overload, such as global warming and the erosion of the ozone layer. Diseases like AIDS and the Ebola virus can spread around the world at unprecedented speeds. As one author put it, "A hot virus from the rain forest lives within a twenty-four-hour plane flight from every city on earth. All of the earth's cities are connected by a web of airline routes. The web is a network. Once a virus hits the net, it can shoot anywhere in a day—Paris, Tokyo, New York, Los Angeles, wherever planes fly."[10]

Because of these and other changes, the role of the nation-state has changed significantly in the past four decades. Although internal political processes are increasingly open and media driven, national populations find themselves at the mercy of global forces that they can neither understand nor control. Nation-state boundaries are no longer as significant as they were, as people, economies, and cultures spread across frontiers in defiance of national governments' attempts to maintain their integrity. Boundary regions take on added importance: Miami has much more in common with the Caribbean, and Seattle with Vancouver, than the two U.S. cities have with each other.

The increasingly diverse nation-state is less and less able to meet the emotional needs of its people for community. After World War II, many observers thought the forces of ethnic nationalism would be tamed by the homogenizing effects of industrialization and modernization. But after the collapse of the Soviet Union, the resurgence of long-dormant ethnic disputes, such as the bloody conflict in Bosnia, reminds us that the potential homogenizing effects of industrialization did not materialize to nearly the degree many social scientists predicted in the 1950s.[11] At the same time, the nation-state embedded in global networks of production and consumption is less and less able to meet its citizens' economic needs for material well-being. Around the world, people see themselves as dependent on institutions that are not accountable to them, while those institutions that *are* accountable, national governments, seem inept, corrupt, and overwhelmed by the challenges they face.

Advances in information recording, storage, and transmission; in the mass ownership of information technologies; in system connections; and in the information sector of the economy have produced a global information network that can send images, sound, data, or combinations of all three in the same transmission around the world at virtually the speed of light. The principal cause of these changes is the increase in the accessibility, speed, volume, flexibility, and diversity of the media of communication and transport and the consequent decrease in the cost of using them—in other words, an improved global bulk flow capability for information. As a result, more people can experience the world as a single place than ever before and virtually in real time.

Electrons and photons are not the only things being moved via bulk flow; matter and energy are also moving in unprecedented volumes, speeds, and distances thanks to the information revolution. People (tourists, business travelers, refugees, immigrants) are on the move in numbers and at speeds heretofore unknown. Manufactured goods are also being moved in huge volume because of air cargo and containerized freight. Thanks to the transformation of global transport, the world's food network has been fundamentally restructured to bring virtually any food product thousands of miles from the field to our plate.[12] Supertankers achieve nearly the same mobility with energy resources.

All of these systems rely on information technologies and information workers to manage and coordinate them. Air traffic controllers and airlines reservations systems need computers and reliable global communications. Air cargo companies need computers to track the millions of packages they handle daily. Immigrants and refugees rely on global telephone services to keep in touch with their homeland and on cable and satellite television networks to keep fresh their culture and language. Oceangoing cargo vessels need satellite telecommunications to be in contact with their controlling home office and they need computers to plot their safest and fastest routes.

The commodification of cultural objects such as music, film, food, and clothing has been promoted by a global capitalism that exploits people's desire to identify with a community tradition that transcends their own individual limits.[13] Global information networks have also made a huge impact on world politics by transmitting around the world in real time scenes from wars, insurgencies, and the struggles for democracy.

As society becomes more global and its component parts become more interconnected, several important changes occur: Social and technological systems expand (they increase the territory they cover and the number of their component parts), connections become more complex (in the sense of becoming more difficult to see, understand, explain, and predict), change spreads more rapidly, and effects are experienced at greater and greater distances from the initial cause. What we do (or fail to do) therefore affects more people, faster, and farther away than ever. And vice versa—we are affected more by the actions (or inactions) of more people, farther away, faster. Moreover, the connections between cause and effect become increasingly ambiguous (we lack necessary information to understand them) and knowledge dependent (only certain people with certain information are privileged to understand them).[14] Thus, in the words of Paul Kennedy, "As the twenty-first century approaches, the people of the earth seem to be discovering that their lives are ever more affected by forces which are, in the full meaning of the word, irresponsible."[15] And the place where all these forces have converged is the city of the Information Age, the informational city.

❧   ❧   ❧

In his book *Megalopolis,* written in the early 1960s, Jean Gottman observed that the great eastern cities of the United States—New York, Philadelphia, Boston, Baltimore, and Washington—all were built along the fall line, near the edge of the North American continent, poised between land and water at the juncture of otherwise unconnected modes of transport and communication:

> As the American economy grew, each of the main seaside cities developed a network of trade relationships on the continent and on the high seas. Standing at the contact of these two realms, the seaports assumed the role of *hinges,* linking the development of these two foundations of the national economy. From period to period, the main weight of this seaboard's interest has oscillated from sea trade and overseas ventures to continental development and back again. Whether the general circumstances threw the door of the American economy open toward the outside or closed it to turn the main endeavors inland depended on decisions made in that *hinge,* the string of eastern cities.[16]

The central role of the cities of the megalopolis was, and still is, to provide the transactions necessary to link modes of commercial intercourse, to smooth the flow of people, merchandise, capital, technology, and information from one bulk flow system to another. The cities of the U.S. eastern seaboard performed this historic function of the "economic hinge" by tying together interior resources, coastal markets, and oceanborne trade and immigration. By providing the work sites, residences, amenities, and social services for the people who offered these hinge services, cities like New York and Philadelphia prospered and expanded swiftly as the young country grew and industrialized.

If the economic hinge is an appropriate metaphor for cities in general, it is even more accurate as a description of cities in the Information Age. These cities are special places because they provide work and consumption sites and residences for the workers who perform the critical hinge functions in a complex global society, connecting the various information media and facilitating the flow of information from city to city and throughout the global communications network. Cities are, of course, much more than hinges connecting disparate bulk flow systems. A city is also a locus of production and consumption, a site for the reproduction of industrial labor, a center for control and domination by some groups over others, and a set of institutions for the distribution and allocation of the costs and benefits of society. The city is, in short, the manifestation in space of all manner of human relationships.

For Manuel Castells, contemporary cities are the site for the "informational mode of development," which he described in 1989 as a "new technological paradigm" characterized by two fundamental features.[17] First, the new technologies deal principally with information processing—that is, information is not only the raw material; it is also the finished product of the system. Second, the principal effects of technological innovations are felt on processes, not products. New products do emerge from the process, but the primary impact of technological change is felt in the ways people and organizations do things. Because the new paradigm is based on information processing, which is an activity rooted in culture, the informational mode of development is much more than simply another way to produce goods and services. It is a powerful tool transforming our entire culture, including the way we communicate, manage and motivate others, entertain ourselves, consume objects and experiences, educate ourselves and others, and so forth. Of special importance to this study, the Information Age affects the way we experience the world as well.

✦   ✦   ✦

The information revolution confronts us with a fundamental dilemma that is built into our systems of production, consumption, knowledge, and control. To put it simply, our ability to construct complex, rapidly changing global systems for production and consumption has far outdistanced our ability to monitor, explain, comprehend, predict, or control their behavior. Because of this imbalance between the construction of systems and their control, we are beset by problems without precedent in human experience. High rates of change give us insufficient time to react to impending system failures, which become more frequent and costly as we build systems of increasing complexity and nonlinearity. The tight interconnecting of these system components produces the well-known "global problematique," a web of mutually aggravating worldwide problems, including food, energy, population, and pollution. The counterintuitive behavior of complex systems places great pressure on analysts and decisionmakers to develop models that replicate reality as closely as possible; demands for information and coordination frequently overload both the analysts and the information system within which they work. Support networks of energy, communications, and so forth become increasingly vulnerable to sabotage, human error, or natural calamity.

This dilemma has its roots in the interplay of two features of global societies. One is what Alain Touraine described as "society's ability to produce itself," by which he meant the ability of society to construct itself in any shape or form it desires.[18] The increased mobility of the factors of production, especially capital, technology, and information, makes the production process much more responsive to rapidly changing market demands and consumer tastes. An unprecedented increase in worker productivity over the past five decades has led to an explosion in individual affluence, not only in the postindustrial countries but in the growing middle classes of otherwise poor countries, such as India, Mexico, and Brazil. A level of affluence unimaginable even a generation ago gives the consumer the power to demand more and more from the production system and provides for the increased mobility not only of people and goods but of ideas as well. A shift from manufacturing to services as the basis of national and global economies occurs as affluent consumers shift their consumption patterns from manufactured goods to experiences and services. A system of identifying and manipulating consumer preferences and marketing products to respond to those preferences ensures constantly rising demand despite a leveling off of population growth in Europe, Japan, and North America. Cultural fragmentation of even the most homogeneous societies is caused by worldwide population shifts of unprecedented scale and scope. Such cultural diversity encourages niche marketing, the design of highly specialized products intended for tiny segments of the consuming public. Developments in manufacturing make possible the mass production of highly specialized, nearly customized goods and services. Several general features of postmodern culture, including the commodification of many objects and relationships that were previously outside the market process, all lead to increased consumption.[19] Finally, the global spread of all of the above magnifies their impact and significance, as well as the speed with which their effects are felt in distant locales.

Running against this tide of production and consumption is "postrationality," or our inability to understand, predict, or control the behavior of complex systems, particularly once they have exceeded parameters such as size, complexity, nonlinearity, or speed of change. Extraordinary changes in the world of scientific thought, led by scholars like Ilya Prigogine, have made us increasingly aware of the ultimately unknowable nature of our physical world.[20] Chaos theory and other ways to describe complex systems cast doubt on the mechanistic and deterministic nature of the Newtonian model of the world.[21] Postmodernism rejects the possibility of universally true values, universally valid perceptions, or universally correct interpretations of reality, all of which heightens our uncertainty as we face the natural and social worlds. Transience, or the ephemeral nature of our material and experiential worlds, heightens our sense of impermanence and relativism. Systems constructed to meet the consumption demands cited above are so complex, so nonlinear, so rapidly changing, and so tightly coupled and interconnected that accidents become normal.

There appear to be three solutions to this dilemma, but this is only an appearance, since one of these is not really available and the second is only partially successful at conquering complexity. The first alternative—to make society less complex—is not really feasible since to do so would imply a return to a lower material standard of living, something unlikely to happen in the absence of some extraordinary disaster. The second solution—improving organizational decisionmaking by means of new intellectual approaches, technologies, or management techniques—appears to be somewhat more feasible than the first. But although solutions of this second type may have some applicability to problems of limited scope, they fail to deal with the rapidly changing environment faced by most global institutions.[22] We are left with the third solution: to make organizations more responsive to rapid changes without necessarily improving our understanding of complex system behavior. The key word here is flexibility, an attribute that many now see as the imperative of global institutions.

Some writers have called for a radical transformation in manufacturing to enable national economies to keep pace with the global economy. These changes go by many names: workplace democracy, the Japanese model, flexible-system production, and others. They all involve the decentralization of production units into many small, autonomous teams, together with a move away from large centralized assembly line models of production. These writers use terms like "flexibility" or "flexible-system production" in a way that focuses almost entirely on the technological innovations introduced in the manufacturing process to make a firm more nimble in responding to changes in consumer taste, factor costs, environmental demands, and so forth.[23]

Many observers are highly critical of industrial firms for pursuing flexibility at the expense of their workers. Far from being neutral as to consequences, flexible production concentrates on improving a firm's responsiveness to rapid change to promote corporate interests, regardless of the effects of such changes on workers, the environment, or society in general. In his book *The Condition of Postmodernity*, David Harvey uses the term "regime of flexible accumulation" to describe "post-Fordist" organizations that adapt to rapid and unexpected change without really trying to understand such change, much less predict or control it.[24] "Flexibility" is the system imperative here; the "contingent economy" is the regime designed to yield such responsiveness.

Global institutions have emphasized some or all of the following in their search for flexibility: (1) labor flexibility (part-time, temporary workers; declining union power; large-scale layoffs and plant closings; contracting out for peripheral services), (2) infrastructure flexibility (leasing office space rather than building; leasing computer and communications equipment rather than purchase), (3) market flexibility (demographic segmentation and the exploitation of market "niches"), (4) production flexibility (the use of robotics, just-in-time inventories and other manufacturing techniques to make production more responsive to rapidly changing demand), (5) institutional flexibility (the "hollow coporation," which does not actually produce anything itself but instead contracts out its most important production activities), and (6) political flexibility (privatization, or the withdrawal of the state from most economic activities except those necessary to maintain the stability of the overall system).[25]

If the imperative of global institutions is to respond quickly to rapid, large-scale, unexpected change, then the distinctive crisis of our era is brought on by the need to steer complex systems through rapidly changing, largely incomprehensible surroundings. As the old industrial system has declined in the face of the flexibility imperative, the result has been a "control revolution" that has seen the emergence of new professions and technologies to handle the daunting tasks of coordinating and controlling complexity. One can regard these control mechanisms as the contemporary version of the hinge functions Gottman identified as performed by the cities of the megalopolis.

James Beniger has argued that the control revolution dates from before the Industrial Revolution in the United States and indeed made the industrialization of the United States possible. The control infrastructure of U.S. society was not invented as a response to the nineteenth century's control crisis, but rather accompanied the emergence of manufacturing institutions or even preceded it. As Beniger describes it, the Industrial Revolution of the 1830s and 1840s involved two changes: "increasing levels of energy utilization or *power* and the progressive translation of this power into the increasing *speed* with which matter, energy and information moved through the system. All else being equal, increases in power will always result in increases in speed, which in turn increases the need for *control* and hence for communication, information processing, programming, and decision."[26]

Once in motion, the control revolution has continued to the present day. There are significant differences, however, between the control crisis of the nineteenth century and that of today. Today's control crisis is global in scope and unlimited as to the realm of life it affects. Today's systems operate at speeds several orders of magnitude greater than those of the nineteenth century, and the systems themselves are much more complex and their components much more tightly interconnected than those of a century earlier. Finally, today's crisis involves primarily information and images rather than the movement of raw materials and manufactured products. Increased speed is achieved not by increasing the power of manufacturing processes and technologies but by exploiting the information transmission capabilities of computers and telecommunications. Because of the fundamental dilemma we have just described, postindustrial society places a premium on rapid change, the high mobility of the factors of production, and the need for flexibility. Central to these transformations is the bulk flow of high quality, timely information. The workers charged with accomplishing these tasks are the symbolic analysts, to whom we now turn.

❦   ❦   ❦

If our only concern was with the professional activities of symbolic analysts, we could simply describe their organizational roles and leave the matter at that. The fact is, however, that symbolic analysts have special values and lifestyles that have decisively shaped the cities and other institutions of the Information Age. They are well educated, affluent, mobile, consumption oriented, and connected principally to an economy and a world of images that are more global than national or local. Their cultural values are derived primarily from postmodernism.[27] Their affluence, mobility, family structure, lifestyle, and image orientation impose a huge demand for personal services on their surrounding society; this demand in turn calls for a large personal services sector.

Since the late 1980s, a number of scholars have drawn attention to the steady polarization of U.S. society.[28] Along with the decline of the old industrial middle class, the income gap between rich and poor grew steadily after 1980. This polarization is reflected in the spatial arrangements of U.S. cities, for as the dividing line between rich and poor grows wider and deeper economically and socially, it grows territorially as well. To understand the contradictions in U.S. postindustrial cities, we must begin with the duality of those cities' workforce and the city form that such duality has produced.

Just as cities in earlier stages of industrialization called forth new professions to guide and facilitate their transactions, so the postindustrial city also has its distinctive professions. The workers who populate this sector have been given many names: "information workers"; "knowledge workers"; "occupational tertiarisation"; "quaternary sector"; or more simply, "office workers," "white-collar workers," or "nonproduction workers."[29] In an advanced industrial country, such workers may account for as much as 40 to 50 percent of the total workforce. Marc Porat, studying the U.S. economy in the 1970s, concluded that some 46 percent of the country's gross national product originated in information-related activities and nearly half of all U.S. workers could be classified as information workers.[30] Mark Hepworth discovered much the same proportions in both Great Britain and Canada.[31]

In their book on the information society, Herbert Dordick and Georgette Wang summarized trends in these data for twenty-one countries from 1970 to 1989.[32] Their findings: In the high income countries (e.g., United States, Japan), the information sector increased from about 39 percent of the total to 45–55 percent; in the middle-income countries (e.g., Brazil, South Korea), from about 25 percent to 35–40 percent; and in the low-income countries (e.g., Egypt, Philippines), from less than 20 percent to 25–30 percent.

Information workers are not only the largest single sector in the postindustrial workforce but also the fastest growing. The reason for this expansion has to do with the high transaction costs of an increasingly complex society as well as the different rates of technological progress in the manufacturing and information sectors.[33] As a society becomes postindustrial, processes of production become increasingly complex and require increased coordination. As the task of coordination grows, the number of transactions within and between the production enterprises grows as well and the overall transaction costs associated with production rise. But the tasks of information handling and processing are not easily or quickly improved simply by the introduction of bulk flow systems. Much of the information sector remains labor intensive, especially at the point where information technologies connect with human operators, that is, at the level of clerical functions. Because worker productivity grows more slowly in the information services sector than in manufacturing, the emergence of information as the leading sector has brought about a rapid increase in the number of workers needed to handle and process the newly available mountains of information. At least this was the case during the first three decades of the Information Age. The recession of 1990–1992 in the United States may have signaled the first real reversal of this trend, since many firms and public bureaucracies chose to deal with the economic slowdown by firing large numbers of clerical workers and mid-level managers, replacing them with new generations of more powerful information-handling technologies.

Hepworth describes the information sector with a five-sector model of the workforce: the primary, secondary, and tertiary sectors, which handle the extraction, processing, and distribution of matter and energy; the quaternary sector (finance, insurance, and real estate) to control the first three; and the quinary sector (law and government) to control the fourth.[34] In Hepworth's model, "information workers" consist of four groups: information *producers* (scientific and technical, market search and coordination, information gatherers, consultative services, health-related consultative services); information *processors* (administrative and managerial, process controls and supervisory, clerical and related); information *distributors* (educators, public information disseminators, communications workers); and information *infrastructure* (information machine workers, postal and telecommunications workers). Many of these information workers are the symbolic analysts who figure so prominently in the work of Robert Reich.[35]

According to Reich, symbolic analysts perform three tasks. *Problem-identifiers* track rapidly changing technologies and social, economic, and political trends and alert their organizations to the problems and opportunities presented by these changes. *Problem-solvers* innovate solutions that enable their organizations to adapt to rapid change; they are also frequently called upon to market these solutions or convince third parties to consume, adopt, or otherwise acquire them. If left isolated, problem-solvers and problem-identifiers would be much less responsive to the postindustrial imperative of flexibility. Hence the importance of the third set of symbolic analysts, the *brokers* who connect the other two groups.

Symbolic analysts are the new professional class of Information Age economies. As such, they have become steadily more significant in the workforce of the United States and other advanced industrial countries throughout the twentieth century. In 1900, writes Steven Sass, just 4 percent of all employed persons in the United States were "professional, technical and kindred" workers; by 1950 the ratio had doubled to 9 percent; and it doubled again to 18 percent by 1988.[36] Not only has their proportion grown, but these new professionals of the United States have expanded their role in a wide variety of industries, ranging from health care and education to advanced technology and business services to government and entertainment. Professionals are now more than one-fifth of the workforce in such industries as aircraft, chemicals, and mining.

The rise of the new professional class has had a major impact on the way global organizations are structured and on the way an advanced industrial economy operates. "What distinguishes professionals from other workers," according to Sass,

> is their vocational relationship to formal bodies of knowledge. Industries employing large numbers of professionals thus depend on the productivity of knowledge workers, the evolution of formal knowledge systems, and the movement of ideas into practice. This close relationship to conceptual systems typically differentiates the management of work and the sources of change in professionalized industries from patterns observed elsewhere in the economy.[37]

In institutions dominated by information professionals, the management and supervision functions are weakened. Professionals are typically involved in the customized application of knowledge or expertise to individual cases rather than the routinized application of rules to standardized objects. Because this knowledge or expertise resides with the professional and because the work is nonrepetitive, managers must delegate significant authority to professional employees. Since measurement of work outputs is usually quite difficult, managers find it hard to monitor the performance of professionals. With managerial authority diluted, the management of professionalized organizations becomes more costly, more difficult, and less exact.

A second important difference between professionalized industries and the rest of the economy is the way professionals have institutionalized, adapted to, and even routinized high rates of change. Professionals are accustomed to—indeed, they depend on—routinizing change through seminars and laboratories, journals and associations, and public and private regulatory bodies. The pace and direction of change of these industries remain quite unpredictable. Change has been incorporated into the professional sector as one of its central values. Long-term investment decisions become much more difficult and as Sass puts it, "Enterprises must remain flexible to accommodate disruptions flowing as a matter of course from professional activities."[38]

The sector of information professionals is only one part of the bifurcated U.S. workforce. To understand the emerging dual labor system of postindustrial cities, we must consider the other end of the economy: routine personal, or basic, services, that is, services of a routine nature that must be delivered face to face. Symbolic analysts demand a very high level of direct personal services. In their production-related lives, information professionals require the services of clerical, secretarial, janitorial, and similar workers to carry out the labor-intensive tasks associated with the gathering and processing of huge quantities of information (e.g., manuscript and graphic display preparation). In their consumption-related lives, information professionals require the services of real estate, retail trade, restaurant, hotel, travel, health care, entertainment, automobile servicing, child care, and similar workers to carry out the labor-intensive tasks associated with a lifestyle of comfort and convenience. In a postindustrial city, the routine personal services sector of the workforce may be twice the size of the symbolic analysts' sector. Because of the flexibility imperative of global institutions, these workers must be as nearly "disposable" as possible. Among these employees, unionization is discouraged, fringe benefits are rare, and job protection is not well established. This sector is made up largely of young women, teenagers, immigrants, and members of minority groups. Although symbolic analysts leave their stamp on the culture and values of the postindustrial city, it is the personal service workers who make the city function efficiently, cheaply, and conveniently.

One momentous consequence of the role of symbolic analysts in the postindustrial United States has been the changing shape of its cities. Information professionals are rebuilding their cities on the periphery of the old downtown core, seeking thereby to distance themselves from their central city. Observers of U.S. suburbia such as Robert Fishman, Kenneth Jackson, and Michael Danielson agree that one of the most important social forces that led to the suburb was the desire of members of the middle class to separate themselves and their families from what they saw as the dirty and corrupting influences of the industrial central city.[39] Between 1850 and 1920, this force led the middle class to relocate its residences on the city periphery. After World War II, mass ownership of the automobile enabled centers of retail trade to move away from the core as well, and after 1960, a number of converging factors, including telecommunications and interstate highways, made possible the massive shift of employment centers similarly to the periphery. "In the fifties," writes Nicholas Lemann in his description of the Chicago suburb Naperville, "the force driving the construction of residential neighborhoods in the suburbs was that prosperity had given to young married couples the means to act on their desire to raise children away from the cities"; in contrast, "in the eighties in Naperville there is still some of this, but the real driving force is that so many jobs are there."[40] Thus, the already strong preference of suburban dwellers to isolate themselves from their core city is reinforced by the fact that they no longer have to go downtown to work. Their entire life can be spent in the urban periphery.

Thus, the postindustrial city consists of two population centers that have only tenuous connections with one another. The core, or central business district, is usually portrayed as decaying and abandoned, but it continues to play an important role by housing the headquarters of many key institutions, including the control centers for a growing number of global firms. In addition, the urban core increasingly serves to house the country's underclass, as well as to provide amenities (shielded from the former group) for the entertainment of information professionals, such as restaurants; tourist attractions; hotels; sports stadia; and restored sites that offer multiple uses, including shopping, museums, and cultural events.[41] The periphery houses the symbolic analysts and their institutions and technologies in a mixture of office "parks," shopping malls, and upscale residences.

Living on the periphery of the core city, symbolic analysts are connected to their local context in only the most superficial ways. The postindustrial city is a suburban population center that has been transformed into a relatively self-contained society and economy where people live, work, and shop; where they are educated, entertained, and cured of their illnesses, all with relatively few connections to the core city. Economically, a postindustrial city is a relatively self-contained mixture of high-density concentrations of traditionally urban jobs and services and lower-density commercial and residential development. These areas are disconnected from their core city because of both inadequate mass transportation facilities and the automobile commuting patterns of the information workers.

In contrast to their local disconnectedness, symbolic analysts are closely connected by telecommunications, the mass media, entertainment and consumption networks, and air travel to their counterparts clustered in similar cities around the world. Indeed, without these global connections these workers could not perform their crucial functions or support their lifestyle. These connections define for the symbolic analysts much of their identity and absorb much of their attention, increasing their local disconnectedness even more.

The preference of information professionals to live on the urban periphery has produced the "urban village," a term used by Christopher Leinberger and Charles Lockwood to describe "business, retail, housing and entertainment focal points amid a low-density cityscape."[42] These mixed-use sites combine office and commercial space with a sizable resident population, usually living in spacious and dispersed surroundings. The automobile, telecommunications, and the shopping mall are the technologies that connect these components and make the urban village possible.

Leinberger and Lockwood identified five factors that have brought about the urban village. The first is the shift of the nation's economy from manufacturing to services. Since most of the business of the United States now is conducted in clean offices rather than dirty factories, middle-class employees are less reluctant to live close to where they work. A second reason has to do with changes in transportation patterns. Trucks have largely replaced railroads for the bulk shipment of manufactured items and the automobile is overwhelmingly preferred by commuters to travel between home and work. Advances in telecommunications are the third factor, since they have made the choice of work site essentially independent of communications considerations. Fourth, the lower cost of land in the suburbs means that office buildings and their associated structures, especially parking lots and garages, can be constructed far more cheaply on the periphery than in the core. Finally, urban villages respond to two U.S. middle-class values: the desire to enjoy the concentration of services afforded by large cities and the wish to enjoy these services without having to drive far to reach them.

What must an urban village have, or be, to support the work of a large population of symbolic analysts? More than two decades ago, Jean Gottman identified nine factors that distinguished what he called "transactional centers," his term for the urban village.[43] First is accessibility—the technologies and infrastructure that make it easy and cheap for people, goods, and ideas to get into, out of, and around the metropolis. The second, information flows, is essential because the transactional city lives on information. Transactional performance, the third factor, is the summary term Gottman used to describe the productivity of the transactional sector. This factor sums up all the things employers must provide to raise the transactional productivity of their organization. Fourth, the labor market includes not only the transactional workers themselves but the less-skilled service workers needed to keep them productive (clerks, secretaries) and contented with their lifestyle (restaurant waiters, car mechanics, and so forth). These last-named workers are needed because the highly paid and well-educated transactional workers demand a city rich in factor five, amenities and entertainment. Sixth, expert consultation and high-quality specialized services support the affluent transactional workers with the kind of professional services they demand, particularly in higher education and health care. Closely related to the need for rich information flows is the seventh factor, the market for money and credit and a highly skilled financial community. Specialized shopping facilities, factor eight, are an important component of the urban amenities cited earlier. Last but not least, educational facilities are a key factor in the transactional city. At the elementary and secondary levels, schools provide a superior education to the children of transactional workers; at the university level, the facilities offer not only intellectual stimulation but a steady flow of well-trained graduates who can step into an expanding transactional job market. Expressed in the terms of this book, Gottman was referring to bulk flow information systems, the personnel needed to manage them, and the service workers needed to attend to the needs of the information professionals.

The function of the postindustrial city, then, is to provide a habitat for symbolic analysts: a work site that links them comfortably to one another and to their counterparts in similar cities around the world; residential areas that signal their affluence and level of consumption; urban amenities and entertainment facilities that mark their affluent lifestyle; dense concentrations of high-quality services, ranging from child care and restaurants to universities, hospitals, and residences for older persons; and transportation and communications infrastructure that enable them to move themselves and their ideas quickly and easily from one part of the global econoculture to another.

↔   ↔   ↔

For about 1 million years, the genus *Homo* has labored to free itself from the bonds of entropy and the second law of thermodynamics. First, our distant ancestors, *Homo erectus*, tried to migrate to more fertile lands, followed by our species, *Homo sapiens*, about 100,000 years ago. When that measure failed, we tried to exploit local resources more intensively by means of the Neolithic Revolution, and when that proved inadequate, we established trade routes, first across the Mediterranean and the Indian Ocean, then overland via the Silk Road, and then across the Atlantic and Pacific Oceans. Eventually, these efforts led to large-scale global migration of Europeans and Africans (the latter against their will) and the establishment of the first primitive global systems. When the Industrial Revolution showed us how to liberate the energy stored in fossil fuels—first coal, then petroleum—we applied those discoveries to the problems of bulk flow and invented systems for moving large quantities of matter and energy great distances at relatively fast speeds. The most recent stage of these efforts has seen the application of bulk flow technology to the global transport of information.

Despite our spectacular successes of technological and social inventions, we have failed to achieve our broader objective. After each episode of globalization, we responded by increasing our number, the density of our population centers, the consumption level of the more fortunate of us (a number also increasing, in some places and in some historical periods faster than in others), and the complexity of the systems of production and consumption required to support all of the above. We have also, in the process, spread ourselves across the Earth. We, our technological systems, and our plant and animal companions have grown to fill most of the habitable recesses of our world. By means of dissipative structures, we have, in James Beniger's words, "persisted counter to entropy."[44] But we have not conquered the second law, nor shall we ever do so, as A. J. McMichael reminds us: "Increasingly, we understand that human cultures have introduced many types of 'evodeviation' that have distorted ecological relationships and reduced the capacity of ecosystems to support health and life. Because of our powers of adaptation we have often been able to modify or defer such problems—and sometimes seemingly sidestep them. But it is in the nature of ecological systems that debts are finally called in."[45]

So, as we near the limits of our rich, yet finite, planet, we confront the question that was inevitable from those first days on the East African savanna: Where do we go from here?[46]

Notes

Introduction: Why Globalization?

1. Roland Robertson, *Globalization: Social Theory and Global Culture* (London: Sage, 1992), Chapters 3 and 8. Anthony King, "Architecture, Capital and the Globalization of Culture," in Mike Featherstone, ed., *Global Culture: Nationalism, Globalization and Modernity* (London: Sage, 1990). Roland Robertson, "Globalization Theory and Civilizational Analysis," *Comparative Civilizations Review*, vol. 17 (1987), pp. 20–30.

2. Garret Hardin has coined the term "ecolacy" to be added to "literacy" and "numeracy" as one of the perspectives we need to appreciate our world. To the mastery of words (literacy) and numbers (numeracy) he adds ecolacy, the mastery of connections. See Garret Hardin, *Living within Limits: Ecology, Economics, and Population Taboos* (New York: Oxford University Press, 1993), pp. 14–16.

3. Albert Einstein, "Religion and Science," *The World as I See It*, trans. by Alan Harris (New York: Citadel Press, 1993), p. 26.

4. Bruce Mazlish and Ralph Buultjens, eds., *Conceptualizing Global History* (Boulder, Colorado: Westview Press, 1993). Michael Geyer and Charles Bright, "World History in a Global Age," *American Historical Review* (October, 1995), pp. 1034–1060.

5. James R. Beniger, *The Control Revolution: Technological and Economic Origins of the Information Society* (Cambridge, Massachusetts: Harvard University Press, 1986), p. 64.

6. John Fenn, *Engines, Energy and Entropy: A Thermodynamics Primer* (San Francisco: W. H. Freeman, 1982), Chapter 12. D.S.L. Cardwell, *From Watt to Clausius: The Rise of Thermodynamics in the Early Industrial Age* (Ithaca, New York: Cornell University Press, 1971). Philip Stehle, *Order, Chaos, Order: The Transition from Classical to Quantum Physics* (New York: Oxford University Press, 1994), pp. 27–33. Paul Davies and John Gribben, *The Matter Myth* (New York: Simon & Schuster, 1992), pp. 122–134. Ilya Prigogine and Isabelle Stengers, *Order out of Chaos: Man's New Dialogue with Nature* (New York: Bantam, 1984), Chapter 4.

7. Quoted in Joseph Tainter, *The Collapse of Complex Societies* (Cambridge: Cambridge University Press, 1988), p. 45.

8. Kenneth Boulding, *The Meaning of the Twentieth Century: The Great Transition* (New York: Harper & Row, 1964), Chapter 7, esp. p. 137.

9. *Ibid.*, p. 138.

10. Nicholas Georgescu-Roegen, *The Entropy Law and the Economic Process* (Cambridge, Massachusetts: Harvard University Press, 1971), Chapter 10.

11. Herman Daly, "Consumption and the Environment," *Philosophy and Public Policy*, vol. 15, no. 4 (Fall, 1995), pp. 6–7.

12. Grégoire Nicolis and Ilya Prigogine, *Exploring Complexity: An Introduction* (New York: W. H. Freeman, 1989), Chapters 1, 2. Prigogine and Stengers, *op. cit.* Erich Jantsch, "Autopoiesis: A Central Aspect of Dissipative Self-Organization," in Milan Zelany, ed., *Autopoiesis: A Theory of Living Organization* (New York: North Holland, 1981), Chapter 5.

13. Boulding, *op. cit.*, p. 139.

14. Murray Gell-Mann, *The Quark and the Jaguar: Adventures in the Simple and the Complex* (New York: W. H. Freeman, 1994), pp. 223–224.

15. Davies and Gribben, *op. cit.*, pp. 125–128.

16. Stuart Kauffman, *At Home in the Universe: The Search for the Laws of Self-Organization and Complexity* (New York: Oxford University Press, 1995), Chapter 4.

17. Jack Cohen and Ian Stewart, *The Collapse of Chaos: Discovering Simplicity in a Complex World* (New York: Viking, 1994), Chapter 8, p. 249.

18. Kauffman, *op. cit.*, p. 92.

19. Cohen and Stewart, *op. cit.*, p. 252. Emphasis added.

20. Georgescu-Roegen, *op. cit.*, pp. 191–192. Emphasis in the original.

21. A. J. McMichael, *Planetary Overload: Global Environmental Change and the Health of the Human Species* (New York: Cambridge University Press, 1993), p. 73.

22. Peter Rowley-Conwy, "Shell Middens: The Rubbish Dumps of History," in Göran Burenhult, ed., *People of the Stone Age: Hunter-Gatherers and Early Farmers* (New York: HarperCollins, 1993), p. 62. Donald Johanson, Lenora Johanson, and Blake Edgar, *Ancestors: In Search of Human Origins* (New York: Villard Books, 1994), p. 273.

23. Clive Ponting, *A Green History of the World* (New York: St. Martin's Press, 1991), Chapter 1.

24. Clive Gamble, *Timewalkers: The Prehistory of Global Colonization* (Cambridge, Massachusetts: Harvard University Press, 1994). Ernest Schusky, *Culture and Agriculture: An Ecological Introduction to Traditional and Modern Farming Systems* (New York: Bergin & Garvey, 1989), Chapter 3.

25. Jantsch, *op. cit.*, p. 83. Emphasis in the original.

26. Abel Wolman, "The Metabolism of Cities," in *Cities* (New York: Alfred A. Knopf, 1966), pp. 156–174. James Trefil, *A Scientist in the City* (New York: Doubleday, 1994), Part One.

27. Lester Brown and Jodi Jacobson, "The Future of Urbanization: Facing Ecological and Economic Constraints," *Worldwatch Paper 77* (Washington, D.C.: Worldwatch Institute, May 1987), p. 35.

28. I am aware of the heavily charged emotions that one sometimes associates with words like "center" and "periphery." I am not asserting here that one region or area of the world has privileges that others lack, that one region takes precedence over others, or that one region is the "engine" that has driven world history. I adopt these terms as simple metaphors to aid in visualizing what happens when one system dissipates its entropy to another. For more on these issues, see J. M. Blaut, *The Colonizer's Model of the World: Geographical Diffusionism and Eurocentric History* (New York: Guilford Press, 1993). Also, Christopher Chase-Dunn, *Global Formation: Structures of the World-Economy* (Cambridge, Massachusetts: Blackwell Publishers, 1989).

29. McMichael, *op. cit.*, p. 97.

30. William McNeill, *Plagues and Peoples* (New York: Doubleday, 1977).

31. Tainter, *op. cit.*, p. 23.

32. Daniel Dennett, *Darwin's Dangerous Idea: Evolution and the Meanings of Life* (New York: Simon & Schuster, 1995). George Johnson, *Fire in the Mind: Science, Faith, and the Search for Order* (New York: Alfred A. Knopf, 1995).

33. Ian Stewart, "Does Chaos Rule the Cosmos?" *Discover* (November, 1992), pp. 56–63. The quote is from pp. 61–62.

34. Carl Sagan and Ann Druyan, *Shadows of Forgotten Ancestors: A Search for Who We Are* (New York: Random House, 1992), Chapter 8.

35. John Holland, *Hidden Order: How Adaptation Builds Complexity* (Reading, Massachusetts: Addison-Wesley, 1995), Chapter 2.

36. Cohen and Stewart, *op. cit.*, Chapter 4, pp. 104–106, and Chapter 5, pp. 134–141. The quote is from p. 136. Emphasis in the original. See also Brian Arthur's brief essay, "Why Do Things Become More Complex?" *Scientific American* (May, 1993), p. 144. On the other hand, scholars from many fields dispute the inevitability of increasing complexity. See Carol Kaesuk Yoon, "Biologists Deny Life Gets More Complex," *New York Times,* March 30, 1993.

37. Gell-Mann, *op. cit.*, p. 229.

38. Tainter, *op. cit.*, pp. 91–92.

39. Donella Meadows, Dennis Meadows, and Jorgen Randers, *Beyond the Limits: Confronting Global Collapse, Envisioning a Sustainable Future* (Post Mills, Vermont: Chelsea Green Publishing Company, 1992). Theodore Modis, *Predictions: Society's Telltale Signature Reveals the Past and Forecasts the Future* (New York: Simon & Schuster, 1992).

40. David Ruelle, *Chance and Chaos* (Princeton, New Jersey: Princeton University Press, 1991), p. 102.

41. McMichael, *op. cit.*, pp. 260–263.

42. As I use the term here, "global city" is much more inclusive than such similar terms as "world city" and "mega-city." A global city is one for which survival depends on being connected to global systems of energy, food, information, population, and so forth. For the latest conceptualizations on the other terms, see two papers prepared for the 'World Cities in a World System' Conference, Center for Innovative Technology, Herndon, Virginia, April 1–3, 1993: John Friedman, "Where We Stand: A Decade of World City Research"; and Janice Perlman, "World Cities and Mega-Cities in the New Urban Configuration." See also, Saskia Sassen, *The Global City: New York, London, Tokyo* (Princeton, New Jersey: Princeton University Press, 1991).

43. Robertson, *Globalization, op. cit.*, p. 54.

44. Clark Kerr, *The Future of Industrial Societies* (Cambridge, Massachusetts: Harvard University Press, 1983).

45. Michael Ignatieff, *Blood and Belonging: Journeys into the New Nationalism* (New York: Farrar, Straus, & Giroux, 1993). Benjamin Barber, *Jihad vs. McWorld* (New York: Random House, 1995). David Rieff, "Multiculturalism's Silent Partner: It's the Newly Globalized Consumer Economy, Stupid," *Harper's* (August, 1993), pp. 62–72.

46. Steven Vogel, *Vital Circuits: On Pumps, Pipes, and the Workings of Circulatory Systems* (New York: Oxford University Press, 1992).

47. Beniger, *op. cit.*

48. Nigel Harris, *The End of the Third World: Newly Industrializing Countries and the Decline of an Ideology* (New York: Penguin, 1986), esp. Chapter 4. David Rieff, *Los Angeles: Capital of the Third World* (New York: Simon & Schuster, 1991).

49. David Harvey, *The Condition of Postmodernity: An Enquiry into the Origins of Cultural Change* (Oxford: Basil Blackwell, 1989), esp. Part Two.

50. Donald Janelle, "Global Interdependence and Its Consequences," in Stanley Brunn and Thomas Leinbach, eds., *Collapsing Space and Time: Geographic Aspects of Communication and Information* (London: HarperCollins, 1991), Chapter 3.

Episode One: Out of Africa

1. Claude Allègre, *The Behavior of the Earth: Continental and Seafloor Mobility*, trans. by Deborah Kurmes Van Dam (Cambridge, Massachusetts: Harvard University Press, 1988). A. Hallam, *A Revolution in the Earth Sciences: From Continental Drift to Plate Tectonics* (Oxford: Clarendon Press, 1974).

2. Alfred Wegener, *The Origin of Continents and Oceans*, trans. by John Biram (New York: Dover Publications, 1966).

3. Stephen Hall, *Mapping the Next Millennium: The Discovery of New Geographies* (New York: Random House, 1992), Chapter 4.

4. The exact number of tectonic plates is still being debated by earth scientists. Early models suggested between seven and nine but the current model divides the earth into thirteen. See Allègre, *op. cit.,* p. 101, Figure 39.

5. We should note that the Earth's landmasses have been more or less constantly on the move since their formation. Before they constituted Pangaea, they were also fragmented, although in patterns we would not recognize from today's formations. See Ian W.D. Dalziel, "Earth before Pangea," *Scientific American*, vol. 272, no. 1 (January, 1995), pp. 58–63.

6. Steven Groak, *The Idea of Building* (London: E & FN Spon, 1992), p. 29.

7. Alfred Crosby, "Metamorphosis of the Americas," in Herman Viola and Carolyn Margolis, eds., *Seeds of Change* (Washington, D.C., and London: Smithsonian Institution Press, 1991), pp. 74–76.

8. Alfred Crosby, *The Columbian Exchange: Biological and Cultural Consequences of 1492* (Westport, Connecticut: Greenwood Press, 1972). The quote is from p. 3.

9. Roger Lewin, *The Origin of Modern Humans* (New York: Scientific American Library, 1993), Chapter 3. C. B. Stringer, "*Homo Sapiens:* Single or multiple origins?" in John Durant, ed., *Human Origins* (Oxford: Clarendon Press, 1989), Chapter 5.

10. Luigi Luca Cavalli-Sforza and Francesco Cavalli-Sforza, *The Great Human Diaspora: The History of Diversity and Evolution*, trans. by Sarah Thorne (Reading, Massachusetts: Addison-Wesley, 1995), Chapters 1–3.

11. Yves Coppens, "East Side Story: The Origin of Humankind," *Scientific American*, vol. 270, no. 5 (May, 1994), pp. 88–95. Michael Day, "Fossil Man: The Hard Evidence," in Durant, *op. cit.,* Chapter 2.

12. Clive Gamble, *Timewalkers: The Prehistory of Global Colonization* (Cambridge, Massachusetts: Harvard University Press, 1994).

13. Lewin, *op. cit.* While this book was in preparation, however, a new fossil discovery was announced that pushes our knowledge of early ancestors back to about 4.4 million years ago. See John Noble Wilford, "New Fossils Take Science Close to Dawn of Humans," *New York Times*, September 22, 1994.

14. Donald Johanson, Lenora Johanson, and Blake Edgar, *Ancestors: In Search of Human Origins* (New York: Villard Books, 1994).

15. Adrienne Zihlman, "Common Ancestors and Uncommon Apes," in Durant, *op. cit.*, Chapter 6.

16. R. E. Passingham, "The Origins of Human Intelligence," in Durant, *op. cit.*, Chapter 8.

17. Nicholas Toth, "The First Technology," *Scientific American*, vol. 256, no. 4 (April, 1987), pp. 112–121.

18. John Pfeiffer, *The Emergence of Man* (New York: Harper & Row, 1969), pp. 137–140.

19. Gamble, *op. cit.*, p. 100.

20. Vaclav Smil, *Energy in World History* (Boulder, Colorado: Westview Press, 1994), Chapter 2.

21. Lewin, *op. cit.*, pp. 21–25.

22. Johanson, Johanson, and Edgar, *op. cit.*, pp. 204–205. Passingham, *op. cit.*

23. Richard Leakey, *The Origin of Humankind* (New York: Basic Books, 1994), pp. 54–55.

24. Smil, *op. cit.*, p. 11. In measuring human food energy requirements in calories, I am following customary usage, even though in fact the correct unit of measurement is the kilocalorie, abbreviated kcal.

25. Johanson, Johanson, and Edgar, *op. cit.*, pp. 183–184.

26. *Ibid.*, p. 118. In a conversation following her lecture at the Smithsonian Institution on November 10, 1994, Kathleen Gordon, research associate at the National Museum of Natural History, observed that as a large and very active animal *Homo erectus* needed at least as much food energy as modern humans and perhaps as much as 2500 calories per day.

27. For more on human diet viewed in evolutionary terms, see A. J. McMichael, *Planetary Overload: Global Environmental Change and the Health of the Human Species* (New York: Cambridge University Press, 1993), pp. 87–95.

28. Smil, *op. cit.*, p. 18.

29. Clive Ponting, *A Green History of the World: The Environment and the Collapse of Great Civilizations* (New York: St. Martin's Press, 1991), pp. 11–12. McMichael, *op. cit.*, Chapter 2.

30. Johanson, Johanson, and Edgar, *op. cit.*, p. 203.

31. Massimo Livi-Bacci, *A Concise History of World Population*, trans. by Carl Ipsen (Cambridge, Massachusetts: Blackwell Publishers, 1992), Table 1.1, p. 27.

32. *Ibid.*, Table 1.2, p. 31.

33. Smil, *op. cit.*, p. 17.

34. Gamble, *op. cit.*, pp. 108–110.

35. Pfeiffer, *op. cit.*, p. 134.

36. Lewin, *op. cit.*, p. 150.

37. Marshall Sahlins, *Stone Age Economics* (Chicago: Aldine-Atherton, 1972), pp. 33–34.

38. Gamble, *op. cit.*, Figure 6.2, p. 108.

39. Lewin, *op. cit.*, p. 72.

40. Richard Potts, in a lecture at the Smithsonian Institution, December 1, 1994.

41. Rodney Castleden, *The Making of Stonehenge* (London: Routledge, 1993), p. 33.

42. Glynn Isaac, "Cutting and Carrying: Archeology and the Emergence of the Genus *Homo*," in Durant, *op. cit.*, Chapter 7.

43. G. L. Isaac, "The Activities of Early African Hominids," in G. L. Isaac and E. McCown, eds., *Human Origins* (Menlo Park, California: Benjamin Publishers, 1976), pp. 483–514. G. L. Isaac, "The Food-sharing Behavior of Protohuman Hominids," *Scientific American* (April, 1978), pp. 90–108.

44. Richard Potts, *Early Hominid Activities at Olduvai* (New York: Aldine de Gruyter, 1988), Chapter 9. The quotes are from pp. 264, 278.

45. Göran Burenhult, "The Megalith Builders of Western Europe," in Göran Burenhult, ed., *People of the Stone Age: Hunter-gatherers and Early Farmers* (New York: HarperSanFrancisco, 1993), pp. 81–82. See also, Livi-Bacci, *op. cit.*, p. 42.

Episode Two: The Neolithic Revolution

1. V. Gordon Childe, *Man Makes Himself* (New York: New American Library, 1951), Chapter 5.

2. Sonia Cole, *The Neolithic Revolution* (London: Trustees of the British Museum, 1970). Ernest Schusky, *Culture and Agriculture: An Ecological Introduction to Traditional and Modern Farming Systems* (New York: Bergin & Garvey, 1989), Part One.

3. Julian Thomas, *Rethinking the Neolithic* (Cambridge: Cambridge University Press, 1991), p. 13.

4. Clive Ponting, *A Green History of the World: The Environment and the Collapse of Great Civilizations* (New York: St. Martin's Press, 1991), pp. 40–41.

5. Among scholars such as paleobotanists and archeologists, there is some disagreement about the timing of the Neolithic Revolution and considerable disagreement over the causes of these changes. See C. Wesley Cowan and Patty Jo Watson, eds., *The Origins of Agriculture: An International Perspective* (Washington, D.C.: Smithsonian Institution Press, 1992); and Anne Birgitte Gebauer and T. Douglas Price, eds., *Transitions to Agriculture in Prehistory*, Monographs in World Archeology No. 4 (Madison, Wisconsin: Prehistory Press, 1992). Charles Heiser, *Seed to Civilization: The Story of Food* (Cambridge, Massachusetts: Harvard University Press, 1990).

6. Kathleen Kenyon, "Ancient Jericho," in *Ancient Cities: Scientific American Special Issue* (1994), pp. 20–23.

7. Daniel Zohary and Maria Hopf, *Domestication of Plants in the Old World*, second edition (Oxford: Clarendon Press, 1994), Chapter 11, esp. pp. 238–239.

8. Rodney Castleden, *The Making of Stonehenge* (London and New York: Routledge, 1993), p. 29. See also Luigi Luca Cavalli-Sforza and Francesco Cavalli-Sforza, *The Great Human Diaspora: The History of Diversity and Evolution*, trans. by Sarah Thorne (Reading, Massachusetts: Addison-Wesley, 1995), Chapter 6.

9. Peter Rowley-Conwy, "Stone Age Hunter-Gatherers and Farmers in Europe," in Göran Burenhult, ed., *People of the Stone Age: Hunter-Gatherers and Early Farmers* (New York: HarperCollins, 1993), pp. 59–75.

10. Gary Crawford, "Prehistoric Plant Domestication in East Asia," in Cowan and Watson, *op. cit.,* Chapter 2.

11. Emily McClung de Tapia, "The Origins of Agriculture in Mesoamerica and Central America," and Deborah Pearsall, "The Origins of Plant Cultivation in South America," in Cowan and Watson, *op. cit.,* Chapters 8 and 9.

12. David Hurst Thomas, "Farmers of the New World," in Burenhult, *op. cit.,* pp. 178–181.

13. Anne Birgitte Gebauer and T. Douglas Price, "Foragers to Farmers: An Introduction," in Gebauer and Price, *op. cit.,* Chapter 1.

14. Robley Matthews, Douglas Anderson, Robert Chen, and Thompson Webb, "Global Climate and the Origins of Agriculture," in Lucile Newman et al., eds., *Hunger in History: Food Shortage, Poverty, and Deprivation* (Oxford: Blackwell, 1990), Chapter 2.

15. Richard MacNeish, *The Origins of Agriculture and Settled Life* (Norman, Oklahoma: University of Oklahoma Press, 1992), Chapter 1. Table 1.1, p. 5.

16. Mark Cohen, *The Food Crisis in Prehistory: Overpopulation and the Origins of Agriculture* (New Haven, Connecticut: Yale University Press, 1977). The quote is on p. 279. See also Mark Cohen, "Prehistoric Patterns of Hunger," in Newman et al., *op. cit.,* Chapter 3.

17. Rowley-Conwy, *op. cit.*

18. William McNeill, *Plagues and Peoples* (New York: Doubleday, 1977), Chapter 2.

19. Cavalli-Sforza and Cavalli-Sforza, *op. cit.,* Chapter 6, p. 144.

20. David Rindos, *The Origins of Agriculture: An Evolutionary Perspective* (Orlando, Florida: Academic Press, 1984).

21. Rowley-Conwy, *op. cit.,* p. 61.

22. A. J. McMichael, *Planetary Overload: Global Environmental Change and the Health of the Human Species* (Cambridge: Cambridge University Press, 1993), p. 249.

23. Jared Diamond, "How to Tame a Wild Plant," *Discover* (September, 1994), p. 102.

24. Sophie Coe, *America's First Cuisines* (Austin, Texas: University of Texas Press, 1994), p. 122.

25. A recent discovery by archeologists in southeastern Turkey suggests that pigs were domesticated there some 10,000 years ago, 2000 years earlier than previously believed, and 1000 years before sheep and goats. John Noble Wilford, "First Settlers Domesticated Pigs before Crops," *New York Times,* May 31, 1994.

26. Jared Diamond, "Zebras and the Anna Karenina Principle," *Natural History* (September, 1994), pp. 4–10.

27. McMichael, *op. cit.,* Chapter 9.

28. Stephen Budiansky, *The Covenant of the Wild: Why Animals Chose Domestication* (New York: William Morrow, 1992). Stephen Budiansky, "In from the Cold," *New York Times Magazine,* December 22, 1991, pp. 18–23.

29. Rindos, *op. cit.*

30. Ponting, *op. cit.,* p. 52.

31. Cole, *op. cit.,* pp. 32–63. T. K. Derry and Trevor Williams, *A Short History of Technology from the Earliest Times to A. D. 1900* (New York: Dover Publications, 1993), Chapters 2 and 3. M. G. Lay, *Ways of the World: A History of the World's Roads and of the Vehicles That Used Them* (New Brunswick, New Jersey: Rutgers University Press, 1992), pp. 6–12.

32. Lewis Mumford, *The City in History: Its Origins, Its Transformations, and Its Prospects* (New York: Harcourt, Brace & World, 1961), pp. 15–16.

33. Theya Molleson, "The Eloquent Bones of Abu Hureya," *Scientific American*, vol. 271, no. 2 (August, 1994), pp. 70–75.

34. Lionel Casson, *Travel in the Ancient World* (Toronto: Hakkert, 1974), pp. 23–25, 51–52.

35. Brian Fagan, "Herding Fields of Ancient Ireland," *Archaeology*, (November/December, 1994), pp. 60–63.

36. Massimo Livi-Bacci, *A Concise History of World Population*, trans. by Carl Ipsen (Cambridge, Massachusetts: Blackwell, 1992), pp. 37–44.

37. Ponting, *op. cit.*, p. 37. Livi-Bacci, *op. cit.*, Table 1.2, p. 37.

38. Castleden, *op. cit.*, Chapters 5 and 6, and Appendix E.

39. Robert Adams, "The Origin of Cities," *Ancient Cities, op. cit.*, pp. 12–13.

40. Jane Jacobs, *The Economy of Cities* (New York: Random House, 1969), Chapter 1, esp. pp. 18–39.

41. Marshall Sahlins, *Stone Age Economics* (Chicago: Aldine-Atherton, 1972). The quotes are from pp. 97 and 135.

42. Childe, *op. cit.*, p. 74.

43. Castleden, *op. cit.*, p. 74.

44. Rindos, *op. cit.*, p. 278.

Episode Three: Ancient Cities and Trade Routes

1. Fernand Braudel, *Civilization and Capitalism, 15th–18th Century: Volume III, The Perspective of the World*, trans. by Siân Reynolds (New York: Harper & Row, 1984), p. 27.

2. Philip Curtin, *Cross-Cultural Trade in World History* (Cambridge: Cambridge University Press, 1984). Jerry Bentley, *Old World Encounters: Cross-Cultural Contacts and Exchanges in Pre-Modern Times* (New York: Oxford University Press, 1993). For a description of the trade diaspora in the pepper trade in India, see Anthony Disney, *Twilight of the Pepper Empire: Portuguese Trade in Southwest India in the Early Seventeenth Century* (Cambridge, Massachusetts: Harvard University Press, 1978), Chapter 3. For a description of the diaspora of Venetian merchants, see Frederic Lane, *Venice: A Maritime Republic* (Baltimore: Maryland: Johns Hopkins University Press, 1973), Chapter 11.

3. Lucile Newman, Alan Boegehold, David Herlihy, Robert Kates, and Kurt Raaflaub, "Agricultural Intensification, Urbanization, and Hierarchy," in Lucile Newman et al., eds., *Hunger in History: Food Shortage, Poverty, and Deprivation* (Oxford: Blackwell, 1990).

4. William McNeill, *The Rise of the West: A History of the Human Community* (Chicago: University of Chicago Press, 1963, 1991), pp. 132–133.

5. A. J. McMichael, *Planetary Overload: Global Environmental Change and the Health of the Human Species* (Cambridge: Cambridge University Press, 1993), pp. 84–87.

6. Newman, et. al., "Agricultural Intensification," *op. cit.*, pp. 118–121. The quote is on p. 119.

7. McMichael, *op. cit.*, pp. 209–210.

8. Charles Redman, "Early Mesopotamian Cities and the Environment," in Göran Burenhult, ed., *Old World Civilizations: The Rise of Cities and States* (New York: HarperSan Francisco, 1994), p. 21.

9. Arie Issar, "Climate Change and the History of the Middle East," *American Scientist*, vol. 83 (July–August, 1995), pp. 350–355, esp. p. 354.

10. Lionel Casson, *Travel in the Ancient World* (Toronto: Hakkert, 1974).

11. Trevor Hodge, "A Roman Factory," *Scientific American*, vol. 263, no. 5 (November, 1990), pp. 106–111.

12. Michael French, *Invention and Evolution: Design in Nature and Engineering*, second edition (Cambridge: Cambridge University Press, 1994), p. 6.

13. Peter Warren, "Minoan Palaces," *Ancient Cities: Scientific American Special Issue:* (1994), pp. 49–50.

14. Vaclav Smil, *Energy in World History* (Boulder, Colorado: Westview Press, 1994), pp. 49–54. Arnold Pacey, *Technology in World Civilization* (Cambridge, Massachusetts: MIT Press, 1990), pp. 6–12.

15. Anna Marguerite McCann, "The Roman Port of Cosa," *Ancient Cities, op. cit.*, pp. 92–99.

16. Casson, *op. cit.*, pp. 153, 216–217.

17. Peter Garnsey, *Famine and Food Supply in the Graeco-Roman World: Responses to Risk and Crisis* (New York: Cambridge University Press, 1988). Peter Garnsey, "Responses to Food Crisis in the Ancient Mediterranean World," in Newman et al., *Hunger in History, op. cit.*, Chapter 5. McNeill, *op. cit.*, pp. 201, 272–273.

18. Curtis Runnels, "Environmental Degradation in Ancient Greece," *Scientific American*, vol. 272, no. 3 (March, 1995), pp. 96–99.

19. McNeill, *op. cit.*, pp. 64–65.

20. Ying-shih Yü, *Trade and Expansion in Han China: A Study in the Structure of Sino-Barbarian Economic Relations* (Berkeley, California: University of California Press, 1967).

21. McNeill, *op. cit.*, p. 174.

22. P. M. Warren, "Crete, 3000–1400 B.C.: Immigration and the Archaeological Evidence," in R. A. Crossland and Ann Birchall, eds., *Bronze Age Migrations in the Aegean: Archaeological and Linguistic Problems in Greek Prehistory* (Park Ridge, New Jersey: Noyes-Press, 1974), pp. 41–47.

23. Rodney Castleden, *Minoans: Life in Bronze Age Crete* (London: Routledge, 1990).

24. *Ibid.*, p. 68.

25. Warren, "Minoan Palaces," *op. cit.*, pp. 46–56. R. W. Hutchinson, *Prehistoric Crete* (Baltimore, Maryland: Penguin, 1962), Chapter 9.

26. Castleden, *op. cit.*, Chapter 5. Hutchinson, *op. cit.*, Chapter 4.

27. Peter Warren, *The Aegean Civilizations* (New York: Peter Bedrick Books, 1989), p. 8.

28. Hakan Wahlquist, "The Silk Road," in Burenhult, *op. cit.*, pp. 120–121. M. G. Lay, *Ways of the World: A History of the World's Roads and of the Vehicles That Used Them* (New Brunswick, New Jersey: Rutgers University Press, 1992), pp. 45–48. Norma Martyn, *The Silk Road* (North Ridge, Australia: Methuen Australia, 1987). Casson, *op. cit.*, pp. 123–124.

29. Yü, *op. cit.*, pp. 150–167.

30. Casson, *op. cit.*, Chapter 6.

31. *Ibid.*, pp. 54–55.

32. Bamber Gascoigne, *The Dynasties and Treasures of China* (New York: Viking Press, 1973), Chapter 3.

33. Yü, *op. cit.*, pp. 135–138. McNeill, *op. cit.*, p. 295.

34. McNeill, *op. cit.*, Chapter 7.

35. Bentley, *op. cit.*, Chapter 2.

36. William McNeill, *Plagues and Peoples* (New York: Doubleday, 1977), Chapter 3. The quotes are from pp. 97, 129.

37. Sechin Jagchid and Van Jay Symons, *Peace, War, and Trade along the Great Wall: Nomadic-Chinese Interaction through Two Millennia* (Bloomington, Indiana: Indiana University Press, 1989).

38. William Denevan, ed., *The Native Population of the Americas in 1492* (Madison, Wisconsin: University of Wisconsin Press, 1976), Table 0.1, p. 3. William Denevan, "The Pristine Myth: The Landscape of the Americas in 1492," *Annals of the Association of American Geographers*, vol. 82, no. 3 (September, 1992), pp. 370–371.

39. René Millon, "Teotihuacán," *Ancient Cities, op. cit.*, pp. 138–148. Richard Blanton, "The Emergence of Civilization in Mesoamerica," in Göran Burenhult, ed., *New World and Pacific Civilizations: Cultures of America, Asia, and the Pacific* (New York: HarperSan Francisco, 1994), p. 33.

40. David Hurst Thomas, "Farmers of the New World," in Göran Burenhult, ed., *People of the Stone Age: Hunter-Gatherers and Early Farmers* (New York: Harper-San Francisco, 1993), p. 173. Daniel Gade, "Landscape, System, and Identity in the Post-Conquest Andes," *Annals, op. cit.*, pp. 461–477.

41. Michael Coe, *The Maya*, fifth edition (London: Thames and Hudson, 1993), p. 93. The quote is from p. 128. Note that B. L. Turner argues that the available evidence does not support a Malthusian explanation for the collapse of the Maya population and suggests that a more plausible explanation would have to consider the complex interconnectedness of agricultural systems and technology, climate, and other factors. See B. L. Turner, "The Rise and Fall of Population and Agriculture in the Central Maya Highlands: 300 BC to Present," in Newman, et. al., *op. cit.*, Chapter 7.

42. Richard Townsend, *The Aztecs* (London: Thames and Hudson, 1992).

43. Richard Blanton, "The Rise of the Aztecs," in Burenhult, *New World and Pacific Civilizations, op. cit.*, p. 63.

44. Thomas Whitmore and B. L. Turner, "Landscapes of Cultivation in Mesoamerica on the Eve of the Conquest," *Annals, op. cit.*, pp. 403–409.

45. Ross Hassig, *Trade, Tribute, and Transportation: The Sixteenth-Century Political Economy of the Valley of Mexico* (Norman, Oklahoma: University of Oklahoma Press, 1985), Part One.

46. *Ibid.*, pp. 20–21.

47. Sophie Coe, *America's First Cuisines* (Austin, Texas: University of Texas Press, 1994).

48. Bernard Ortiz de Montellano, *Aztec Medicine, Health, and Nutrition* (New Brunswick, New Jersey: Rutgers University Press, 1990), p. 119.

49. *Ibid.*, pp. 86–89. Sophie Coe, *op. cit.*, pp. 89–91.

50. McCann, *op. cit.*, p. 97.

51. Sophie Coe, *op. cit.*, p. 89.

52. T. K. Derry and Trevor Williams, *A Short History of Technology from the Earliest Times to A.D. 1900* (New York: Dover Publications, 1993), Chapter 6. Casson, *op. cit.*, pp. 23–24.

53. Smil, *op. cit.*, pp. 40–49.

54. Lay, *op. cit.*, Chapter 3.

55. Casson, *op. cit.*, pp. 68–70.

56. *Ibid.*, Chapter 10.

57. *Ibid.*, Chapters 11–13.

58. James Burke, *The Day the Universe Changed* (Boston: Little, Brown, 1985), pp. 95–97.

59. Hassig, *op. cit.*, pp. 56–64.

60. Castleden, *op. cit.*, pp. 114–116.

61. Casson, *op. cit.*, pp. 149–152.

62. Pacey, *op. cit.*, p. 15.

63. Castleden, *op. cit.*, pp. 100–102.

64. Pacey, *op. cit.*, Table 2, p. 42.

65. Simon Berthon and Andrew Robinson, *The Shape of the World: The Mapping and Discovery of the Earth* (Chicago: Rand McNally, 1991), Chapters 1, 2.

Episode Four: The Age of Discovery

1. Eric Wolf, *Europe and the People without History* (Berkeley, California: University of California Press, 1982). Urs Bitterli, *Cultures in Conflict: Encounters between European and Non-European Cultures, 1492–1800*, trans. by Ritchie Robertson (Stanford, California: Stanford University Press, 1989). Philip Curtin, *Cross-Cultural Trade in World History* (New York: Cambridge University Press, 1984).

2. The phrase is from Alfred Crosby, *Ecological Imperialism: The Biological Expansion of Europe, 900–1900* (Cambridge: Cambridge University Press, 1986).

3. Eviatar Zerubavel, *Terra Cognita: The Mental Discovery of America* (New Brunswick, New Jersey: Rutgers University Press, 1992).

4. Daniel Boorstin, *The Discoverers: A History of Man's Search to Know His World and Himself* (New York: Vintage Books, 1985), Chapters 25, 26. The quote is from p. 201.

5. Louise Levathes, *When China Ruled the Seas: The Treasure Fleet of the Dragon Throne, 1405–1433* (New York: Simon & Schuster, 1994).

6. Arnold Pacey, *Technology in World Civilization: A Thousand-Year History* (Cambridge, Massachusetts: MIT Press, 1990), pp. 62–70.

7. Crosby, *op. cit.*, Chapter 3.

8. Massimo Livi-Bacci, *A Concise History of World Population*, trans. by Carl Ipsen (Cambridge, Massachusetts: Blackwell, 1992), Table 1.3, p. 31, pp. 44–50.

9. Fernand Braudel, *Civilization and Capitalism, 15th–18th Century: Volume III, The Perspective of the World*, trans. by Siân Reynolds (New York: Harper & Row, 1984), Figure 10, p. 93.

10. Livi-Bacci, *op. cit.*, pp. 44–45.

11. Henry Hobhouse, *Forces of Change: An Unorthodox View of History* (New York: Little, Brown, 1989), Chapters 1 and 2. The quote is from p. 11.

12. William McNeill, *Plagues and Peoples* (New York: Doubleday, 1976), Chapter 4.

13. Fernand Braudel, "The Mediterranean Economy in the Sixteenth Century," trans. by Siân Reynolds, in Peter Earle, ed., *Essays in European Economic History, 1500–1800* (Oxford: Clarendon Press, 1974), pp. 30–31.

14. Clive Ponting, *A Green History of the World: The Environment and the Collapse of Great Civilizations* (New York: St. Martin's Press, 1991), Chapter 7.

15. Ernest Schusky, *Culture and Agriculture: An Ecological Introduction to Traditional and Modern Farming Systems* (New York: Bergin & Garvey, 1989), Chapter 6. John Post, "Nutritional Status and Mortality in Eighteenth-Century Europe," in Lucile Newman et al., eds., *Hunger in History: Food Shortage, Poverty, and Deprivation* (Oxford: Blackwell, 1990), Chapter 9.

16. Göran Burenhult, "The Iron Age in Europe," in Göran Burenhult, ed., *Old World Civilizations: The Rise of Cities and States* (New York: HarperSan Francisco, 1994), pp. 202–207.

17. Crosby, *op. cit.*, pp. 26–27. For more on the evolution of lactose tolerance in neolithic Britain, see Julian Thomas, *Rethinking the Neolithic* (Cambridge: Cambridge University Press, 1991), p. 24.

18. *American Demographics* (January, 1995), pp. 47–48.

19. Hans Eberhard Mayer, *The Crusades,* second edition, trans. by John Gillingham (Oxford: Oxford University Press, 1988). William McNeill, *The Rise of the West: A History of the Human Community* (Chicago: University of Chicago Press, 1963, 1991), pp. 545–547. Crosby, *op. cit.*, Chapter 3.

20. Frederic Lane, *Venice: A Maritime Republic* (Baltimore, Maryland: Johns Hopkins University Press, 1973).

21. Lionel Casson, *Travel in the Ancient World* (Toronto: Hakkert, 1974), pp. 61–64.

22. Ralph Davis, *The Rise of the Atlantic Economies* (Ithaca, New York: Cornell University Press, 1973), Chapter 1.

23. Braudel, *Civilization, op. cit.*, Chapter 2.

24. Mary Kilbourne Matossian, *Poisons of the Past: Molds, Epidemics, and History* (New Haven, Connecticut: Yale University Press, 1989).

25. Hobhouse, *op. cit.*, pp. 119–123.

26. Casson, *op. cit.*, p. 124.

27. Anthony Disney, *Twilight of the Pepper Empire: Portuguese Trade in Southwest India in the Early Seventeenth Century* (Cambridge, Massachusetts: Harvard University Press, 1978), p. 26.

28. Hobhouse, *op. cit.*, p. 119.

29. Boorstin, *op. cit.*, p. 195.

30. Braudel, *Civilization, op. cit.*, Chapter 2.

31. Bitterli, *op. cit.*, pp. 64–65.

32. Braudel, "The Mediterranean Economy," *op. cit.*, p. 17.

33. Davis, *op. cit.*, Chapter 11.

34. Braudel, *Civilization, op. cit.*, p. 143.

35. *Ibid.*, p. 150. Lane, *op. cit.*, Chapter 20.

36. Disney, *op. cit.*, esp. Chapters 4–6, 9.

37. Alfred Crosby, *The Columbian Exchange: Biological and Cultural Consequences of 1492* (Westport, Connecticut: Greenwood Press, 1972). Alfred Crosby, *Germs, Seeds and Animals: Studies in Ecological History* (Armonk, New York: M. E. Sharpe, 1994).

38. Davis, *op. cit.*, Chapter 8.

39. B. W. Higman, *Slave Population and Economy in Jamaica, 1807–1834* (Cambridge: Cambridge University Press, 1976).

40. Bitterli, *op. cit.*, pp. 36–37.

41. Karl Butzer, "The Americas before and after 1492: An Introduction to Current Geographical Research," *Annals of the Association of American Geographers*, vol. 82, no. 3 (September, 1992), Table 1, p. 358.

42. Crosby, *Columbian Exchange, op. cit.*

43. George Lovell, "'Heavy Shadows and Black Night': Disease and Depopulation in Colonial Spanish America," in *Annals, op. cit.*, pp. 426–443.

44. Ross Hassig, *Trade, Tribute, and Transportation: The Sixteenth-Century Political Economy of the Valley of Mexico* (Norman, Oklahoma: University of Oklahoma Press, 1985), Chapters 10 and 11.

45. Samuel Wilson, "On the Matter of Smallpox," *Natural History* (September, 1994), pp. 64–69.

46. Crosby, *Columbian Exchange, op. cit.*

47. Nelson Foster and Linda Cordell, eds., *Chilies to Chocolate: Food the Americas Gave the World* (Tucson, Arizona: University of Arizona Press, 1992).

48. Pierre and Huguette Chaunu, "The Atlantic Economy and the World Economy," trans. by Elizabeth Mortimer, in Earle, *op. cit.*, pp. 119–121.

49. Crosby, *Germs, op. cit.*, Chapter 9. The quote is on p. 163. Emphasis in the original. For more on the impact of the potato on the British diet, see John Walton, *Fish and Chips and the British Working Class, 1870–1940* (Leicester: Leicester University Press, 1992), Chapter 7, esp. pp. 151–162.

50. William McNeill, "American Food Crops in the Old World," in Herman Viola and Carolyn Margolis, eds., *Seeds of Change* (New York: Smithsonian Institution, 1991), pp. 43–59.

51. Crosby, *Columbian Exchange, op. cit.*, p. 219.

52. Braudel, *Civilization, op. cit.*, pp. 581–586. M. G. Lay, *Ways of the World: A History of the World's Roads and of the Vehicles That Used Them* (New Brunswick, New Jersey: Rutgers University Press, 1992), Chapters 3 and 4.

53. Crosby, *Ecological Imperialism, op. cit.*

54. Boorstin, *op. cit.*, pp. 163–164. See Lane, *op. cit.*, Chapter 10, for a discussion of the impact of the revolution in maritime technology on Venetian traders.

55. Pacey, *op. cit.*, pp. 65–70.

56. Zerubavel, *op. cit.*

57. Boorstin, *op. cit.*, pp. 161–162.

58. Braudel, *Civilization, op. cit.*, Chapters 2 and 3. Davis, *op. cit.*, Chapter 11.

59. Samuel Eliot Morrison, *The Great Explorers: The European Discovery of America* (New York: Oxford University Press, 1978), pp. 43–49.

60. Crosby, "The Demographic Effect of American Crops in Europe," in Crosby, *Germs, op. cit.*, Chapter 9. William Cosgrove et al., "Colonialism, International Trade, and the Nation-State," in Newman et al., *Hunger in History, op. cit.*, Chapter 8. Davis, *op. cit.*, Chapter 15.

61. Lovell, *op. cit.* Davis, *op. cit.*, Chapter 8.

62. Braudel, *Civilization, op. cit.*, pp. 490–491.

63. McNeill, *Rise of the West, op. cit.*, pp. 611–652.

Episode Five: The Partnership of Steam and Coal

1. A. J. McMichael, *Planetary Overload: Global Environmental Change and the Health of the Human Species* (Cambridge: Cambridge University Press, 1993), Chapter 4. Vaclav Smil, *Energy in World History* (Boulder, Colorado: Westview Press, 1994), Chapter 5. James Trefil, *A Scientist in the City* (New York: Doubleday, 1994), Chapter 7.

2. Asa Briggs, *The Power of Steam* (Chicago: University of Chicago Press, 1982). G. N. von Tunzelmann, *Steam Power and British Industrialization to 1860* (Oxford: Oxford University Press, 1978). Donald Cardwell, *From Watt to Clausius: The Rise of Thermodynamics in the Early Industrial Age* (Ithaca, New York: Cornell University Press, 1971). Donald Cardwell, *The Norton History of Technology* (New York: W. W. Norton, 1995), Chapter 5.

3. Smil, *op. cit.*, Figure 5.3, p. 164. Smil rates the thermal efficiency of the Newcomen engine at about 0.5 percent, of the Watt engine at about 3 to 5 percent, and of the best locomotive and steamship engines in the 1930s and 1940s at about 10 to 20 percent.

4. Cardwell, *Norton History, op. cit.*, p. 159.

5. John Harris, "The Rise of Coal Technology," *Scientific American*, vol. 231, no. 2 (August, 1974), pp. 92–97.

6. Smil, *op. cit.*, Chapter 5. The quote is on p. 159.

7. von Tunzelmann, *op. cit.*

8. Terry Reynolds, "Medieval Roots of the Industrial Revolution," *Scientific American*, vol. 251, no. 1 (July, 1984), pp. 123–130.

9. Trefil, *op. cit.*, p. 96.

10. Asa Briggs, *Iron Bridge to Crystal Palace: Impact and Images of the Industrial Revolution* (London: Thames and Hudson, 1979), pp. 61, 90, 111.

11. Briggs, *The Power of Steam, op. cit.*, p. 107.

12. Angus Sinclair, *Development of the Locomotive Engine* (Cambridge, Massachusetts: MIT Press, 1970). The original edition of this book was published in 1907 by the Angus Sinclair Publishing Company of New York. The reissue features annotations by John White.

13. James Beniger, *The Control Revolution: Technological and Economic Origins of the Information Society* (Cambridge, Massachusetts: Harvard University Press, 1986).

14. Eugen Weber, *Peasants into Frenchmen: The Modernization of Rural France, 1870–1914* (Stanford, California: Stanford University Press, 1976). The quote is on pp. 217–218.

15. Daniel Headrick, *The Tools of Empire: Technology and European Imperialism in the Nineteenth Century* (New York: Oxford University Press, 1981), Chapters 13, 14.

16. Michael Adas, *Machines as the Measure of Men: Science, Technology, and Ideologies of Western Dominance* (Ithaca, New York: Cornell University Press, 1989), Chapter 4.

17. Headrick, *op. cit.*, Chapters 1, 2, 8–12. Arnold Pacey, *Technology in World Civilization: A Thousand-Year History* (Cambridge, Massachusetts: MIT Press, 1993), pp. 142–144.

18. Ernest Schusky, *Culture and Agriculture: An Ecological Introduction to Traditional and Modern Farming Systems* (New York: Bergin & Garvey, 1989), Part 2. The quote is on p. 102.

19. McMichael, *op. cit.*, pp. 92–93.

20. John Post, *The Last Great Subsistence Crisis in the Western World* (Baltimore, Maryland: Johns Hopkins University Press, 1977).

21. *Ibid.*, pp. 54–58, 151.

22. Clive Ponting, *A Green History of the World: The Environment and the Collapse of Great Civilizations* (New York: St. Martin's Press, 1991), pp. 68–69, 115–116, 243.

23. John Walton, *Fish and Chips and the British Working Class, 1870–1940* (Leicester: Leicester University Press, 1992), Chapters 1, 3.

24. Smil, *op. cit.*, Figure 5.18, p. 197.

25. Roger Scola, *Feeding the Victorian City: The Food Supply of Manchester, 1770–1870* (Manchester: Manchester University Press, 1992).

26. Sinclair, *op. cit.*, pp. 28–29.

27. Cardwell, *Norton History, op. cit.*, pp. 231–235.

28. Scola, *op. cit.*, Table 2.1, p. 19.

29. *Ibid.*, p. 275.

30. *Ibid.*, Table 3.1, p. 47.

31. *Ibid.*, p. 272.

Episode Six: Petroleum and the Internal Combustion Engine

1. John Fenn, *Engines, Energy and Entropy: A Thermodynamics Primer* (San Francisco: W. H. Freeman 1982). The quote is from p. 191.

2. M. G. Lay, *Ways of the World: A History of the World's Roads and of the Vehicles That Used Them* (New Brunswick, New Jersey: Rutgers University Press, 1992), pp. 148–163.

3. Donald Cardwell, *The Norton History of Technology* (New York: W. W. Norton, 1995), pp. 338–346.

4. Maury Klein, "The Diesel Revolution," *Invention & Technology* (Winter, 1991), pp. 16–22.

5. Lay, *op. cit.*, pp. 131–135. The quote is on p. 133.

6. Rudi Volti, "Why Internal Combustion?" *Invention & Technology* (Fall, 1990), pp. 42–47.

7. Merrill Dennison, *The Power to Go: The Story of the Automotive Industry* (Garden City, New York: Doubleday, 1956), pp. 108–110. Thomas Hughes, *American Genesis: A Century of Invention and Technological Enthusiasm, 1870–1970* (New York: Penguin, 1989), pp. 220–226.

8. Paul Lucier, "Petroleum: What Is It Good For?" *Invention & Technology* (Fall, 1991), pp. 56–63.

9. Dennison, *op. cit.*, pp. 190–194. Hughes, *op. cit.*, pp. 206–220.

10. See, e.g., David Harvey, *The Condition of Postmodernity: An Enquiry into the Origins of Cultural Change* (Cambridge, Massachusetts: Basil Blackwell, 1989), Chapter 8.

11. Eugene Linden, "Megacities," *Time*, January 11, 1993, pp. 28–38.

12. Alan Pisarski, *Commuting in America: A National Report on Commuting Patterns and Trends* (Washington, D.C.: Eno Foundation for Transportation, 1987). "The City, the Commuter and the Car," *The Economist*, February 18, 1989, pp. 19–22.

13. Joel Garreau, *Edge City: Life on the New Frontier* (New York: Doubleday, 1991). Robert Fishman, "Megalopolis Unbound," *Wilson Quarterly* (Winter, 1990), pp. 25–45.

14. Wolfgang Sachs, *For Love of the Automobile: Looking Back into the History of Our Desires*, trans. by Don Reneau (Berkeley, California: University of California Press, 1992), pp. 91–101. The quotes are from pp. 95, 97, 98–99, and 101. See also Martin Pawley, *The Private Future: Causes and Consequences of Community Collapse in the West* (New York: Random House, 1974), pp. 45–51.

15. Alan Durning, "How Much Is Enough?" *Technology Review* (May/June, 1991), pp. 57–64. Lester Brown and Jodi Jacobson, "Assessing the Future of Urbanization," in Lester Brown et al., eds., *State of the World, 1987* (New York: W. W. Norton, 1987), Chapter 3. Abel Wolman, "The Metabolism of Cities," in *Cities* (New York: Alfred A. Knopf, 1966), pp. 156–174. James Trefil, *A Scientist in the City* (New York: Doubleday, 1994), Part One.

16. Lay, *op. cit.*, Chapter 7.

17. John Sedgwick, "Strong but Sensitive," *The Atlantic Monthly*, vol. 267, no. 4 (April, 1991), pp. 70–82.

18. Lay, *op. cit.*, pp. 313–322.

19. T. A. Heppenheimer, "The Rise of the Interstates," *Invention & Technology* (Fall, 1991), pp. 8–18.

20. "Oil's New Order," *The Economist*, July 13, 1991, pp. 67–68. "Oil Brief: The Stuff of Wars," *The Economist*, January 12, 1991, pp. 66–67. "Oil Reserves," *The Economist*, August 1, 1992, p. 89. Allen Myerson, "OPEC Rivals Curb Cartel Impact," *New York Times*, December 27, 1994. Agis Salpukas, "Shift in Insurance to Cover Oil Ships May Disrupt Flow," *New York Times*, December 12, 1994.

21. Alan Altshuler, et al., *The Future of the Automobile* (Cambridge, Massachusetts: MIT Press, 1984). Peter Dicken, *Global Shift: Industrial Change in a Turbulent World* (New York: Harper & Row, 1986), Chapter 9. James Womack, Daniel Jones, and Daniel Roos, *The Machine That Changed the World* (New York: Macmillan, 1990).

22. *The Economist Book of Vital World Statistics* (New York: Random House, 1990), pp. 108–109.

23. "The Endless Road: A Survey of the Car Industry," *The Economist*, October 17, 1992.

24. Kurt Hoffman and Raphael Kaplinsky, *Driving Force: The Global Restructuring of Technology, Labour, and Investment in the Automobile and Components Industries* (Boulder, Colorado: Westview Press, 1988).

25. Elsbeth Freudenthal, *Flight into History: The Wright Brothers and the Air Age* (Norman, Oklahoma: University of Oklahoma Press, 1949).

26. Vaclav Smil, *Energy in World History* (Boulder, Colorado: Westview Press, 1994), Figures 5.9 and 5.20, pp. 176–177, 198–200. The quote is on p. 199.

27. "Broadening the Mind: A Survey of World Travel and Tourism," *The Economist*, March 23, 1991.

28. Lionel Casson, *Travel in the Ancient World* (Toronto: Hakkert, 1974), Chapter 8.

29. "Gone away," *The Economist,* April 3, 1993, p. 40.

30. "Tangled: A Survey of the Airline Industry," *The Economist,* June 12, 1993.

31. Richard Weintraub, "Delivering a Revolution," *Washington Post,* August 28, 1994.

32. "Blue Skies, Red Ink, Black Future," *The Economist,* May 6, 1995, pp. 61–64.

33. Patrick Lyons, "50 Years after D-Day, an Aircraft Industry Remade," *New York Times,* June 5, 1994. Artemis March, "The Future of the U.S. Aircraft Industry," *Technology Review* (January, 1990), pp. 27–36. "Ground Control, We Seem to Have a Problem," *The Economist,* January 26, 1991, pp. 57–60. "Will They Ever Fly Again?" *The Economist,* March 7, 1992, pp. 67–68.

Episode Seven, Part One:
Prelude to the Information Age

1. Arthur Clarke, *How the World Was One: Beyond the Global Village* (New York: Bantam Books, 1992), pp. 3–4.

2. T. K. Derry and Trevor Williams, *A Short History of Technology from the Earliest Times to A.D. 1900* (New York: Dover Publications, 1960), Chapter 22.

3. Dirk Hanson, *The New Alchemists: Silicon Valley and the Micro-Electronics Revolution* (New York: Avon Books, 1982), pp. 15–24.

4. Steven Lubar, *InfoCulture: The Smithsonian Book of Information Age Inventions* (Boston: Houghton Mifflin, 1993), pp. 73–99. Derry and Williams, *op. cit.,* pp. 621–629.

5. Maury Klein, "What Hath God Wrought?" *Invention & Technology* (Spring, 1993), pp. 34–42. The quote is on pp. 34–36.

6. James Beniger, *The Control Revolution: Technological and Economic Origins of the Information Society* (Cambridge, Massachusetts: Harvard University Press, 1986), pp. 221–237. Arnold Pacey, *Technology in World Civilization* (Cambridge, Massachusetts: MIT Press, 1990), pp. 137–138.

7. Clarke, *op. cit.,* Part One.

8. D.J.R. Bruckner, "Yelling 'Stop the Presses!' Didn't Happen Overnight," *New York Times,* November 20, 1995.

9. Peter Baida, "Breaking the Connection," *American Heritage* (June–July, 1985), pp. 65–80. Clarke, *op. cit.,* Chapter 15. Lubar, *op. cit.,* pp. 119–146.

10. Hanson, *op. cit.,* Chapter 1. Derry and Williams, *op. cit.,* pp. 621–628. Clarke, *op. cit.,* Chapter 17. Lubar, *op. cit.,* pp. 213–242.

11. Michael Shrage, "Two Firms Had Unusual Relationship," *Washington Post,* December 15, 1985.

12. Mitchell Stephens, "From Dots and Dashes to Rock and Larry King," *New York Times,* November 20, 1995.

13. John Bardeen, "To a Solid State," *Science 84* (November, 1984), pp. 143–145.

14. Lubar, *op. cit.,* pp. 243–263.

15. Andy Meisler, "Lucy Sure Didn't Start It, But She Has Stuck to It," *New York Times,* November 20, 1995.

16. Derry and Williams, *op. cit.,* pp. 637–643.

17. Lubar, *op. cit.,* pp. 290–301.

18. Hanson, *op. cit.*, Chapter 2.

19. T. A. Heppenheimer, "How Von Neumann Showed the Way," *Invention & Technology* (Fall, 1990), pp. 8–16.

20. Lubar, *op. cit.*, pp. 311–318.

21. Oliver Allen, "The Power of Patents," *Great Inventions That Changed the World*, special issue of *American Heritage of Information & Technology* (1994), pp. 2–11.

22. Beniger, *op. cit.*

23. Lewis Mumford, *Technics and Civilization* (New York: Harcourt, Brace and World, 1934).

24. Everett Rogers and Judith Larsen, *Silicon Valley Fever: Growth of High-Technology Culture* (New York: Basic Books, 1984).

Episode Seven, Part Two: The Information Age

1. Margaret Cheney, *Tesla: Man Out of Time* (Englewood Cliffs, New Jersey: Prentice-Hall, 1981), Chapters 15, 16.

2. John O'Neill, *Prodigal Genius: The Life of Nikola Tesla* (New York: Ives Washburn, 1944), Chapter 12, pp. 209–211. Emphasis in the original. Dirk Hanson, *The New Alchemists: Silicon Valley and the Micro-Electronics Revolution* (New York: Avon, 1982), pp. 24–26.

3. T. R. Reid, "The Chip," *Science 85* (February, 1985), pp. 32–41.

4. Steven Lubar, *InfoCulture: The Smithsonian Book of Information Age Inventions* (Boston: Houghton Mifflin, 1993), pp. 232–234.

5. Rick Cook, "Digital Signal Processors," *High Technology* (October, 1985), pp. 23–30. Nicholas Negroponte, *Being Digital* (New York: Alfred A. Knopf, 1995).

6. Robert Noyce, "Microelectronics," *Scientific American*, vol. 237, no. 3 (September, 1977), pp. 63–69.

7. Hanson, *op. cit.*, Chapter 4.

8. Paul Ceruzzi, "A Few Words about this Picture," *Invention & Technology* (Spring, 1994), pp. 18–22.

9. Lubar, *op. cit.*, pp. 318–350.

10. Arthur Clarke, *How the World Was One: Beyond the Global Village* (New York: Bantam, 1992), Chapter 39.

11. *Ibid.* Burton Edelson, "Global Satellite Communications," *Scientific American*, vol. 236, no. 2 (February, 1977), pp. 58–73.

12. Charles Townes, "Harnessing Light," *Science 84* (November, 1984), pp. 153–155.

13. Emmanuel Desurvire, "Lightwave Communications: The Fifth Generation," *The Computer in the 21st Century: Scientific American Special Issue* (1995), pp. 54–61.

14. Everett Rogers and Judith Larsen, *Silicon Valley Fever: Growth of High-Technology Culture* (New York: Basic Books, 1984), Chapter 6. Manuel Castells and Peter Hall, *Technopoles of the World: The Making of 21st Century Industrial Complexes* (London: Routledge, 1994), Chapter 2. Another important source of technological innovation was the Xerox Corporation's Palo Alto Research Center (PARC). See Elizabeth Corcoran, "Homers, Out of the PARC," *Washington Post*, September 3, 1995.

15. Hanson, *op. cit.*, p. 120.

16. Rene Chun, "Wonders of the Ancient Video-Game World Are Back," *New York Times,* June 18, 1995.

17. Lubar, *op. cit.*, p. 325.

18. *Ibid.*, p. 257.

19. Peter Baida, "Breaking the Connection," *American Heritage,* vol. 36, no. 4 (June–July, 1985), pp. 65–80. Raymond Akwule, *Global Telecommunications: The Technology, Administration, and Policies* (Boston: Focal Press, 1992). Loy Singleton, *Telecommunications in the Information Age: A Nontechnological Primer on the New Technologies,* second edition (Cambridge, Massachusetts: Ballinger, 1986). Mark Landler, "Uncle Sam, Ma Bell and Her Babies: A Timeline," *New York Times,* December 22, 1995.

20. "The Uses of Heaven: A Survey of Space," *The Economist,* June 15, 1991, p. 8. Thomas O'Toole, "Communications Satellites Overcrowded," *Washington Post,* February 1, 1984.

21. Lubar, *op. cit.*, p. 260.

22. *Ibid.*, pp. 153–159. "Planet Internet," *Business Week,* April 3, 1995, pp. 118–124. Gary Stix, "The Speed of Write," *Scientific American,* vol. 271, no. 6 (December, 1994), pp. 106–111. Herb Brody, "Internet@Crossroads.$$$," *Technology Review,* (May/June, 1995), pp. 24–31. "The Accidental Superhighway: A Survey of the Internet," *The Economist,* July 1, 1995.

23. John Burgess, "Internet Creates a Computer Culture of Remote Intimacy," *Washington Post,* June 28, 1993.

24. *The Economist,* April 15, 1995, p. 98.

25. Herbert Dordick and Georgette Wang, *The Information Society: A Retrospective View* (Newbury Park, California: Sage, 1993). Wilson Dizard, *The Coming Information Age: An Overview of Technology, Economics, and Politics,* second edition (New York: Longman, 1985). Howard Frederick, *Global Communication and International Relations* (Belmont, California: Wadsworth, 1993).

26. Manuel Castells, *The Informational City: Information, Technology, Economic Restructuring and the Urban-Regional Process* (Oxford: Basil Blackwell, 1989), Chapter 1. Castells and Hall, *op. cit.*

27. Charles Perrow, *Normal Accidents: Living with High-Risk Technologies* (New York: Basic Books, 1984).

28. Walter Anderson, *Reality Isn't What It Used to Be* (New York: Harper & Row, 1990).

29. Michael Polanyi, *The Tacit Dimension* (New York: Doubleday, 1966). Mark Weiser, "The Computer for the 21st Century," *Scientific American,* vol. 265, no. 3 (September, 1991), p. 94.

30. Vaclav Smil, *Energy in World History* (Boulder, Colorado: Westview, 1994), Figure 5.22, p. 204.

31. Lawrence Tesler, "Networked Computing in the 1990s," *Scientific American,* vol. 265, no. 3 (September, 1991), p. 88.

32. Vinton Cerf, "Networks," *Scientific American,* vol. 256, no. 3 (September, 1991), pp. 74–75. Lubar, *op. cit.*, p. 154.

33. *The Economist Book of Vital World Statistics* (New York: Random House, 1990), pp. 126–127. Gary Stix, "Domesticating Cyberspace," *The Computer in the*

21st Century, op. cit., pp. 31–38. "The Third Age: A Survey of the Computer Industry," *The Economist,* September 17, 1994.

34. Mark Landler, "Multiple Family Phone Lines, A Post-Postwar U.S. Trend," *New York Times,* December 26, 1995.

35. Thomas Miller, "New Markets for Information," *American Demographics,* (April, 1995), pp. 46–54.

36. "What Information Costs," *Fortune,* July 10, 1995, p. 119.

37. "The Death of Distance: A Survey of Telecommunications," *The Economist,* September 30, 1995, p. 6.

Episode Seven, Part Three: Cities and Global Systems in the Information Age

1. Manuel Castells and Peter Hall, *Technopoles of the World: The Making of 21st Century Industrial Complexes* (London: Routledge, 1994).

2. Manuel Castells, *The Informational City: Information Technology, Economic Restructuring and the Urban-Regional Process* (Oxford: Basil Blackwell, 1989), pp. 12–17.

3. Saskia Sassen, *The Global City: New York, London, Tokyo* (Princeton, New Jersey: Princeton University Press, 1991).

4. Nigel Harris, *The End of the Third World: Newly Industrializing Countries and the Decline of an Ideology* (New York: Penguin, 1987).

5. David Rieff, *Los Angeles: Capital of the Third World* (New York: Simon & Schuster, 1991).

6. Robert B. Reich, *The Work of Nations: Preparing Ourselves for 21st Century Capitalism* (New York: Alfred A. Knopf, 1991).

7. *Ibid.* Richard Barnet and John Cavanagh, *Global Dreams: Imperial Corporations and the New World Order* (New York: Simon & Schuster, 1994). Robert Ross and Kent Trachte, *Global Capitalism: The New Leviathan* (Albany, New York: State University of New York Press, 1990). Christopher Chase-Dunn, *Global Formation: Structures of the World-Economy* (Cambridge, Massachusetts: Blackwell, 1989).

8. Herbert Schiller, *Culture, Inc.: The Corporate Takeover of Public Expression* (New York: Oxford University Press, 1989).

9. Charles Perrow, *Normal Accidents: Living with High-Risk Technologies* (New York: Basic Books, 1985).

10. Richard Preston, *The Hot Zone* (New York: Random House, 1994), pp. 11–12. See also Laurie Garrett, *The Coming Plague: Newly Emerging Diseases in a World out of Balance* (New York: Farrar, Straus and Giroux, 1994).

11. Michael Ignatieff, *Blood and Belonging: Journeys into the New Nationalism* (New York: Farrar, Straus and Giroux, 1993).

12. Philip McMichael, ed., *The Global Restructuring of Agro-Food Systems* (Ithaca, New York: Cornell University Press, 1994).

13. David Rieff, "Multiculturalism's Silent Partner," *Harper's* (August, 1993), pp. 62–72.

14. Ulrich Beck, *Risk Society: Towards a New Modernity,* trans. by Mark Ritter (London: Sage, 1992).

15. Paul Kennedy, *Preparing for the Twenty-First Century* (New York: Random House, 1993), p. 64.

16. Jean Gottman, *Megalopolis: The Urbanized Northeastern Seaboard of the United States* (New York: Twentieth Century Fund, 1961), esp. Chapter 3. The quote is from p. 103. Emphasis in the original.

17. Castells, *op. cit.*

18. Alain Touraine, *Return of the Actor*, trans. by Myrna Godzich (Minneapolis, Minnesota: University of Minnesota Press, 1988), Chapter 10.

19. Mike Featherstone, ed., *Consumer Culture and Postmodernism* (London: Sage, 1991).

20. Ilya Prigogine and Isabelle Stengers, *Order Out of Chaos: Man's New Dialogue with Nature* (New York: Bantam, 1984).

21. James Gleick, *Chaos: Making a New Science* (New York: Penguin, 1988). Roger Lewin, *Complexity: Life at the Edge of Chaos* (New York: Macmillan, 1992).

22. Heinz R. Pagels, *The Dreams of Reason: The Computer and the Rise of the Sciences of Complexity* (New York: Bantam, 1988). Alvin Toffler, *The Adaptive Corporation* (New York: Bantam, 1985). William Ouchi, *Theory Z: How American Business Can Meet the Japanese Challenge* (Reading, Massachusetts: Addison-Wesley, 1981), pp. 250–254. Roger Benjamin, *The Limits of Politics: Collective Goods and Political Change in Postindustrial Societies* (Chicago: University of Chicago Press, 1980). Walter Baber, *Organizing the Future: Matrix Models for the Postindustrial Polity* (University, Alabama: University of Alabama Press, 1983), Chapter 1.

23. Frank Hearn, ed., *The Transformation of Industrial Organizations: Management, Labor, and Society in the United States* (Belmont, California: Wadsworth, 1988), esp. David Friedman, "Beyond the Age of Ford: Features of Flexible-System Production," pp. 254–265.

24. David Harvey, *The Condition of Postmodernity: An Enquiry into the Origins of Cultural Change* (Oxford: Basil Blackwell, 1989), esp. Part Two.

25. Many of these strategies of flexibility and a contingent workforce are discussed in Bennett Harrison and Barry Bluestone, *The Great U-Turn: Corporate Restructuring and the Polarizing of America* (New York: Basic Books, 1988).

26. James R. Beniger, *The Control Revolution: Technological and Economic Origins of the Information Society* (Cambridge, Massachusetts: Harvard University Press, 1986), esp. Chapter 5, p. 202, and Chapter 7, pp. 291–292.

27. Mike Featherstone, *op. cit.* Kenneth J. Gergen, *The Saturated Self: Dilemmas of Identity in Contemporary Life* (New York: Basic Books, 1991).

28. Harrison and Bluestone, *op. cit.*

29. Mark Hepworth, *Geography of the Information Economy* (New York and London: Guilford Press, 1990), Chapter 2.

30. Marc Uri Porat, "Global Implications of the Information Society," *Journal of Communication* (Winter, 1978), pp. 70–80.

31. Hepworth, *op. cit.*, Tables 2.8 and 2.9, pp. 25–26.

32. Herbert Dordick and Georgette Wang, *The Information Society: A Retrospective View* (Newbury Park, California: Sage, 1993), Table 7, Appendix B, p. 143.

33. Hepworth, *op. cit.*, pp. 29–33.

34. *Ibid.*, Chapter 2, esp. Table 2.2

35. Reich, *op. cit.*

36. Steven Sass, "The U.S. Professional Sector: 1950 to 1988," *New England Economic Review* (January–February, 1990), pp. 37–51.

37. *Ibid.*, p. 37.

38. *Ibid.*, p. 38.

39. Robert Fishman, *Bourgeois Utopias: The Rise and Fall of Suburbia* (New York: Basic Books, 1987), Chapter 4. Kenneth T. Jackson, *Crabgrass Frontier: The Suburbanization of the United States* (New York: Oxford University Press, 1985). Michael N. Danielson, *The Politics of Exclusion* (New York: Columbia University Press, 1976).

40. Nicholas Lemann, "Stressed Out in Suburbia," *The Atlantic Monthly* (November, 1989), p. 36.

41. Michael Sorkin, ed., *Variations on a Theme Park: The New American City and the End of Public Space* (New York: Noonday Press, 1992).

42. Christopher Leinberger and Charles Lockwood, "How Business Is Reshaping America," *The Atlantic Monthly* (October, 1986), p. 43. See also Christopher Leinberger, "The Six Types of Urban Village Cores," *Urban Land*, vol. 47, no. 5 (May, 1988), pp. 24–27.

43. Jean Gottman, "Urban Centrality and the Interweaving of Quaternary Activities," in Jean Gottman and Robert A. Harper, eds., *Since Megalopolis: The Urban Writings of Jean Gottman* (Baltimore, Maryland, and London: Johns Hopkins University Press, 1990), pp. 56–60. See also Manuel Castells, *op. cit.*, pp. 49–57, for a similar listing.

44. Beniger, *op. cit.*, p. 64.

45. A. J. McMichael, *Planetary Overload: Global Environmental Change and the Health of the Human Species* (Cambridge: Cambridge University Press, 1993), p. 105. "Evodeviation" is defined by McMichael (p. 89) as a condition in which, "for any species, the conditions of life deviate from those of its evolutionary formative natural habitat."

46. Some observers believe that the next "episode" in this saga will inevitably take *Homo sapiens* off this planet in search of new worlds. A "post-global" future thus looms as our destiny, an imperative if you will. As Carl Sagan puts it, "Every surviving civilization is obliged to become spacefaring—not because of exploratory or romantic zeal, but for the most practical reason imaginable: staying alive." *Pale Blue Dot: A Vision of the Human Future in Space* (New York: Random House, 1994), p. 371.

About the Book and Author

Robert Clark delves into 100 millennia of human history to create a unified and consistent explanation for humankind's need to spread itself across the globe. Examining events from different eras, Clark melds them together to form a framework for understanding the process of globalization. Drawing from a variety of academic disciplines, the book reveals the spread of humans and their cultures to be part of an ongoing struggle to supply the needs of an increasingly large and complex society.

❧   ❧   ❧

Robert P. Clark is professor of government and politics at George Mason University.

Index

Printed in the United States
124301LV00015B/139/A